AND SO TO ROME

SUN, CYPRESS, FOUNTAIN AND COLUMN
(Michelangelo's garden, National Museum, Rome)

AND SO TO ROME

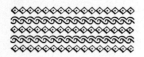

By CECIL ROBERTS

"Come to Rome. It is a scene by which expression
is overpowered; which words cannot convey."
—*Shelley*

"As regards staying at Rome, I shall never be able
to stay anywhere else again."   —*Raphael*

NEW YORK

THE MACMILLAN COMPANY

1950

CONTENTS

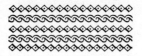

ILLUSTRATIONS

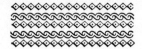

PROLOGUE

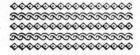

As the train drew into Rome, in the golden light of an autumn evening, I was conscious of some anxiety. I had first come to Rome some thirty years earlier, an eager young man whose means permitted only a visit of three days. I left with a determination to return soon, but except for one brief transit in 1935, the events of a varied life had always defeated this intention; moreover, I had discovered Venice, and through many years it held me with its enchantment, preventing other Italian wanderings.

Nevertheless, that brief vision of Rome had fixed my resolution, and I had faith in the act of throwing a coin into the Fountain of Trevi, duly performed, by which the visitor ensures his return. In the intervening thirty years I had steadily explored a vast bibliography, archaeological, historical, political and social, whose inexhaustible riches are mined from the greatest city in the history of the world. So that now on this autumn evening, as the train drew in through the litter and tawdriness of a railway terminus, I was rather like a lover who, at long last, in the moment of reunion, fears that Time and reality may bring disillusionment.

A friend had procured for me a room. 'I think you will like it,' he said briefly. It was on the top floor of an hotel, a room with a balcony, and in the last flush of golden evening I stepped out on to it. Whatever I had imagined or hoped for was here overwhelmingly fulfilled. I think my friend was

1

aware of this great moment, for he left me alone to survey the city spread out before me.

The sun had not set, and that singular light of a Roman sunset, unforgettably recalled by all who have experienced it, pervaded the sky and touched with its fleeting beauty the hills known to the Caesars, the city streets that had echoed with human traffic through more than two thousand years, and the domes, arches, towers and palaces that evoked memories of emperors, popes, artists and scholars whose lives and genius had created here an unsurpassable pageant of human splendour.

To my left, purple fading into saffron and gold, lay the Alban Hills, with Frascati and Rocca di Papa, terraced and remote, glimmering in the last flush of the dying sun. Nearer, a bright Italian flag fluttered on the tower of the former royal palace of the Quirinale. The level expanse of the Campagna spread duskily beyond the city, visible as far as the Mediterranean. The green, forested Janiculum lifted a crest of tufted pines pierced by the golden west, so that it became a vast cathedral through whose windows the day magnificently waned; it rose, remote and cool, above the Tiber's thronged valley. Its line, continuing to Monte Mario, with its observatory like a white eggshell on the peak, led the eye ultimately to the violet Sabine Hills, haunt of so many ghosts wandering in the shadowy birth of Rome.

Such were the wide and distant prospects glowing under the evening sky wherein a new moon, a sickle wraith, with one brilliant attendant star, awaited the surrender of her domain. Near lay the city itself, a congeries of faded sienna and ochre buildings, speared with dark cypresses, winged with silhouetted quadrigas and spaced with innumerable lanterned and cross-surmounted cupolas.

Immediately below me, astonishing in its expanse and in its umbrageous beauty, was a green oasis from which rose the twin towers of the Villa Medici, through whose arches the crimson sunset burned. A symbol of the magnificence of the

Renaissance, it lay enfolded by the old Aurelian Wall of Rome, that curves by the promenade of the Pincio and the adjacent bosky avenues of the Villa Borghese. Here is history indeed, for this is the site of the former villa and gardens of the patrician Lucullus, the giver of lavish banquets. Here, with a fortune made as a commander of the Roman armies in Asia, he staged his feasts, games and torchlight processions. Here he entertained Cæsar and Pompey, offering such delicacies as lampreys, to which it is said he fed his slaves. The Villa passed to Asiaticus, and was coveted by Messalina, wife of the Emperor Claudius. She persuaded her son's tutor to make licentious charges against the patrician and he was condemned to death. In Roman fashion he bathed, supped and opened his veins. With forethought he had the pyre, prepared for his cremation, removed elsewhere, in order that the flames should not damage the trees in his garden. Messalina's life in this villa became so notorious that the Emperor on his return to Rome put her lovers to death and sent his freedman and some soldiers to the garden to despatch his wife. They found her in the woodland with her mother, and slew her.

In a part of this garden the nuns of the convent of Trinita dei Monti now collect eggs from the farm at the bottom of the orchard. Each morning of my sojourn I awoke to a clucking of hens, so that I might have been miles away in the country, instead of in the very heart of Rome. All the world knows the twin domes of the church beyond the obelisk that cuts the skyline above the great sweep of the Spanish steps. The church holds upon its baroque façade the last light of evening. I looked on the reverse side, with St. Peter's vast dome rising distantly between its towers; the nuns' long garden, partly playground for their pupils, partly orchard and farm, lay beneath me, a thing of endless beauty. Every time a grave nun stooped, with voluminous posterior, I knew it meant another egg in the basket.

Immediately below me the wall, bordering the road that led to the Porta Pinciana, was broken by a gateway, long disused, which once opened on to a straight drive between walls smothered with roses. It ran to the famous Villa Medici, whose double towers rose above a forest of parasol pines, cypresses and ilexes, silhouetted, tall and dramatic, against the evening sky. The gate to this avenue, the back entrance, led to the garden side of the Villa, of which the front commanded a panorama of Rome. The drive had once been a ceremonial one. It had a high arch surmounted by a terrace. On either side of the portal were niches which formerly held statues. Over these niches were marble slabs with Latin inscriptions of welcome and hospitality. Beyond the portal there was a large garden filled with pink and red roses, and a little square house which at first I thought was for a gardener, but was an artist's studio. Behind this rose a great mound covered with a dense ilex wood, beautifully clipped and rounded so that from my balcony it seemed like a green velvet pin-cushion. From this emerged a belvedere with a view of the whole of Rome in the valley below, and of the vast pile of St. Peter's, and the green mount of the Janiculum.

The Villa Medici thus splendidly set before me is the headquarters of the French Academy of Art, and here the fortunate winners of the Prix de Rome have their studios, many of them built into the thick recesses of the great wall raised by the Emperor Aurelian in the third century A.D. for the defence of Rome. The Villa has a history stretching far beyond its present use. The pin-cushion wood that I saw below me, with its belvedere, was called the Boschetto, I discovered later, and it was reached by a flight of steps leading to *Il Parnaso*, as the belvedere was called, which rose on the site of an ancient nympheum that had been converted to its present use by Cardinal Ricci. He built the Villa Medici in 1540 with material mostly taken from the temple of Jupiter Capitolinus above the Forum. A subsequent owner was Cardinal Alessandro dei Medici, later Pope Leo XI. The Villa thus naturally became the seat of the Tuscan ambassador to the Vatican. It was here that he gave hospitality to Velasquez,

who has left some beautiful pictorial reminiscences of his
sojourn. Here also, while awaiting trial by the Inquisition,
the unhappy Galileo was held in confinement. In 1801
Napoleon coveted the Villa and made a deal, exchanging it
for a palace in the city, since when, French property, it has
been the Academy for French art students.

The garden side of the Villa is magnificent. The fountains,
the loggias, the avenues leading to arcades and porticos with
statues, make it an enchanted domain. Over it all there is the
melancholy patina of faded grandeur, helped somewhat by
Italian *dolce far niente*, for when visiting the gardens, later, I
remarked that they seemed somewhat neglected, the reply
was: 'Yes, but the gardener is an Italian, a poet at heart, with
the most beautiful hands, and one cannot chide him.'

It was singular that only a few hours before my journey to
Rome I had bought in a Riviera town a battered little Tauch-
nitz edition of Henry James's *Foreign Parts*. In a chapter
headed 'From a Roman Notebook,' dated January, 1873, he
had evoked a vanished Rome, but not a vanished Boschetto,
for there was a description of the wooded belvedere I found
below my balcony a few hours later. His account of a visit
there may stand unaltered:

'With Mrs. W to the Villa Medici—perhaps on the whole
the most enchanting place in Rome. The part of the garden
called the Boschetto has a kind of incredible, impossible
charm; an upper terrace, behind locked gates, covered with a
little dusky forest of evergreen oaks. Such a deliciously dim
light—such a soft suffusion of tender grey-green tones—such
a company of gnarled and twisted little miniature trunks—
dwarfs playing with each other at being giants—and such a
shower of golden sparkles playing in from the glowing west!
At the end of the wood is a steep, circular mound, up which
the little trees scramble amain, with a long, mossy staircase
climbing to a belvedere. . . . I should wish one was not
obliged to be a Frenchman to come and live and dream and
work at the Académie de France. Can there be for a while a

happier destiny than that of a young artist, conscious of talent, with no errand but to educate, polish and perfect it, transplanted to these sacred shades?'

In line with the gardens of the church of Trinita del Monti and the Villa Medici, by the wall that bounded the road to the Pincian Gate, I looked down upon the Villa Malta, whose Byzantine-Gothic columned tower soared above the cypresses and palms. It had been the last home of Prince von Bülow, the German statesman, who, with Wilhelm II, contributed by persistent irresponsibility to the destruction of Europe, from which it never really recovered. It is a more sinister though less disastrous figure whose name is now evoked by this Villa, Count Cagliostro, the eighteenth-century charlatan. He held his séances here, and here came his dupes, foolishly believing he could turn water into wine—a rather unnecessary miracle in Italy—and metal into gold.

Cagliostro began life in a humble monk's habit, as Brother Giuseppe Balsamo, but abandoned it, becoming in turn a 'marquis,' in Naples, and the grandiloquent Count Alessandro Cagliostro in London, in 1776. Expelled from Russia, he triumphed at Warsaw and Strasbourg. The friend of Cardinal Rohan, shut up in the Bastille, released, acclaimed, driven from Paris, he eventually arrived at Rome and settled in the Villa Malta in September, 1789, founding there an Egyptian magic rite. Three months later he was arrested, tried by the Inquisition for fraud and necromancy, and condemned to death. The death sentence was commuted by the Pope to a life sentence. He died in the prison of the fortress San Leo five years later. He had created legends, and legends persisted regarding him after death, as that he had murdered the priest who came to confess him, donned his clothes and escaped.

This much of history, and more still to be comprehended, lay below me in the gathering dusk. In the higher sky, where crimson cirrus floated in the amber-and-emerald vault, there was a ceaseless criss-cross of innumerable small swallows, scavengers of the air, whose evening task had kept Rome habitable for thousands of years. The flaming disk of the sun fell swiftly behind a black lace-work of pinewoods, the glow faded, the myriad lights of the city twinkled in the valley and along the eternal hills. I waited while the curtain of night fell on the stage of Rome. I knew then that fulfilment, more ample than hoped for, was the reward of the waiting years. Month after month, through long days of excitement and patient pursuit of data, I came home to my balcony, anxious never to miss this pageant of the day's end, ever varied, ever superlatively lovely. For that is Rome, whose folly, vanity, passion and splendour, through two thousand years of vicissitude, march in a pageant to undertones of the sad destiny of Man. If Greece has taught us that marble bleeds, Rome shows us that the dust flowers.

Here and there let us pluck a bouquet from Time.

I

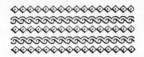

THE CASTLE OF ST. ANGELO

I

Day after day in Rome, at some street corner, on some slope of its many hills, in a valley filled with ruins of the city of the Caesars, in parks shaded by dark ilexes and dramatic parasol pines, or on the banks of the old brown Tiber, one is suddenly caught up in ecstasy by a sense of colour, form and history, blended in panoramic beauty.

Where most does one experience this sudden exaltation of the spirit, arising from the scene? One might say it comes on first seeing Rome from the belvedere of the Pincio, above the great Piazza del Popolo, with its gentle hills, palaces, churches and bridges, backed by the vast dome of St. Peter's in the rose-and-violet dusk of evening. Here is the Rome we know from a hundred engravings, an open book of more than two thousand years of turbulent history, the eternal Rome.

Some of us would choose as the most memorable impression the view down the ancient Forum, along the Sacred Way, beyond the Arch of Titus, where rises the great Coliseum on the horizon, a long-familiar friend, though seen now for the first time. And yet much could be said for the astonishing sight that greets the traveller who steps suddenly into the wide Piazza before St. Peter's, with Bernini's twin colonnades, vast wings to its central façade. Here are epitomised

8

the majesty and power of the Christian faith. The dome soars
into the azure sky, where the uplifted Cross is the symbol of
the devout, and a challenge to the sceptical, throughout the
world.

For myself, reviewing a crescendo of enchantments never
ceasing in the pageant of Rome, it is not any one of these
scenes, the view from the Pincio, down the Forum, before St.
Peter's, memorable as they are, that creates the supreme moment. This occurs for me when, emerging from a shadowed
street, and looking beyond the old Tiber, there suddenly con-
fronts me the tremendous vision of the Castle of St. Angelo,
crowned with the angel towering in the sky. The castle is,
first, a monument of history, seen in the vivid Roman air. It
stands across the bridge, sturdy and immense, yet with an
aerial quality born of sunshine and sky, so that it might suddenly vanish in the impalpable air.

I know many who have experienced this same sensation,
and they, too, have never quite analysed how much of the
magic is derived from the majesty of this mausoleum-fortress
and its setting in the ambient air, or from the all-pervading
sense of its history through the stormy vicissitudes of eighteen
centuries.

Possibly the magic arises from a blend of both. Few things
in Rome, it seems to me, are more arresting than this building, whose impressiveness owes little to size or beauty, though
it has something of both. The great mole rises from the Tiber's
bank, amber in hue, corbelled, bastioned, lightened by a
graceful loggia, the whole mass crowned by the silhouetted
angel that hovers, wings spread, dominant in the luminous
blue sky. This angel, sword in hand, represents the legend we
have known since childhood. As a work of art the bronze
statue has no particular merit, yet here, one feels without
question, is the mighty archangel Michael poised, not for
flight but alighting from Heaven. Thus he was seen by Pope
Gregory the Great when, leading a procession to offer prayers

at St. Peter's for staying the terrible pestilence that followed
the inundation of A.D. 589, he looked up, as the dying fell
around him, and above the great mausoleum saw the archangel sheathing the sword of Death while a celestial choir
chanted the anthem that has sounded so often since in the
church's vesper service[1]—

*Regina coeli laetare—quia quem meruisti portare—resurrexit,
sicut, dixit, Alleluia.*

to which the Pope solemnly responded—

Ora pro nobis Deum, Alleluia.

An angel surmounts the castle,[2] but the building has seen
enacted within its walls a terrible story of assassination, hanging, beheading, strangulation, poisoning and torture, with
grim variations in the mode of murder and execution, such as
death by starvation in its dungeons, or swift exit from the
living world by its dreadful *oubliettes*. It has witnessed more
continuous wickedness than perhaps any other place on earth.
The murder of the Princes in the Tower of London, and the
dire processions to the headsman's block, which give to that
grim fortress its sinister air, are pale incidents compared with
the colour and passion of the crimes that stain the record of
the popes who made the castle their refuge in the Dark Ages
and through the Renaissance.

Its history begins as a mausoleum built by the gifted and
enlightened Emperor Hadrian. He threw across the Tiber a
bridge and planned the great sepulchre that was to receive

[1] The onset of the plague was marked by fits of sneezing and yawning. Pope
Gregory VII decreed that 'God bless you' should be said to those who sneezed,
and the sign of the Cross be made over the mouths of those who yawned. From
the former decree descends the practice of saying 'God bless you,' 'Dio ti
benedica,' 'Gesundheit,' to a person who sneezes.

[2] Looking at the Angel it is difficult not to recall the ludicrous exploit of a
crazy Early Victorian English squire, Charles Waterton, who stood on one
leg on its head.

THE CASTLE ST. ANGELO AND ST. PETER'S

A FLORENTINE CASSONE OF 1452

The wedding chests (cassoni) of the Renaissance had friezes of gilded carving and painted panels and lids. They achieved high artistic merit, particularly in the Florentine School. They are of great historical interest since they often depict contemporary scenes. The lid of the cassone above shows three episodes. Right: The entrance of the Emperor Frederic III of Austria and King of the Romans into Rome, by the Ponte St. Angelo, showing the castle in the background. Centre: The meeting of Pope Nicholas V and his cardinals with the Emperor at the gate of Rome. Left: The marriage of the Emperor with Elena of Portugal, and his coronation by the Pope on March 16, 1452. These chests were highly prized and were carried by servants in the wedding procession to the bride and bridegroom's home.

his ashes. Not only Rome, but the whole world, civilised and barbarian, knew the fame of this complex man, poet, soldier, architect, statesman and traveller. He was capable of capricious cruelty, yet had the grand manner that put its indelible stamp upon the world. He was an incessant builder. His rule throughout the Roman Empire was marked by the labour of the trowel as much as by the power of the sword. The ruins of his vast villa at Tivoli have been one of the great quarries of the classical world, and the statuary found there enriches every museum of note. At the chill and misty outposts of his Empire, across Britain from Tyne to Solway, he threw a wall that seventeen centuries have not wholly demolished. He took Agrippa's Pantheon, rebuilt it and made of it the most perfect pagan building in Rome, and to this day one of its finest monuments. In the singular warp and woof of the loom of Time it was destined, after fifteen centuries, that Pope Urban VIII, another great builder in Rome, should ravish 450,250 lb. of bronze from the Pantheon, to make, among other things, eighty cannon for the Castle of St. Angelo. He also took from this pagan temple of a Roman emperor the bronze for the canopy over the high altar in St. Peter's.[3]

Unwittingly Hadrian contributed much to the building schemes of the popes. The tomb of Gregory XIII, the parsimonious old pontiff who rejoiced in the Massacre of St. Bartholomew and gave his name to the New Calendar, was made of marble plundered from the walls of the Castle of St. Angelo, in which he took refuge and where, at eighty-three, he died.

Hadrian was not the first Roman emperor to have the idea of building himself a grandiose sepulchre on the banks of the

---

[3] A contemporary wrote: 'Our good Pontiff could not bear the idea that such a mass of metal designed for loftier purposes should humble itself to the office of keeping off forever the rain from the portico of the Pantheon. He raised it to worthier destinies because it is becoming that such noble material should keep off the enemies of the Church rather than the rain.'

Tiber. One hundred and fifty years earlier, on the opposite bank, in meadows where the Roman youths met for martial exercises and games, Augustus Caesar, founder of the Empire, built a mausoleum, inspired by his travels in Asia Minor. It rose in three diminishing tiers, flanked by gardens planted with cypresses, to a lofty marble tower. Its interior was honeycombed with chambers for the reception of the ashes of the imperial family, together with those of their thousands of slaves and freedmen. Augustus himself slept in its core, his colossal statue shining above the place of his cremation. On the day of this ceremony the conflagration on his funeral pile was so great that his wife and the Roman senators had to watch by it for five days before his ashes had cooled sufficiently for collection.[4]

Marcellus, son of the unhappy Octavia, nephew of Augustus, the glorious youth immortalised in Virgil's lines—
Heu pietas heu prisca fides invictaque bello dextera! . . . was the first to be entombed there, in 23 B.C. Later came Agrippa and Octavia, Marc Antony's widow, and sister of Augustus. The mausoleum rapidly filled, violent deaths augmenting natural ones — Drusus, poisoned by his wife; Agrippina starved to death; Tiberius; Caligula murdered; Claudius murdered; his son Britannicus poisoned by Nero, and finally the Emperor Nerva, in A.D. 98. The mausoleum was the scene, centuries later, of the burning of the body of Rienzi, liberator and brief dictator of Rome, after having been publicly exposed on the order of his enemy, Colonna.

The circular form of the ancient mausoleum of Augustus is still visible. On July 17th, 1787, Goethe went to a bull-baiting there. 'It held from four to five thousand persons. The spectacle was not edifying for me.' In 1935 it achieved a new use as the scene of splendid orchestral concerts inaugurated

[4] In 353 B.C. the widow of Mausolus, Satrap of Caria, erected a vast rotund sepulchre for her husband that became one of the Seven Wonders of the World. Fragments of this are now in the British Museum. Any large sepulchre subsequently derived its name from this.

in its arena. Thus the tombs of the Caesars have become the boxes of the concert patrons.

Alas, to-day, around the old mausoleum, standing between the Tiber and the Corso, the modern note is struck with a harshness born of Fascism's brutal passion for modernity. The vogue of factory-like blocks of masonry is here triumphant. Amid these rectangular piles of offices I found Roman boys kicking a football in the very shadow of the mausoleum of the great Augustus, while from façades carrying statuary similar to the pseudo-Assyrian creations of Epstein that afflict the London scene, the young Romans were admonished by flamboyant edicts, legacy of an era of Fascist declamation. One runs: 'The Italian people are an immortal people who always find Springtime for their hopes, their passion and their greatness.'

Augustus Caesar's mausoleum constituted a challenge to Hadrian. No dynasty would carry his name. His deeds therefore must be memorialised by himself. So Hadrian crossed the Tiber to build something more grandiose. He succeeded. His mausoleum no longer holds his ashes, which, like those of Augustus, were scattered and lost. His gigantic statue no more crowns the great mole. In the place of the pagan emperor the archangel Michael now commands the heavens. Hadrian's mausoleum has been transformed through successive ages, and now even his name no longer belongs to it. Gone are the hanging gardens, the sixty-five marble statues that adorned it, the gigantic gilt effigy of the Emperor. Gone the great bastions of its front, the circular storey with fluted Ionic columns, and the second tier with Corinthian columns. It was stripped of its original facing of Parian marble, its statues were scattered. Centuries later they found here the Barberini *Faun*, now in Munich, the *Dancing Faun*, now in Florence, and the bust of Hadrian, now in the Vatican. The epitaphs of the Antonines on the walls of the sepulchral chamber were intact until 1572, when Gregory XIII cut them out and used the marble for decorating St. Peter's. Denuded of its early splendour, the castle is to-day more gravely clothed with the patina of its history, and lovely in its mellowed strength set against the vivid blue sky.

Hadrian, like Augustus, was not the first occupant of this mausoleum which he had built for himself. His adopted son, Aelius Verus, predeceased him and was interred there. Hadrian died at Baiae, on the Gulf of Naples, tired of a life that had nothing more to offer.[5] His body was transported to Rome from its temporary sepulchre by his successor, Antoninus Pius, who completed the mausoleum in A.D. 180. After death Antoninus was interred there, followed by Lucius Vero, Marcus Aurelius, Commodus and Septimius Severus, the last, in an urn of gold enclosed in a vase of alabaster. Thus it chanced that two Roman emperors who had stepped upon the soil of England—Hadrian and Septimius Severus—were interred there. Part of Hadrian's sarcophagus survives. It was removed and used as a tomb for Pope Innocent II, in A.D. 1143. This was destroyed in a fire at the Lateran two centuries later. The lid, of Egyptian porphyry, after use on the tomb of the Emperor Otho II, is now, if legend does not lie, the font in St. Peter's. So a child is now baptised in the Christian faith with water from the lid of a pagan emperor's coffin!

Hadrian's ashes have long vanished, but the colossal head from his statue on the mausoleum can be seen in the Vatican Museum, where it stands near the bust of his beloved Bithynian page, the beautiful Antinous. The great central chamber where the urns were kept is now empty. It was discovered and reopened in 1825.

By a niche of the chamber which probably held his sarcophagus the authorities have put a commemorative tablet, aptly quoting the sad little poem Hadrian wrote in his weary old age.

[5] 'In the thousands of years which followed the birth of Christ, there was no era in which the external conditions of life were so favourable to the happiness of mankind as in the reign of the Emperor Hadrian' (H. H. Asquith in *The Legacy of Rome*).

Animula vagulla blandula
Hospes comesque corporis,
Quae nunc abibis in loca
Pallida, rigida, nudula,
Nec ut soles dabis jocus?[6]

It was a pagan's simple question, devoid of Christian promise.

In the centre of the castle two terrible dungeons, the Gemelli (twins), were found, constructed in the time of Alexander VI, from which no one emerged alive. A tomb, a fortress, a prison, a palace, the mausoleum is honeycombed with dark chambers, winding stairs and corridors, black dungeons and dreadful *oubliettes* that hid from the light of day a succession of known and unrecorded crimes in the medieval and Renaissance eras.

Sixty years after the mole had ceased to be a sepulchre, Septimius Severus, who died at York, A.D. 211, being the last emperor interred therein, it was converted into a fortress by the Emperor Aurelian, builder of the great road that runs along the Italian and French Rivieras. He foresaw the military uses to which the castle-tomb could be put. He was the builder of the wall around Rome, the last development in antiquity of the science of fortification. He knew the danger to the city from the barbarian invasions, that he only just succeeded in stemming, in northern Italy in the third century. Rome had outgrown the early walls of the fourth century B.C. Aurelius built seventeen principal gates in a total circumference of eleven miles.

Honorius added to the strength of the castle by building outer bastions and repaired the Aurelian walls. It was a timely work. The fury from the north, Alaric and his Goths,

---

[6] Soul of me, vague, debonnair,
Guest of this body, and friend,
Say whither now wilt thou fare,
Pallid and rigid and bare,
Little soul, all thy jests at an end?
trans. Marcus S. Dimsdale.

laid a trail of ruin through Italy, sacked and burned Rome, and stormed the castle. The Emperor Theodosius made the great stronghold also a prison.

It was not until A.D. 537 that the castle suffered any serious damage, when the terrible Ostrogoths and Vitiges stormed the castle and a scene of carnage ensued. The Ostrogoths raised their scaling-ladders against the walls, and the desperate Roman defenders took the marble columns and statues, broke them up and poured a rain of torsos, legs, arms and heads of Greek and Roman masterpieces down upon the enemy. The great Belisarius was the master of the castle, but he lost it to Totila eight years later. Some thirty years passed, and the day came when Pope Gregory the Great, seeing the archangel Michael alighting upon the fortress during the visitation of the plague, caused it to be known ever afterwards as the Castle of St. Angelo. Thenceforward the darkness of the Middle Ages engulfed it, fitfully breaking to reveal terrible chronicles of blood. Its last marbles were stripped from it, and it no longer bore any resemblance to the magnificent sepulchre planned by Hadrian.

There is in Rome to-day a grim-looking street near the Pantheon called the Via de' Crescenzi. The dark and bloody events of the tenth century seem still remembered in this street, which takes its name from the Crescenzi family. The city was ruled in A.D. 904 by Theodora. From this ruthless woman descended five Popes and a line of counts, among whom rose the great house of Colonna. She had a daughter, Marozia, and these two infamous women took paramours and bred bastards who were made popes. It was in keeping with the age that Marozia's son rebelled, and imprisoned his mother in the castle she had so befouled.

In A.D. 965 Peter the Lion, prefect of the city, and his twelve captains, seized Pope John XIII. They threw him first into the castle prison and then drove him into exile. A year later the Emperor Otto the Great descended upon the re-

bellious city and restored John to his papal throne. He hanged
the twelve captains from the castle battlements and took a
terrible vengeance on the prefect. Bound naked on an ass, he
was flogged through the city and put to death. His mutilated
body was hung by the hair from the head of the bronze horse
bearing the figure of Marcus Aurelius, long believed to be the
Emperor Constantine, which then stood opposite the Pope's
door at the Lateran, and now commands the square of the
Capitol. Pope John died peacefully, not then a customary end.
He was buried in the basilica of St. Paul's outside the Walls.
This magnificent church was built in A.D. 386 by three emperors, Valentinian II, Theodosius and Arcadius, with the intention of rivalling St. Peter's in grandeur. The emperors'
creation is most curiously confirmed on the ancient tag of a
dog's collar found near the church a century ago, inscribed,
'I belong to the basilica of St. Paul the Apostle, and our three
sovereigns, and am in charge of Felicissimus the shepherd.'
What, one wonders, was the name of the dog, and was he
there to wag his tail when the funeral cortege of Pope John
arrived in A.D. 972? We can still read this Pope's epitaph. The
church, built on the supposed site where Paul was beheaded,
was under the protection of the sovereigns of England until
the break with Rome, in witness of which the emblem of the
Order of the Garter is still retained in the cloister there, which
also contains the sarcophagus of Peter the Lion. Thus the two
enemies, the Pope and the prefect, take their long sleep in the
same church, which was almost totally destroyed by fire in
1823. It has been restored, and a long nave with eighty massive granite columns recalls the lost splendour of this old
church to whose reconstruction the whole world contributed.

Benedict VI succeeded John XIII. He was strangled in the
castle by a Crescenzi who raised the anti-Pope Boniface VII
in his place. He fled later to Constantinople with many of the
treasures of the Vatican. The battle never ceased between
these two factions. Each, in turn triumphant, dominated the

city from the castle. Later Boniface was killed by the Roman mob. Then came young Otto III with Pope Gregory V. Crescenzi shut himself up in the castle, believed by all to be impregnable. A desperate siege followed. Catapults, battering-rams and scaling-towers were all turned on the fortress. Assault after assault failed. The Imperial forces caught the anti-Pope, John XVI, and vented their savage rage on him. They cut out his tongue, put out his eyes and sliced off his nose. He was then placed backwards on an ass and conveyed to a dungeon, from which he never emerged. Meanwhile the assault on the Castle of St. Angelo grew more desperate, until finally, a handful of soldiers having made a small breach, the enemy poured in. The fortress was forcibly taken, a thing that had never happened before in its history, and never happened again in its future of almost a thousand years. The carnage was tremendous, and soon the decapitated bodies of Crescenzi and his captains were dangling from the battlements.

It is a very different Pope who comes upon the scene in the latter half of the eleventh century. This is Hildebrand, who, on election, took the name of Gregory VII. A man of great piety, all his labours were devoted to the restoration of the damaged prestige of the Church. He was sixty years of age when he was made Pope in 1073. He wrote to William the Conqueror, King of England, thanking him for his good wishes, 'We are tossed about in the stormy sea by the violence of the waves.'

The visitor to St. Peter's will find in the north aisle a figure of a queen standing in a niche. It is a monument to one of the most striking women in the history of the world, the Countess Matilda, whose whole life was tirelessly devoted to supporting the Church. Her kingdom, her wealth, and a courage unsurpassed on the field of battle even by Jeanne d'Arc, made her memorable. It was at her fortress of Canossa in the hills that one of the great events of papal history took place. This is commemorated on her marble sarcophagus in St. Peter's by the scene in which Henry, Emperor of Germany, prostrates himself before Pope Gregory at Canossa.

When Gregory assumed the tiara the Castle of St. Angelo was held by a noble named Cenci, a violent man who robbed and murdered his uncle. He had been excommunicated, and in revenge he offered his services to Germany. With this powerful ally he laid tolls upon and pillaged all pilgrims who crossed the St. Angelo Bridge on their way to St. Peter's. The champion of an anti-Pope, he ravaged the domains of the Countess Matilda, whose loyal Tuscan troops repulsed him again and again. It was the custom for the pontiff to say Mass in the great church of St. Maria Maggiore on Christmas Eve. There Cenci and his band of assassins went. A tremendous storm smote Rome that night, but nothing, neither the warnings he received of possible violence nor the gale, deterred Gregory from officiating at the Mass. Suddenly the service was interrupted by the inrushing of Cenci and his murderous followers. A wild scrimmage took place at the altar, where the Pope was severely wounded in the head and stripped of his pontifical vestments. He was then forcibly hustled out of the church, thrown across a horse, bound, and in this humiliating fashion taken to the Castle of St. Angelo, where he became Cenci's prisoner. But the ruffian had not reckoned with the anger of the Roman populace, who armed themselves, rushed through the castle gates and up the stairs into the great hall, where they would have killed Cenci had not Gregory pleaded for the man prostrate at his feet.

Cenci lost no time in fleeing to the Court of Henry IV, Emperor of Germany, another enemy of the Church. The ban of excommunication fell upon the young monarch. The consequences were so dire, threatening the crown he wore, that he was compelled to seek remission of the ban by confession of error and repentance. 'If the sun should go down on February 23rd, 1077, and he was not forgiven, his crown was to be transferred to another,' wrote a counsellor, warning the obdurate King. Action was essential. He resolved to humble himself before Gregory. He was summoned to meet the Pope at the Countess Matilda's castle at Canossa.

The journey from Germany entailed the crossing of the Alps, and to avoid his enemies Henry had to make the passage via the Jura to Lake Geneva. There followed the tremendous ordeal of the St. Bernard Pass in which hundreds perished in the snow or in the yawning abysses. The Queen and her child, who accompanied the King, were tied up in hides, and, braving the wintry blasts, were dragged up the nine thousand feet of the great barrier. The sufferings of the royal party were intense. At last they reached the castle of Canossa. The gates were opened, but only the Queen was allowed to pass into the interior, where she threw herself at the Pope's feet. He received her with the greatest tenderness.

Henry was not permitted to take his followers into the inner courtyard of the castle lest he resort to treachery. Nor was he allowed to enter the castle. He abased himself by laying aside his robes and wearing only a simple woollen garment. For three days he paced up and down the outer courtyard, awaiting the summons to the Pope's presence. In those long hours the iron entered into his soul, but he kept a mask of humility. Barefooted, cold, in humble attire, the proud young King waited and waited. Finally he was admitted, and flung himself at the feet of Gregory, who, in tears, raised him up, saying, 'It is enough, it is enough!' The ban of excommunication was revoked. But it was soon evident that Henry was dissembling. The Pope watched him depart in sorrow and apprehension.

Within a few years, in March, 1084, the vengeful Henry was at the gates of Rome. They treacherously opened to his army. In the Castle of St. Angelo the Pope, with the defiant Countess Matilda to support him, faced what seem inevitable defeat. The King began to build a great wall around the castle, prelude to a grim siege. He was determined to repay the Pope for the humiliation he had suffered at Canossa. The end of Gregory seemed inevitable despite the strength of the castle. Henry seized the empty throne at St. Peter's and placed his nominee upon it, as Pope Clement III.

Then help came from an unexpected source. Robert Guiscard, the Norman Duke of Naples, had driven the Saracens before him, and after a brilliant victory over the Byzantine forces, stood before the walls of Constantinople. At this moment he received a letter from Pope Gregory appealing for his help. Leaving his army in the hands of his son, he started immediately for Rome. All Italy, Normans, Apulians and Tuscans, rose behind him. With thirty thousand horse and sixty thousand foot Guiscard approached Rome. At the threat of this force Henry and his anti-Pope fled. The Norman knight 'appeared like a lion in the Christian capital of the world,' said a chronicler. Soon his banner waved before the Castle of St. Angelo, which opened to him joyously. Guiscard severely punished the treacherous Romans, and the city was looted by his troops. More damage to ancient monuments was done by his army than in all the centuries since the downfall of the Roman Empire.

In the midst of this state of affairs Henry returned with new forces. Flight became imperative, and Gregory, with Guiscard, retreated to the Duke's feudal territory of Apulia. In that sad journey the Benedictine Pope paid a visit to his beloved monastery at Monte Cassino and was overwhelmed at the sight of the narrow cell in which his youth had been spent, before the cares of his great office had broken him. Then on he went again, to the Duke's fortress at Salerno, in a country rich with oranges, palms and vines. There the Duke left him to rejoin his army in the East. Gregory, worn out by his trials, died within a short time at Salerno.

Seventy years later the master of the Castle St. Angelo was an Englishman, Nicholas Brakspeare, called Pope Adrian IV, formerly Bishop of St. Albans. Elected in 1154 through the

influence of the Emperor Barbarossa, he was the only Englishman who ever occupied the Pontiff's chair.[7] He crowned
the Emperor a year after his own election, in times marked
by violent upheavals. Arnold of Brescia, an ascetic reformer,
led a crusade against the growing temporal power of the
popes. He was captured, brought to Rome, imprisoned in the
castle, and finally burnt alive, whereupon his ashes were
scattered in the Tiber. When Adrian died the state of Rome
was so menacing that the cardinals held their Conclave for
the election of his successor inside the walls of the castle.

Through the next three centuries the old fortress was a
storm centre. Rienzi the Tribune sought refuge there, and
fled in disguise from it to Bohemia in 1347. Its possession was
incessantly contested by popes and anti-popes. It suffered
heavy damage when the anti-Pope Clement VII refused to
surrender it to the papal troops. What remained of the
marble casing was stripped from the walls for street pavements. The popes, constantly on the run for safety from St.
Peter's to the castle, constructed a private passage upon a
battlemented wall. It was finished by Alexander VI, fortunately for Clement VII, who, when the Constable of Bourbon
broke into Rome in 1527 with his cut-throat German and

[7] Rome, the mother of superstition and fable, believed firmly for many centuries in a popess, who was an Englishwoman. In olden times the pope after
his enthronement at St. Peter's went in solemn procession to take possession
of his palace at the Lateran. The route lay via the St. Angelo bridge, past the
Colosseum and up the steep Via di San Giovanni. It was in this street that an
episode occurred regarding the persistent legend of a female pope. The Popess
Joan was said to be an Englishwoman who, disguised in the Benedictine habit,
rose by her great theological learning to the highest standing in the Church,
and on the death of Leo IV in A.D. 855, was elected Pope, and for two years
reigned in disguise at St. Peter's. Then one day, proceeding to San Giovanni
in Laterno along the Via di San Giovanni, the steep hill precipitated the birth
by her of a baby. The horrified crowd assaulted the Popess and her infant on
the spot. Nothing could kill this legend, and in the cathedral of Siena, in the
long series of sculptured portraits of the popes that decorate the nave, a portrait
inscribed 'Johannes VIII, Femina de Anglia' was visible until 1600, nearly
seven hundred and fifty years after it was declared she had been elected pontiff,
when it was changed into a head of Pope Zacharius, at the request of
Clement VIII.

Spanish troops, fled along it, with thirteen cardinals, from the Vatican to the castle.

Pope Clement is the most disastrous figure in the varied history of the popes. It is to his credit, however, that he encouraged the arts. He sent Michelangelo to work on the Medici tombs in Florence, and for the ten years of his papacy never lost interest in his favourite artist. In administrative affairs he showed no insight. Vacillating, treacherous, he always made the wrong decision. Under his rule the Church lost millions of its adherents. He quarreled with Henry VIII, and by his obduracy caused the loss of England as a Catholic country. With a little tact in dealing with Queen Elizabeth, who it is alleged made overtures to Rome on her accession, he might have won it back. But the most serious charge against him was that by his duplicity in playing off France against Charles V he brought the army of the latter, under the Constable of Bourbon, to the gates of Rome.

The sack of the city in 1527 is one of the most horrible stories in history. It may be said that Rome never recovered from it. The carnage continued for three days and nights. The most atrocious tortures were visited upon the inhabitants. The city which saw a great renaissance of art under Raphael and Michelangelo was put to the sword and the torch. Cardinals, princes and the common people suffered alike at the hands of the pitiless soldiers. Cardinal Numalio, unlucky enough not to get into the Castle of St. Angelo before its portcullis fell, was taken from his bed, dressed in his robes, put into a hearse and paraded through the burning city, while a horde of drunken soldiers and prostitutes shouted blasphemous songs in imitation of the Church's canticles. In the end he was lowered into the crypt of a church, to be buried alive unless a ransom was paid. Cardinal Ponzetta was seized in his house, held to ransom for twenty-six thousand ducats and then, with his hands tied behind his back and a rope round his neck, the old Cardinal was dragged through the streets of Rome. He died soon afterwards in abject poverty.

There was an old scholar in Rome, Fabio of Ravenna, who had once lived in the house of Raphael when the great artist had turned his attention to the preservation of the antiquities of Rome. Fabio repaid his kindness by translating Greek and Latin texts. They worked together on a book which was ready to appear in 1527. Fabio had been a tutor of the young prince from Mantua, Federico Gonzaga, to whom he had shown the statue of Laocoön, discovered in 1516. The old scholar, now penniless, was not spared by the murderous soldiers of Charles V. As he could not pay the ransom demanded, he was left to die of his wounds in a wayside hostel. In the sack of Rome thirteen thousand houses were put to the torch, thirty thousand inhabitants lost their lives, and after the ordeal of the sword and the torch the terrible plague followed.

On his flight along the covered way from the Vatican to the castle the terrified Pope had seen through the loopholes the foreign soldiers pursuing his subjects and slaughtering them without quarter.

In the castle, along with Clement and his cardinals, there was a remarkable man of genius in that age of Da Vinci, Raphael, Michelangelo and the shining stars of the Renaissance—one Benvenuto Cellini, goldsmith, sculptor, inventor, murderer, on his own confession, liar by his own proof, and man of letters as well as of arts, by witness of his entrancing autobiography. He told his own arresting story of the part he played in the siege of the castle, which, if a quarter be true, is still sufficiently exciting. He narrates how from the battlements of 'The Angel' he fired a culverin at a Spaniard down in the meadow and cut him in two, which greatly astonished the Pope, who had witnessed it.

'Whereupon the Pope raising his hand, made the sign of the Cross broadly over my face, gave me his blessing, and his pardon for all homicides I had committed, or ever should commit, in the

service of the Church Apostolic. So I left him and on the rampart
again I went on firing without stopping and hardly was shot of
mine in vain. My drawing, my fine studies and my skill in music
were all drowned in the roar of those guns; and were I to tell
minutely all the fine things which I did in that infernally cruel
'business, I should strike the world with wonder.'

Earlier in his career Pope Clement received money from
Henry VIII, who promised him support during a time when
the powerful Colonna had threatened the Pope's supremacy.
But now he had no friends. It happened, however, that the
Constable of Bourbon, in the act of leading his men up a
scaling-ladder, had been killed. Cellini claimed credit for the
fatal shot, but Cellini claimed to have done many wonderful
things. The infuriated soldiers redoubled their efforts, yell-
ing, 'Blood and Bourbon!' The mailed Spaniards, drunk with
blood and crazed for loot, spread terror around them. They
stripped the churches, divided among them the nuns in the
convents, and diced for the captive daughters of Roman senators. From the ramparts of the castle Clement watched the
city swept by flames. In the end he could do nothing but sue
for peace. The terms were stiff. With his thirteen cardinals
the Pope was to remain a prisoner in the castle until a ransom
of four hundred thousand ducats of gold had been paid, after
which he might leave. Within seven months of the sack of
Rome, in the dark of a December night, Clement, disguised as
a market gardener, was allowed to slip out of the Castle of St.
Angelo and to seek refuge at Orvieto. Thus, with a plague following the famine and devastation, Rome was brought to
ruin in the height of the Renaissance, at a time when Leonardo da Vinci and Raphael were recently dead, when Titian
was painting in Venice and Michelangelo was hiding in
Florence.

The tale of blood continues within those dark walls. Cardinal Caraffa was strangled after the judge had spent eight
hours summing up his crimes. In the hour of his death his
brother was beheaded. The prisons of the castle are there

to-day, and one wonders what is the story of these walls, though one would shudder to hear it. The rack, the strangler's cord, the headsman's axe, and death in far worse forms, by slow starvation in the dark *oubliettes*, drew its victims from these grim cells. Benvenuto Cellini himself was destined to be a prisoner in a cell still shown, and from which he made the sensational escape he so vividly described in his memoirs.

II

The long tale now brings us to the episode of the Cenci. The fate of Beatrice Cenci provided Shelley with his great drama, and thus made known to English readers the tragedy familiar to all Italians. Goaded by the devilish cruelty and lusts of Count Francesco Cenci, his daughter Beatrice, together with his second wife, hired assassins to kill him in his sleep. Tormented on the rack, the wife confessed, but Beatrice withstood the torture. They were sentenced by the Pope to be tied to horses' tails, dragged through the streets, and then beheaded. Beatrice's two brothers, also charged, were similarly sentenced. Against these terrible sentences the cardinals and princes of Rome made appeal. The most notable advocate, Faranacci, undertook their defence. He made a speech of four hours' duration, and of such eloquence, in the Council Hall within the castle, that the Pope, greatly moved, spent the whole night studying the papers with a cardinal. He contemplated pardoning the four accused when news was brought to him of matricide in a noble Roman family. Exasperated, and having in mind also the confiscation of the vast Cenci estates, he ordered all the Cencis to be executed, granting a reprieve to the younger brother, Bernardino, an adolescent, who owed his life to the Confraternity of St. Marcello, which had the yearly privilege of liberating two prisoners condemned to death. The Pope ordered Bernardino to be present on the scaffold to witness the execution of his mother, brother and sister.

Throughout the trial the beauty and nobility of Beatrice had moved all beholders. On a May morning, on a high scaffold built in the square before the bridge of St. Angelo, mother, son and daughter met their doom on the executioner's block. A beautiful portrait, said to be that of Beatrice Cenci, erroneously attributed to Guido Reni, greatly moved Shelley on his visit to Rome, after he had been given a manuscript version of the story. On seeing this portrait he called Beatrice Cenci 'one of the loveliest specimens of the work of Nature.' He went to look at the vast and gloomy palace of the Cenci, sinister to this day, and decided to write his drama. This portrait similarly moved Dickens when he saw it thirty years later. Shelley had hopes that his great play would be produced in London, but the subject of incest was taboo. It was not until 1886 that it was performed before three thousand people, and made a tremendous impression. But the play, like the story itself, remains 'too ideal and too terrible for ordinary occasions'—as the leading actress said.

A belief in magic was still strong in the seventeenth century, and another prisoner here, Giacinto Centini, was accused of exercising his evil powers in order to procure the death of Pope Urban VIII. He was arrested, thrown into a cell in the castle, and after torture was beheaded by the papal headsman. The bell that was tolled for these executions still hangs above the battlements. Centini was not the last magician to be incarcerated there. After a long career of humbug Cagliostro was arrested and flung into prison, where all his arts failed to effect his release.

Ironically, the cells adjoin a little court much used in the time of Leo X for elaborate theatrical performances. Ariosto's *Suppositi* was acted here, and the scenery was painted by Raphael. While Pope Leo was examining with his magnifying glass the artist's designs, Cardinal Petrucci was being strangled to death a few yards away. The cells retain the memory of only their most tragic or illustrious occupants. Here is the one that held the brave Giordano Bruno, whose thought was in advance of his day. He was taken from one of these cells and burnt for heresy. The first cell was the scene of the strangling of Cardinal Caraffa. One observes here, as in all the successive cells, the shaft for the swift disposal of the corpse, in view, and in mind therefore, of the wretched victim. Centuries later, when the Italian Government began fresh excavations in the castle, these deep shafts were found loaded with skeletons. The second cell once held the condemned wife of Count Cenci, and in the next cell young Beatrice, unbroken in spirit, passed her last night on earth before mounting the scaffold across the bridge, on September 11th, 1599.

The fourth cell held Benvenuto Cellini, accused of having stolen jewels from the papal treasury, probably during the sack of 1527, when he helped the Pope to pick off the jewels from the papal tiara and hide them. His cell had enough light for him to work by, and on the wall is shown the cross he drew in gratitude, he declares, for the holy apparition that came to console him. It was from this cell he made his sensational flight. Side by side with this misery the popes and cardinals worked, feasted and slept in their sumptuously decorated apartments.

It is an odd fact that Clement VII gave the castle its first and only bathroom, decorated with mythological frescoes.[8] The great artists of the Renaissance, Raphael, Michelangelo, Giulio Romano, del Vaga and others, designed and decorated the papal suites and council chambers, all within a few yards of the dungeons, the cells, and the *oubliettes* concealed, even, in the reception-rooms. The Hall of Apollo has a trap-door in its pavement covering a cellar at the bottom of a forty-foot chute. The next room is the chapel of Leo X, for the altar of which Raphael painted a Madonna. One room has decora-

---

[8] Pius XII has advanced with the times in his toilet. A Rome newspaper of August 16th, 1948, describing the Pope's day at Castle Gondolfo, recorded— 'La mattina si alza alle 6 e dopo essere personalamente fatto la barba col rasorio elletrica, celebra la messa.'—He rises at six in the morning, and, after shaving himself with an electric razor, celebrates Mass.

tions devoted to the story of Cupid and Psyche, in ten panels, by Pierin del Vaga, presenting twelve amorous episodes of that great pagan love-story.

It was in an adjacent suite that Pope Alexander VII entertained Christina, the ex-Queen of Sweden, an apostate. During her visit she fired the great octagonal cannon called La Spinosa,[9] taken from the army of the Constable of Bourbon. One of the balls struck the iron gates of the Villa Medici on the Pincio, where the dint it made in the bronze left door is still visible. She held fantastic artistic seances, fancied herself as a connoisseur of the arts, and left funds for the performance of military symphonies. But she left almost nothing to her relations or dependents. She lived regally in the Corsini Palace, which had been occupied in turn by Catherine Sforza, by the Poet-Cardinal di S. Giorgio, who entertained Michelangelo for a year, but gave him no commission, 'being of small understanding in art,' explained Vasari, and by Erasmus. It contained a deadly *oubliette*. The trap-door in the salon floor shot the victim who stood on it down a hudred feet, out of sight forever. When Prince Corsini was making repairs in the nineteenth century the bones of the nameless victims were found in a large heap at the bottom of the chute.

Europe rang with stories of the amazing conduct of the ex-queen of Sweden. Even the Romans found her too much for their strong stomachs, and when she died in 1689 Pasquino, the public satirist, fired one of his squibs:

Regina senza Regno,
Christiana senza Fede,
E donna senza Vergogna.[10]

[9] The cannon of the castle thundered again on New Year's Eve, 1720, when, in the Roman palace of the Old Pretender, Bonnie Prince Charlie was born. It was claimed that a new star appeared in the heavens that night. It must have been an unlucky one. He died sixty-eight years later, the wreck of a man, in the arms of his illegitimate daughter, the Duchess of Albany, in the palace in which he had been born.

[10]   Queen without a Realm,
   Christian without a Faith,
   And a Woman without Shame.

With the oncoming of the eighteenth century the cells of the castle held political rather than criminal prisoners. The fight for the liberation of Italy against her oppressors was beginning. Near to the chapel of Clement XII, where the condemned were taken for their last confession, there is the courtyard in which innumerable victims last saw the light of day. It carries the ominous name of 'The Shooting Court.'

In the next hundred years the old castle witnessed a rapid series of revolts. A pope fled, Napoleon promised Italy freedom, and then enslaved and sacked it. The flag of a rabble evoked by the French Revolution waved from the turret. Throughout the reign of Pope Sixtus V the castle had been the repository of the vast wealth hoarded by that Pope. The jewels, mitres, triple crowns, with gold and silver, amounted in value in 1586 to a million golden scudi. Every year five millions were added in current coin. All this treasure was kept in three iron-bound chests that are still visible. In 1796 this wealth—thirteen million gold francs—was given by Pius VI to pay the ransom demanded by the French. It was paid in vain.

Later Murat, briefly Governor of Rome, placed his banner there, to give place to that of the liberating English, which in turn was lowered for the restored papal flag. But the days of the temporal power of the popes were numbered. Napoleon captured and exiled the gentle, intelligent and devout Pius VI, and later he captured and exiled his successor, Pius VII, who, in 1814, came back to Rome. Under the wise rule of his enlightened Secretary of State, Cardinal Consalvi, it looked as if a liberal policy would heal stricken Italy. But the reactionary Leo XII followed, and the evil days returned. The castle cells were again filled, the shootings were renewed. Niggardly, avaricious, yet a good administrator, Leo XII was notorious for his love affairs. Handsome and elegant in manner, he was a dangerous Don Juan, the father of several illegitimate children. The former Pope, anxious to remove him

from temptation during his early career, sent him as Nuncio
to Cologne, for it was known that one of his mistresses was
the wife of a captain in the Papal Guard. When, in 1823, Leo
was elected Pope at sixty-four years of age, his health had
been greatly impaired by his excesses. 'You have elected a
dead man,' he said to the cardinals after the Conclave, and
showed them his legs, fearfully swollen. His first act was to
summon and dismiss the enlightened Consalvi, whom he detested. The Cardinal gave an account of this interview to his
friend, the Duchess of Devonshire. He had gone to it in sound
health. He returned a broken man, and in four days he was
dead. The ugliest rumours were at once current in Rome.

Under Pope Leo's rule, and that of his new prefect of
Rome, flogging was re-established as a punishment. The old
feudal days seemed to have returned. Severe laws were passed
against the Jews. They were placed under the surveillance of
the Holy Inquisition, and they were forbidden to have servants or to hire Christian nurses, to make love to a Catholic, to
have membership in any society or club, to possess property
or land, to change dwelling-places or live outside the
crowded, insanitary Ghetto, in which they had to be at a pre-
scribed hour or suffer arrest. Other indignities and oppres-
sions were devised for them at a time when a young English
Jew named Benjamin Disraeli was starting a career that led
to the premiership of the richest and most powerful country
in the world. The Roman Jews had been treated with great
liberality under Sixtus V, since, as he said, they 'were of
the family from whom Christ came.' Now Leo XII restored
the orders of Gregory XIII, made two hundred and fifty years
earlier, compelling the Jews to attend a service and to listen
to the preaching of a Catholic priest. Crushed together and
overcome by heat, they were watched over by an official who
laid an ox-whip on the shoulders of anyone who nodded or
showed inattention. Under Gregory XIII they had suffered
severely. Montaigne was in Rome in 1581, and remarked on
his enjoyment of the Lenten sermons.

'There were many excellent preachers, for instance the renegade Rabbi who preached to the Jews on Saturday afternoons in the church of the Trinita. Here was always a congregation of sixty Jews who were bound to be present. This preacher had been a famous doctor amongst them, and now he attacked their belief by their own arguments out of the mouths of their rabbis and from the words of the Bible. He had admirable skill and knowledge of the subject, and of the languages necessary for the elaboration of the same.'

All that was in 1581. Now, in 1823, under Leo XII, the evil days of this kind of persecution had returned. Leo restored Latin as the language of the civil as well as the ecclesiastical courts. He restored to the barons their feudal rights and renewed the law of asylum, another relic of feudal times, with the result that throughout the papal domains the churches harboured brigands and assassins. Capital punishment was re-established in the odious form of *morte esemplare*, so that when the murderer of a Monsignore had been flogged and hanged in the Piazza del Popolo, he was quartered and his dismembered body was displayed upon stakes. Leo restored to the Jesuits the care of all the seminaries and ecclesiastical institutions, discharged the professors from the Collegio Romano, and filled their places with Jesuits with increased stipends. Science was frowned upon, and vaccination was abolished, so that small-pox raged and thousands of Romans were disfigured for life.

Leo's ministers reflected their master's intolerance. The Holy Inquisition sentenced its victims to perpetual imprisonment in the dungeons of the Castle of St. Angelo. When the Roman Republic temporarily triumphed in 1849, fifteen forgotten prisoners came out to the light of day twenty years after their committal. Yet Pope Leo had virtues. He was honest, he reduced taxation, controlled the administration wisely, and, according to his narrow views, administered justice speedily. But the groaning public feared and hated him.

When he died, following an operation, no one lamented him and there was an outbreak of scurrilous epigrams:

> *Tre dispetti ci feste, O Padre Santo:*
> *Accettare il Papato, viver tanto,*
> *Morir di Carneval per esser pianto.*[11]

A simple, harmless old man succeeded Leo as Pope. Pius VIII reigned for only twenty months. Austria, and Cardinal Albani, dominated him. He easily burst into tears. When he died in 1830 Rome scarcely knew he had been and gone. Gregory XVI proved to be of sterner stuff. He suppressed the last vestiges of medieval cruelties and privileges. Floggings, tortures, secret enquiries, proscriptions, the rights of asylum, were all abolished. Political prisoners were treated with more humanity, but the effect of years of coercion remained. Macaulay was in Rome in 1838, and wrote a scathing denunciation of the social and political atmosphere in which he found himself:

'I can conceive nothing more insupportable than the situation of a layman who should be a subject of the Pope. In this government there is no avenue to distinction for any but priests. Every office of importance, diplomatic, financial and judicial, is held by clergy. A prelate armed with the most formidable powers, superintends the police of the streets. . . . Corruption infects all public offices. Old women above, liars and cheats below—that is Papal administration. The States of the Pope are, I suppose, the worst governed in the civilized world; and the imbecility of the police, the venality of the public servants, the desolation of the country, and the wretchedness of the people, force themselves on the observation of the most heedless traveller. It is hardly an exaggeration to say that the population seems to consist chiefly of foreigners, priests, and paupers.'

Something of the old tyranny returned with Pius IX in

---

[11] Three things, O Holy Father, thou didst wrong:
Accept the Papacy and live so long,
Then die and check the Carnival's gay throng.

1846. The prisons filled, the Castle of St. Angelo again played
its sinister role. On the surface there never was a more pleasing pope. Well-born, as a youth he had come to Rome to join
the Noble Guard, but because of epilepsy found himself rejected. He became for a time a cafe-haunter and was popular
in the *salons*. He was endowed from birth with a radiant
beauty that never left him. To this natural asset he added the
technique of a born actor. Voice, gesture, looks, conquered
all who came near him. The disappointed youth owed his
career in the Church to Pius VII, a distant relative, who assured him his epilepsy could be overcome by prayer. He believed then that he had a call. The epilepsy vanished and he
took holy orders.

A gift for extempore preaching revealed itself. To a beautiful presence and voice he added a sense of theatre. With his
fine head shining in the gloom of the church, a skull on the
cushion beside him, a thigh-bone steeped in spirits and set
alight to illustrate the terrors of Hell, he created a sensation.
To this theatrical production he added a real devotion to
duty. He worked hard among the poor, he undertook a mission to Chile that would have daunted the strongest spirit
with its ardours of travel, stormy seas, torrid plains and fever
jungles. Pure in every act of his life, he was doomed to become a beautiful nonentity, dominated by his sinister Secretary of State, Cardinal Antonelli, who amassed great wealth
and was so hated that on his death he had to be secretly
buried at night to avoid the ire of the public.

Pope Pius had no judgment. Vain, weak, vacillating, faced
in 1848 by the angry populace he had deserted in its struggle
against the foreign oppressor, he fled from Rome. Under the
calculating Antonelli's rule terror walked abroad again on
the return of the Pope after the fall of the abortive Roman
Republic of 1849. The Holy Inquisition was renewed. Sudden arrests, indictments without witnesses or the right of defence, shootings, penal servitude in chains, infamous proc-
esses and merciless sentences were the order of the day. The

liberty of all who dared to criticise the papal rule was menaced. Spying and private vengeance resulted in savage sentences of exile against which there was no appeal. The cells
of the Castle of St. Angelo were full to overflowing in the
years 1850–70. All this was supported by the hated French
troops backing the papacy. For twenty years their flag flew
over the city.

On the anniversary of the revolt of 1849 some young art
students were caught preparing to celebrate the day with
fireworks. They were sentenced to imprisonment for twenty
years for no other crime than demonstrating against the Austrian oppression, tacitly supported by the Church. But this
tyranny was doomed. Led by King Victor Emanuel, in whose
veins there was not a drop of Italian blood, and by Garibaldi,
Liberty was on the march. Young patriots slipped out of
Rome to enlist under the King's banner. The exiles and emi-
grants flocked to Turin.

One Sunday in 1866, a day of carnival, some young aristo-
crats gathered in Rome for supper. They boyishly rose and
drank to Italy and Victor Emanuel. They were young,
ardent, and the toast was given in the flush of conviviality. It
doomed them. A boy of twenty-four, Count Carpegna, the
oldest at the supper-party, was called upon by the police,
summoned before an official and asked for the names of all
those who had drunk the toast. He refused to give them. He
was ordered to leave the Papal States forthwith. He was sun-
dered from his home and his friends. A special audience with
the Pope was of no avail. A friend, Prince Paolo Borghese,
who came to say good-bye to him, also carried his passport in
his hand. He likewise had to leave within three days.

Their exile was not to be of long duration. Garibaldi and
his volunteers crossed the papal frontier in the autumn of
1867, and stood under the walls of Rome. They were defeated, but returned three years later and triumphed. On the
memorable September 20th, 1870, the Italian soldiers opened
a breach in the old Aurelian wall near the Porta Pia and

entered the Eternal City. The next day the papal banner was lowered on the Castle of St. Angelo after a thousand years, and the fortress with its long and bloody history became a monument, incomparable in the richness of its episodes and in its power to evoke the stormy past.

III

The way to the Castle of St. Angelo is across a comparatively modern bridge, but here again we are walking on the very stones of history as we approach the monumental pile dominating the sky.

When the Emperor Hadrian planned his sepulchre in the Gardens of Domitia, as the site was then called, there was a bridge that crossed the Tiber about a hundred yards downstream, built by Nero, but destroyed later by Aurelian, as it weakened the orbit of his defensive wall. Hadrian built a new bridge, and called it the Pons Elius, using one of his names. It originally had eight arches.[12] It was intended solely as an approach to the mausoleum. This bridge existed almost wholly in its original form until 1894, when it was grossly mutilated, in the era of vandalism, by the public authorities intent on the 'improvement' of Rome at the cost of some of its finest monuments. The river-side bastions of the castle were demolished, and a boulevard was driven along the side of the Tiber in a preposterous imitation of Paris. Although all Europe united in protest, the tower of Nicholas V was swept away and the castle was severed from the river. But no vandalism can divorce what remains of the ancient bridge from its venerable history. It long offered the only and direct approach to the mausoleum and to St. Peter's. Across it for sixteen hundred years millions of pilgrims from all over the earth have journeyed to worship at the shrine of St. Peter.

[12] Visitors from Newcastle-upon-Tyne have a particular interest in this bridge. Their city owes its name to the castle built by Henry II but there was a settlement in Roman times that was connected with Hadrian's Wall by a bridge called Pons Aelius. This Roman colony created the first coal port of any importance in the ancient world.

What a pageant of history has flowed across this bridge, of which four pilons and three original arches remain! Here in the crowd, had stood Dante watching the pilgrims come and go. The throng was so large in the Jubilee Year, 1300, that a barrier was placed down the center of the bridge to divide the up and down traffic. Dante records the time and scene exactly in his *Inferno:*

> Come i Roman per l'esercito molto,
> L' anno del Giubbileo, su per lo ponte
> Hanno a passar la gente modo colto,
> Che dall' un lato tutti hanno la fronte
> Verso il castello, e vanno a Santo Pietro,
> Dall' altra sponda vanno verso il monte.[13]

It was here in Rome that the heaviest blow of his life fell upon him. He had been sent on a mission from his beloved Florence. His party, the Whites, were in power, and they despatched an embassy to protest against the papal policy directed at the suppression of the Republic. While Dante was in Rome, Charles of Valois arrived in Florence, made peace with the Pope, and espoused the cause of the Blacks. Restored to power, they immediately outlawed the rival party, and, charging Dante with fraudulent conversion of public funds, condemned him and his embassy to be burnt alive if caught.

Never again was Dante to set foot in his native Florence, and there now began the sorrowful twenty years spent in exile, mostly in poverty, that ended only with his death in Ravenna.

'I have gone about as a beggar, showing against my will the wound of fortune,' he wrote. 'Verily, I have been a ship without sails and without rudder, driven to various harbours and shores by the dry wind which blows from pinching pov-

[13] 'Thus the Romans because of the great throng in the year of Jubilee, upon the bridge have taken means to pass the people over. So that on the one side all have their faces towards the Castle, and go to St. Peter's; at the other ledge, they go towards the Mount' (*Inferno,* Canto XVIII, 28–33).

erty. And I have appeared vile in the eyes of many who, perhaps from some report of me, had imagined me in a different
guise.'[14]

With what mounting ecstasy the religious pilgrims crossing the bridge, and turning left through the Porta S. Pietro,
must have approached the end of their long, perilous journey
through foreign lands, over dangerous mountains with all
the hazards of robbery and pestilence. Among the most celebrated and beautiful of ancient bridges, it was to them, after
perilous months of journeying on foot, almost as the gateway to
Paradise. The pilgrims represented every land to whose far
corners the names of Christ and His disciple Peter, rock of the
Church, had penetrated. Soon at the high altar of the great
basilica they would prostrate themselves, where St. Peter lay
in his sarcophagus of gilt bronze. The dream of all Christians,
having crossed the bridge and passed the castle, was fulfilled
here. Young, old, lame, blind, poor, rich—somehow, through
time and distance, they arrived.

Here came in A.D. 728 the King of Wessex, who abdicated,
stayed and founded a hostel for English pilgrims. Here came
a little boy from England, with his father on a pious errand,
destined to be famous as Alfred the Great. Possibly he lingered on the bridge to look in boyish wonder at the wares
displayed in its booths, much of it doubtless tourist junk.
Those booths obstructing the bridge were demolished in 1449
by Nicholas V, who strengthened the parapets which had
broken under the pressure of the crowds, resulting in the
drowning of one hundred and seventy persons. He built two
little chapels on the bridgehead, removed by Clement VII,
who put in their place the statues of St. Peter and St. Paul.

[14] It is probable that the writing of *The Divine Comedy* began shortly before
this visit to Rome. The first lines are—

> *Nel mezzo del cammin di nostra vita*
> *mi ritrovai per una selva oscura.*

'In the middle of the journey of our life I found myself in a dark wood.' Dante
was thirty-five in 1300, and the Vision that opens the *Inferno* takes place in the
early morning of the Friday before Easter, in that year of the pilgrimage.

The bridge was always a scene of vivid life, of processions coming and going from St. Peter's or the Castle of St. Angelo. Frederick II dubbed a hundred knights on it in 1452. Leo X hanged forty conspirators there in 1517. Raphael, Michelangelo and Cellini, on their way to work, must have seen the swinging corpses. In 1669 Clement IX had the fine idea that 'an avenue of the heavenly host should be assembled to welcome the pilgrims to the shrine of the great apostle.' So Pope Alexander VIII called in his beloved Bernini, who designed for him the ten angels with such gusto that ever since they have been called 'the breezy maniacs of Bernini.'

The cheering crowd and the murderous mob have swarmed across the bridge, century after century. The great warrior-cardinal, Vitelleschi, who won back the papal throne for the treacherous Eugene IV, was hacked to death here by his hired assassins. The brother of Benvenuto Cellini, grievously wounded by an *arquebusier* in a street brawl, reached the bridge, to sink in his life's blood. Cellini boasts of avenging his brother by stabbing the soldier to death in the doorway of his house nearby. It was across this bridge that the pompous funeral of Clementina Maria Sobieski, wife of the Old Pretender, self-styled King of England, made its way to St. Peter's, where her mosaic portrait, held by marble cherubs, looks down on Canova's beautiful memorial of the three last Stuarts.

Even to-day, the old bridge can add a memorable footnote to history. When, for the first time, the pageantry of its story in my mind, I stood upon it, I found my path barred by officious soldiers opening a way for an oncoming cavalcade. Trumpets sounded, banners waved, hoofs clattered and cheers filled the air as a squadron of plumed *cuirassiers*, their breastplates gleaming, rode by, six abreast. Following at a distance, superbly mounted on a white horse, came a sturdy, black-uniformed man, arrogantly impressive. Behind him, against the brilliant sky, like a drop scene of history, stood the old castle. And while I looked at the crowd cheering their idol,

Benito Mussolini, none of us could foresee that within a decade his corpse would dangle, head downwards, a victim of mob fury, like so many others whose bodies had swung from the battlements behind him.

II

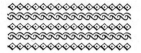

LUTHER AND FEDERICO GONZAGA

I

ONE perfect Sunday morning in the late autumn, when the sun vividly played amid the dark parasol pines behind the Pincio, I went down into the Piazza del Popolo. The crowd was coming out of the church where Luther heard his last Roman Mass. Across the square a cafe had lowered its awning. I took a chair and watched the pageant flowing over the old cobbles. Near me, flanking the opening of the Corso, were the domed and colonnaded twin churches of S. Maria di Monte Santo and S. Maria dei Miracoli, Pope Alexander VII's commission carried out by Fontana and Bernini. Since they were ordered at the same time and built by the same builders, why, I wondered, should they differ minutely in height and shape? But why, I wondered again, were two such churches built so near to each other? Was it so that they might open for worship in shifts, for just now the well-dressed Romans, with their exquisite and perfectly laundered children, were drifting in and out of the right-hand church, while the left was closed.

The waiter brought me a vermouth and a *specialité de la maison*, a hot, succulent pasty, sugared, with a spiced-macaroni interior. A very decrepit old man stood before me with a basket of flowers that was a cascade of colours. I wanted to buy the lot for the pleasure of both of us, but I contented myself with a bunch for my companion. The old man raised his battered hat with the gesture of a cavalier. A smart little boy in the shortest and tightest of lavender shorts, with the perfectly shaped brown legs of Italian children, his fair front lock fixed by a hairpin, led a black poodle, as graceful as himself, to his young mother waiting in a car. His mission was to carry three ice-cream cones from the cafe, one for mother, one for himself, one for the poodle. All three slowly consumed them, whereupon a patient young father drove them all away. I looked across to the old obelisk, *circa* 1300 B.C., an alien from Heliopolis, once set up on the *spina* of the Circus Maximus. Moses may have seen it by the Nile in the reign of Rameses II. Eighteen centuries have passed since its journey to Rome, and certainly the Roman crowd, cheering the charioteers along the race-track, saw its slender shadow fall across the rutted sand. The obelisk was moved to the Piazza in 1589 by Sixtus V.[1]

Beyond it rose the Pincio, from whose balustrade all visitors view Rome. By this hill Nero was buried in a porphyry tomb. Legend said that out of his grave grew a great walnut-tree, the home of a multitude of crows. Pope Paschal (1099–1118) dreamt they were demons and that the Virgin commanded him to cut down the tree and build a church in her honour. It was made a parochial (*populus*) church, and so it was named Santa Maria del Popolo. It was restored later by Piranesi.

The crowd now on its steps was having a good gossip after Mass. In my mind's eye I reclothed these gay Romans with sixteenth-century costumes, stomachers and parti-coloured hose. It became the crowd that once gathered to greet Pope Alexander's daughter, Lucrezia Borgia, coming out of church after returning public thanks at her betrothal to her third

---

[1] It was for long a favourite diversion of the joyous Romans to walk with closed eyes from the Obelisk in an attempt to reach the opening of the Corso. You make that journey to-day, with both eyes open, at the peril of your life. It is on the fountain round this obelisk that the visitor encounters his first Roman lions. They are all over Rome, the most amiable beasts in happy repose with fascinating folded paws. It is difficult to believe they could ever have eaten the Christians.

husband, Alfonso d'Este. She was twenty-one, and was only thirteen when she married Giovanni Sforza, Lord of Pesaro, on June 12th, 1493. Her father, Pope Alexander VI, gave a great banquet in her honour at the Castle of St. Angelo. The Pope and all the cardinals each had a lady beside him. There was the performance of a comedy, indecent, and games and dancing till daylight. An agent sent an account of it to the Court at Ferrara: 'We spent the whole night there. I leave it to Your Excellency to judge whether well or ill.' The Pope escorted the newly-wedded couple back to their palace. Four years later he had other plans. A divorce was sought on the grounds of Sforza's impotence. Two cardinals, after enquiry, affirmed the marriage had never been consummated. The Mantuan envoy swore it had been consummated. The divorced husband also swore he had cohabited with his wife, and openly charged that this was all Pope Alexander's scheming in order that he might himself enjoy Lucrezia. This was the basis of the incest charge, never proved, brought against the Borgia pope. Lucrezia became a bride again. She married in 1497 Alfonso d'Aragona, Duke of Bisceglia. She was twenty when this young man she loved was foully murdered by her brother Cesare. Since he would not die of his wounds from a stabbing affair, Cesare went to his sick room and had him strangled in his bed. In 1501 a marriage was arranged for her with Alfonso d'Este, eldest son of the Duke of Ferrara. The announcement of the betrothal was celebrated by Lucrezia gaily proceeding to return thanks to S. Maria del Popolo. The guns at the Castle of St. Angelo thundered. In the procession to the church she was escorted by the French and Spanish ambassadors, four bishops, three hundred horsemen, Spanish grooms in black and gold and buffoons in fancy attire. In the church there was a solemn Mass, and when the beautiful Lucrezia stepped out on to the platform before the church on this morning of September, 1501, the crowd in the Piazza del Popolo deliriously acclaimed her. The festivities lasted a month pending the arrival of the escort to take her to Ferrara. They ended on October 31st, when fifty courtesans were entertained at dinner at the Vatican. Cesare Borgia also entertained fifty at his palace, courtesans of a lower order. The Pope and Lucrezia with some cardinals came on to Cesare's banquet, and were much entertained after supper by the ladies taking off their clothes and in a state of nudity crawling on the floor between candles, in competition for chestnuts placed there by the guests.

This Piazza witnessed other spectacles connected with the betrothal. On December 23rd, 1501, there passed through its gate the cavalcade sent to escort Lucrezia to Ferrara. It was headed by the handsome Cardinal Ippolito d'Este, her brother-in-law, a blade of twenty-two. Cesare Borgia with four thousand troops and nineteen cardinals, together with two hundred liveried servitors, awaited him. Cesare embraced the young Cardinal and escorted him to the Vatican. A few days later, with the Pope on his throne in the Sala Paolina, Lucrezia was married by proxy.

On January 6th, 1502, the wedding cavalcade, with Cardinal Ippolito escorting Lucrezia, passed across the Piazza out through the gate en route to the expectant Alfonso at Ferrara. She carried with her the Pope's endorsement of her chastity and high moral behaviour. Strange to say, from that day she became a loving wife, an excellent mother and a Duchess beloved by her people. But the leopard cannot change its spots. She had lovers on the side—the man of letters, Cardinal Pietro Bembo, and the soldier, Francesco Gonzaga, Marquis of Mantua, the father of young Federico. Her son Ippolito in due course became a cardinal, came to Rome and built the renowned Villa d'Este, at Tivoli, where three hundred years later Liszt lived and composed for many years as the guest of Cardinal Hohenlohe.

Towards the end of her life Lucrezia became very religious. She reformed her court, and in her last ten years wore a hair shirt and confessed daily. She had much to confess. She was thirty-eight years old. The mother of this terrible brood,

Vanozza Catanei, predeceased her by three months. Leo X
sent his chamberlains to Vanozza's funeral and honoured her
as if she were Pope Alexander's widow, which she was in fact
if not in name. Sanudo recorded the death of this mother of
the assassinated Duke of Gandia, of Cesare and Lucrezia: 'Yesterday she was buried in S. Maria del Popolo, whither she
was borne with great splendour, almost like a cardinal.'[2]

There was yet another scene that came crowding in my
memory as I sat at the cafe on the Piazza. Little more than a
year after Lucrezia, with her first husband, the Lord of
Pesaro, had departed through the gate, and Cesare Borgia, a
youth of eighteen, had been created a cardinal, a vicious
young man of twenty-three, Charles VIII of France, began
to create trouble for Alexander VI. He longed to be a conqueror. At first he was minded to lead a crusade against the
Turks, but the throne of Naples being in dispute, and he the
heir of the Angevins, he decided to claim it. This aroused
Pope Alexander. He had other plans and warned Charles to
leave Naples in peace, whereupon the King gathered an army
and invaded Italy. He came on like a prairie fire. In September, 1494, he was in Asti, a few weeks later he sacked Rapallo
and massacred the inhabitants. Soon he entered Florence,
welcomed as a deliverer by Savonarola, at loggerheads with
the Pope. On the last day of the year Charles marched into
Rome through the Porta del Popolo. His troops began to cross
the Piazza at three in the afternoon, and the procession of
soldiers lasted until nine o'clock, marching by the lurid light
of torches. Rome had never seen anything like it. In the
Piazza the treacherous Romans gave him the keys to the city,

[2] In a restoration of the church in the seventeenth century the stones of
Vanozza Catanei's tomb were removed together with a painting in which she
had been depicted as Saint Lucia. But things are never quite lost in Rome.
Lunching one day at Prince Doria's, a fellow guest, a young Italian admiral,
surprised me by saying that he knew where the lapidary inscription on her
tomb was. Later he escorted me to the porch of San Marco, adjoining the
Palazzo Venezia, and there on the right hand wall showed me the stone in
which Vanozza was named as the mother of Cesare and Lucrezia. For many
years it had lain, inscription downwards, as a paving-stone, and during street
repairs it was discovered and placed in the porch of the church.

they lit bonfires, put the emblem of the French lilies on their balconies, and cried 'Francia! Francia!' as the hideous little hunchback King rode by with his army of Germans, Switzers, Scottish bowmen, five thousand heavy cavalry, the flower of France, and thirty-six enormous guns. The King billeted himself in the Piazza San Marco. Alexander VI, terrified, retreated to his fortress, the Castle of St. Angelo.

After much parleying, terms were arranged and Charles went to the Vatican. The Pope came out of hiding, along the covered walk from the castle, and kissed the King. But the two men watched each other like tomcats. When Charles marched on to Naples he took with him as a hostage Cesare Borgia, who gave him the slip. Before leaving, the King founded the church of S. Trinita dei Monti, above the Piazza di Spagna, as a memorial of his visit. His conquest of Naples crowned an incredible march through Italy 'with only a piece of chalk (for billeting) and spurs.' It was not long before Charles was retreating precipitately, seriously threatened in the north. Again his army, gravely diminished by disease and loot, marched out of the Porta del Popolo in a desperate race to safety, leaving behind a fell legacy, the *mal francese*—syphilis.[3]

This square before us had probably the most famous gate in the world, for on this route the Caesars, coming from their triumphs in the barbarian north, the emperors, soldiers and saints, have passed its portal, Rome-bound, for the last seventeen centuries. Here inside the great gate in the Aurelian Wall the later multitudes had watched the execution of criminals. In 1698 Count Guido Franceschini, the villain of Browning's *The Ring and the Book*, was beheaded here while his four hired assassins were hanged. On that February day the Piazza was filled with a vast concourse on stands draped with

---

[3] One of the earliest books printed by Aldo Manuzio on his famous press at Venice, in 1497, was a work by N. Leonicenus, entitled *Libellus de morbo gallico*, dealing with the *Epidemia quam vulgo morbum Gallicum vocant*. A copy of this book, the first printed in Italy on the malady, is in the San Marco Library, Venice.

tapestries and flags. In the centre of the Piazza was a high platform with a double gallows and a block in the middle. The death procession started from the prison of the Tor di Nona, opposite the bridge leading to the Castle of St. Angelo. It made a slow progress. Each of the four assassins occupied separate tumbrils. After them came Count Guido, who, because of his rank, would go to the block instead of the gallows. They were all pinioned. A pious Father accompanied each criminal, holding a crucifix before him while the mob following joined in their contrite prayers for a blessed end. At the Piazza Pasquino, before the church of the Agonizzanti, the tumbrils halted while the Host was exposed and, as was the custom, the Benediction was pronounced upon the condemned men. Then the procession went on its way, passing the scene of the murder. At last it entered the thronged Piazza. The four assassins were hanged on the gallows, after which the axe severed the head of Guido Franceschini. As the executioner held up the Count's grisly head the face looked towards the gateway through which he and his assassins had come on Christmas Eve, 1697, to murder his young wife Pompilia and her parents. An eye-witness wrote:

'They exhibited the same signs of contrition as they had shown while being prepared for death; and just as the youngest had given special tokens during life, so it pleased God that these should appear again at death; for as the hangman was casting him off he clasped to his bosom the crucifix—that emblem of mercy by which they had just been assured of Divine pardon.'

At carnival time they brought criminals to the Piazza and executed them as a form of popular entertainment. The hangman and his assistants were clad in the costume of harlequins and punchinellos to add gaiety to the occasion. The preferred bag was a mixed one of nobility and clergy, as a spice to common criminals. Thus on Shrove Tuesday, 1650, they executed Count Soderini; in the carnival of 1720 the Abbe Volpini; and in 1737 Count Trivelli. As late as 1854 six robbers

were executed publicly here by being beaten to death before
the crowd.

II

Turning from the church of S. Maria del Popolo, let us look
at the Augustinian convent adjoining. It was here, in a former convent, that an unknown German, Martin Luther, had
his lodging in the autumn of 1510 or 1511, for the friar, recol-
lecting his visit ten years later, was never sure of the date.
'Anno Domini (if I am right) 1510, I was in Rome,' he recorded in his *Table Talk*. It is generally considered, on a
basis of relevant details, that he was there in 1511. He had
started on foot from Germany, possibly on a mission that had
something to do with Augustinian politics. The journey was
a long one in those days, and occupied some six or seven
weeks. The ten golden *gulden* he took with him were not for
travelling purposes but to fee an advocate in the papal courts.
It is possible that he journeyed through Switzerland. His ex-
penses were light, for in those days poor scholars and friars
found hospitality in a chain of monasteries throughout the
civilised world. We are apt to think of ourselves as living in
an era of enlightenment and liberty, but a medieval traveller
would be appalled by the official checks and irritations to
which the worried traveller is subject to-day.[4]

[4] A serious question is raised by the arbitrary currency controls often capri-
ciously interpreted by anonymous bureaucrats. It is difficult to assess the loss
inflicted on English scholarship and literature by the current virtual ban on
foreign travel entailed by currency restrictions. Our literature and that of
the world have been enormously enriched by writers who have been economically
free to travel and reside in foreign places for the purpose of their work. The
nineteenth century provides an impressive array of books written by devoted
scholars and leisured men of letters. Living for long years in Italy, they were
enabled, by virtue of their private incomes or earnings, to devote their whole
lives to the production of books requiring lengthy research. If such hampering
restrictions had been enforced in the post-Napoleonic period as have been
enforced in the post-Hitlerian, nineteenth-century English literature would be
seriously impoverished. Byron could not have written *Childe Harold's Pilgrimage,* Shelley *The Cenci, The Ode to the West Wind, Prometheus Unbound*
and some forty other memorable poems, Elizabeth B. Browning *Casa Guidi
Windows,* Robert Browning *The Ring and the Book, Pippa Passes,* and the best
part of his work, Ruskin *The Stones of Venice,* George Eliot *Romola,* John

Martin Luther did not have to ask for Treasury permission to use his own money. He did not have to satisfy officials, anonymous deities unapproachable except through bankers' agents, as to his purpose for travel. He filled in no forms, he required no passport, he queued at no bank or Customs barrier, nor was he asked where he was going and for how long he would stay, nor, having arrived there, was he spied upon by his Government's detectives, or the odious informers to whom it offered bribes. In Italy's famed markets he could buy a silk shirt or a timepiece without being punitively taxed, and again taxed for it—luxurious indulgence—on his return. He would not at every frontier and in every halting place be asked to produce his passport for it to be stamped and re-stamped and scribbled in. He would have smiled derisively at the preamble of that document wherein a Foreign Secretary requests all those whom it may concern (and what a legion they are!) to allow the bearer to pass freely without let or hindrance. He would probably have been rendered inarticulate had he lived in an age in which an heroic people, after two great wars for liberty, had suffered the deprivation of their freedom of movement while the political arenas rang with a babble of voices prating of Atlantic Charters, the Four Freedoms and the Bill of Human Rights. To such liberty and enlightenment Luther was not an heir. He walked across Germany, Switzerland and Italy, unrestrained, spending as and where he would, free in the great commonwealth of scholarship.

He was impressed by Italy, as every traveller must be when first he reaches this smiling land of light, of Nature's

Addington Symonds his great study of the Renaissance in Italy, among many glories of our literature. If the travel ban had existed in the eighteenth century Gibbon would not have been inspired to write *The Decline and Fall of the Roman Empire*. The influence of Italian travel alone has been enormous. To-day an author labours under the greatest difficulties, severely restricted in the length and scope of his researches, and unable to finance such legitimate assistance as he is in need of. The harvest of our intellectual achievement is being imperilled by myopic bureaucratic control, at a time when more money is squandered on useless propaganda than at any other in the world's history.

fertility and man's astonishing craftsmanship. He noted the clustering vines, the ripe pomegranates, the olives with their dowry of oil. He was struck by the richness of the monasteries, whose fasts were more luxurious than the feasts at home. The hospitals and foundling asylums impressed him with their cleanliness and efficiency. He admired, after the grossness of his own countrymen, the soberness of the Italians, though aware of their less admirable proneness to deceit, lust and crime, general everywhere, but taking a special vigour from the Italian sun.

Luther entered Rome by the Porta del Popolo, from the ancient Via Flaminia. Upon the first sight of its walls, towers and domes he had flung himself upon his knees, crying, 'Hail, Holy Rome! thrice sacred for the blood of the martyrs shed here!' and remained, it would seem, in a mood of spiritual ecstasy throughout his visit. There is a general belief that Luther became antagonistic to the Church during the time of his visit. It was not so; the Protestant was not born there. Many years were to elapse before he became its most powerful enemy and shook the Roman Church by the sweeping flood of the Reformation as no emperor, assailing it physically, had ever shaken it. When his reforming zeal was at its height and he was thundering against the occupant of the Fisherman's Chair he could not clearly remember exactly in which year he had visited Rome. 'I was like a mad saint in Rome,' he said in 1530. 'I ran through all the churches and holes; believed everything that is lied and stunk there.'

These bitter words were not on his lips in 1511. Immediately upon his entrance by the Porta he went into the church on his left, Santa Maria del Popolo, confessed, and heard the Mass, not knowing he was to become the most formidable enemy of his Church. He was in Rome at a time of great activity. Raphael was in the full flood of his power; Michelangelo, painting the ceiling of the Sistine Chapel, reached the peak of his achievement in the long life of a man of incomparable genius. All Rome was a workshop, a court and a

fortress. The young German friar saw in the streets princes
of the Church in cavalcades of state, attended by bodyguards
and courtiers. He saw carnivals and masks, hangings and be-
headings. Rome was not yet sacked. Sixteen years were to
elapse before it suffered that dreadful ordeal from which it
never really recovered.

The gulf between the theoretical sanctity of the Papacy and
its actual wickedness seemed unbridgeable.[5] Great wealth
was amassed by the vilest means. Rome was the populous
centre of the civilised world, though oddly mixed. The Venetians prevailed under Eugenius IV and Paul II, Ligurians
under Sixtus IV, Innocent VIII and Julius II, the Tuscans
under Clement VII, the Spaniards under Calixtus III and
Alexander VI, and the men of the north under Adrian VI.
A new pope meant the rise to power and wealth of a new clan
gathered from his rapacious relatives. Under Alexander VI,
Cesare Borgia had flared horrifically across the sky. The day
of wrath was nigh. In a census of the population it was found
that born Romans were a minority of the population,
that *cortigiane*, otherwise prostitutes, outnumbered honest
women. 'We cannot deny that we Romans form but a minority in this international rendezvous of the world,' wrote a
chronicler on the eve of the sack of Rome. When this event
took place in 1527 the swollen state of the Papacy is shown
by the fact that Clement VII fed 700 retainers, Cardinals
Farnese 306, Cesarini 207, Orsini 200, del Monte 200. Thirteen cardinals sought refuge with the Pope in the Castle St.
Angelo. The less fortunate were murdered, tortured or black-
mailed by the Constable of Bourbon's pikemen. In the Rome
of Julius II Luther visited 'at peril of my life'—the sights of
Rome, the Pantheon, the Colosseum, the Tarpeian Rock, the

---

[5] 'Sixtus IV, Innocent VIII, Alexander VI, Julius II, Leo X, Clement VII
are names that are inscribed in the book of human infamy as a page by themselves. The annals of no secular State can show such a succession of rulers,
profligate, self-seeking, cruel, dead to all higher responsibilities of government;
a succession—except for the few months during which Adrian VI tried to clean
the Augean stable—without a break' (*Martin Luther*, by C. Beard).

Catacomb of St. Calixtus, and the Franciscan convent on the
Capitol. He saw the Pope pass in state, he experienced the
law's delays, waiting in the papal courts. He missed little,
and while the dark infamies of Alexander VI gave place to
those of Julius II, he listened to men making mockery of the
holy mysteries as they gabbled through the Mass and gamed
on the steps of the altars. Yet there were great moments for
this pilgrim. It was not all disenchantment, as every devout
soul learns, visiting Rome. The ancient traditions, the sacred
sights, the majestic assemblies, faith enthroned on the rock of
Peter, lifted his spirit. When Luther left Rome in 1512 it was
not with disgust and denunciation, as is commonly supposed.
That was to well up later, in slow recollection and experience.
He returned to his Augustinian convent at Wittenberg having made, like all good Catholics, the great and rewarding
pilgrimage.

It may be that on a morning early in 1512, if Luther had
been standing by the bridge leading to the Castle of St.
Angelo, he would have seen a gay cavalcade saluted by the
citizens with obvious affection. At its head rode a mere boy
of eleven, beautiful to behold, a smiling face beneath a red
velvet cap, saucily worn, and a slim body, clothed in a doublet of gold damask with blue hose, seated easily on his small
white horse. Young Prince Charming saluted the citizens of
Rome as he went to the castle. He was Federico Gonzaga, son
of the Marquis of Mantua and Isabella d'Este, one of the most
cultured women of the age, whose court at Mantua was
famous as the gathering place of the foremost poets and
philosophers of all Italy. Ariosto sang Isabella's praises,
Castiglione, author of *The Courtier*, Bembo and Machiavelli
graced her court. She scoured the land for great works of art,
the friend of Mantegna, Michelangelo and Titian. In her
library there were choice Aldine editions of Virgil and
Petrarch. Her home was a treasure-house of paintings, medallions, sculpture and musical instruments. She corresponded
with Leonardo da Vinci and commissioned Bellini, Dosso

Dossi, Raphael and Perugino, all happy to serve her. In her little son Federico, whose charm had captivated Julius II, her intense spirit and love of beauty seemed reflected. The Roman public loved the princeling not only for his physical beauty, his easy manners, his bright mind, but it was also moved by the sadness of the event that exiled this child from his home and his adoring mother. On December 10th, 1508, a secret treaty known as the League of Cambray was signed. It was concluded by the Emperor Louis XII, Pope Julius II, Maximilian I and Ferdinand V, and its object was the reduction of the proud Venetian Republic. In May the following year, the Republic was defeated in the field, and lost in one day all she had patiently acquired in eight hundred years. Verona, Vicenza, Padua, all subject cities of her territory, were ravished. By an evil chance it happened, on August 9th, that the Marquis of Mantua was trapped at a farm near Legnano and taken prisoner after the recovery of Padua by the Venetians. They led Francesco Gonzaga in triumph to a prison in Venice. The Pope, hearing of this setback, angrily threw his cap on the ground and cursed St. Peter. Heavy gloom hung over the brilliant court at Mantua, where Isabella d'Este reigned while the Marquis was held in the prison tower of the ducal palace at Venice.

When the stunning news first reached the court at Mantua, Isabella's brother, Cardinal Ippolito d'Este, at once hurried there and had little Federico proclaimed successor in case the Marquis should lose his life. The Pope was implored to effect the release of the prisoner, and after long negotiations terms were arranged. But the allies looked with some suspicion on Francesco Gonzaga, who might go over to the Venetians. They insisted, therefore, before effecting his release, that his son and heir, Federico, a child of ten, should be a hostage in their hands. Vainly the distracted mother protested. She appealed to the Pope, who, satisfied that Venice had been humbled, absolved the erring Republic. In July, 1510, the Marquis was set free, and went to Bologna to meet the Pope.

He was destined to encounter his son there, but only briefly, for after bitter tears Isabella was compelled to consign the boy Federico into the custody of the Pope as a hostage for his father's good behaviour. During this brief meeting of a freed father and a captive son the artist Francia painted a portrait of the little boy. It was finished in twelve days and cost thirty ducats. The delighted father showed it to the Pope and cardinals and allowed it to go with the boy to Rome, to his mother's dismay.

Young Federico was treated kindly by the Pope, and on reaching the Vatican was housed in the Villa Belvedere, now part of the famous Vatican Galleries, with its exquisite view of the Roman Campagna and the Alban Hills. We know something of Federico's appearance by following the strange history of Francia's portrait. After having disappeared for several centuries, it suddenly came to light in an exhibition at the Burlington Fine Arts Club, in 1903. It had come out of a Gloucestershire country house, and was the property of Mr. G. A. Leatham, whose father had purchased it from the Napoleon collection. At first it was thought to be the portrait of a Medici boy, but it was ultimately identified as Francia's quick study of Federico, painted from July 29th to August 10th, 1510. In Francia's well-preserved portrait we see a boy of about ten years of age, holding a dagger in his right hand, and dressed in a black doublet and a white frilled shirt. He has a black cap jauntily set on his small head, and from his neck hangs a red ribbon with a gold medallion by Caradosso. It is a winning, chubby face, intelligent, with bright brown eyes. His long hair is fair, and the whole poise makes an engaging picture of a boy of exceptional grace. It is embellished by its contemporary setting in the romantic Italian landscape. It happened, in the strange working of Chance, that Francia's portrait was discovered, after four hundred years, within a few months of the discovery of a portrait painted by Titian of Federico's mother, from Francia's original.

Young Federico could not have had a more distinguished

background. He was born in the castle at Mantua, in a nursery furnished with tapestries from Ferrara. His father was a rough soldier of many successful campaigns, but the boy's grace and distinction seemed to be inherited from his mother. His uncle, the Duke of Ferrara, married Lucrezia Borgia, his other uncles were the Duke of Milan and Cardinal Ippolito d'Este. His godfathers were the Emperor Maximilian, then rejoicing over his grandson, the future Charles V, destined to be a good friend to Federico; Cardinal Sanseverino; and Cesare Borgia, the Pope's son, who held the child at the font.

Such was the background of the boy, of a princely house, from a court renowned for its culture, son of a gallant soldier and of Isabella, the gifted daughter of the great house of d'Este of Ferrara. It was not long after the boy's advent in Rome before it was obvious that he had wholly charmed Julius II. The old Pope doted on this graceful and intelligent boy. His lodging befitted a young prince, in the spacious villa planned by Bramante, set amid orange-groves, fountains and antiques collected by Julius II. Among these was the famous Laocoön and the beautiful Apollo, soon to be renowned as the Apollo Belvedere.

We have a portrait of the young hostage in Rome. 'His Highness,' wrote the Mantuan agent to Isabella, 'is lodged in the finest rooms of this palace, and takes his meals in a most beautiful loggia overlooking the Campagna, which may well be called the Belvedere.[6] He spends all day walking about these halls amid the gardens of orange-trees and pines, which afford him the greatest delight and amusement, but he does not neglect his singing, often sending for his master himself,

---

[6] It was in some peril from the Corsairs. The Bastion of the Belvedere was made by Paul III. It was begun by Sangallo, and after his death was completed by Michelangelo. It was finished in March 1548, part of a scheme of fortification, its purpose being to protect Rome from invasion by sea by the Barbary pirates who ravished the coast. On August 20th, 1534, a pirate fleet commanded by Barbarossa cast anchor at the mouth of the Tiber, to replenish its water. It could well have sacked Rome and have carried off the Pope into slavery, as happened to many Romans along the coast. After this scare the protecting bastion was completed.

and also repeats the Office every day, and will no doubt attend
to his lessons when Maestro Francesco Virgillio arrives.'

Singing, playing the lute, riding, knightly exercises, thus
the boy's hours were filled. He could repeat long passages
from Ovid. He went about the rooms of the Castle of St.
Angelo singing in his blithe treble voice, and spent there
much time with the old Pope. When they showed him the
papal treasury and playfully put the papal tiara on his head,
he cried, 'No! I will not be Pope, but Captain of the Church!'
a wish later fulfilled. The dark corridors and grim rooms of
the castle rang with his infectious laughter, and his graceful-
ness touched all hearts; he was like a sprig of golden mimosa
in a forest of dark oaks. Whenever he went forth into the
streets of Rome all eyes turned towards the boy Prince. He
rode a richly caparisoned steed. The purple cap jauntily stuck
on his fair curls, his dress of gold-and-white brocade, his
green belt and gilt dagger, the sturdy legs in scarlet hose,
made an enchanting picture of boyhood. The crowd loved
him, and he laughed back at them as the hoofs of his horse
rang out on the bridge of St. Angelo. If Martin Luther saw
him on that morning of 1512 he must have felt this also was
one of the sights of Rome.

Federico was now seldom out of the Pope's sight. He could
amuse and pacify him in his sudden rages. After supping
with the boy, Cardinal Bibbiena wrote to Isabella d'Este: 'O
Madonna! you have indeed a rare son, and I think you will
find more comfort in him than in anything else in the world!'
Pope Julius made him his constant companion when working, out riding or at meals. When any of the cardinals came
to dinner they occupied separate tables in the hall. Federico
always sat at the Pope's small table. In the evenings they
heard music or played backgammon, or the boy would take
his lute and sing to the Pope. Sometimes they went out to
dine with Agostino Chigi, the banker, in his fabulous villa.
The boy was befriended by Raphael, Michelangelo and the
future Pope Leo X. It was at the request of Julius II that

Raphael introduced the young Federico in his great painting *The School of Athens*. It is believed by many critics that he appears behind the Oriental philosopher Averroës in the group on the left, as the youth leaning over while Bramante draws an hexagonal figure on a slate.

The Pope took Federico with him on his visits to Urbino and Bologna, and one day in August 1512 they went hunting at Ostia. The old Pope was delighted when Federico caught a pheasant, laughed loudly and showed the boy's prize to everyone. They returned after a few days, and the Pope attended the unveiling of the central portion of Michelangelo's frescoes in the Sistine Chapel. Three days later he fell ill and seemed to be dying. The physicians could do nothing with him. Already the servants were stripping the papal apartments—traditional loot on the death of a pope. They vainly tried to prevail upon the turbulent old man to take his medicine. 'Throw those cursed medicines out of the window!' he roared. In despair they fetched Federico. 'Everyone was in despair,' wrote the Mantuan agent. 'His Holiness refused to take anything, but Signor Federico took a cup of broth with two yolks of eggs beaten up in it, and carried it himself to the bed of His Holiness, begging him to drink it for his sake. . . . It is said in Rome that Pope Julius will live, thanks to Signor Federico.'

The Pope recovered, and the boy went with him to the opening of the Lateran Council, 'wearing a sword and cuirass and a suit of white satin and gold brocade embroidered with the Greek letters "Alpha and Omega" which his mother had sent him. In his cap he carried the gold medallion of Hercules by Caradosso, which we see in Francia's portrait. The Pope was highly amused by this warlike attire. He flourished his stick at the splendidly arrayed youngster, exclaiming "Are you ready to fight me?" '

Handsome, courteous and bright, generous in his treatment of scholars and artists, the Prince, with his gay fellowship and insouciant air, won the favour and love of the whole city, so that in an atmosphere of bitter rivalries and crime he became the connecting link between all manner of men —the Pope, the cardinals, the ministers and men of genius then bringing such glory to the Renaissance. And since his influence was so great with the irascible Julius, he was regarded as the best approach to the autocrat in the Castle of St. Angelo.

Fabio Calvo, an austere old scholar, was one of the young prince's tutors. A common delight in ruins and excavations cemented a warm friendship between so apparently incongruous a pair. When Federico first saw the Laocoön, discovered in June, 1506, the boy wrote to his mother: 'How I wish I could send you, or at least show you this group, *cosa ecellentissima et opera divina.*' The men of genius in Rome vied with each other in explaining to Federico the wonders of the city. He was a familiar of Bernardo Ascolti, regarded as the foremost poet of the age, who took him to see the ruins of the Forum and the Capitol. The Pope while fortifying the abbey at Grottoferrata discovered the incomparable statue of Apollo. He took Federico to witness its transference to the garden of the Belvedere, from which it subsequently derived its title. He saw also the moving of the so-called Cleopatra—in reality Ariadne—purchased by Pope Julius, and was present at the finding of the colossal statue of 'The Tiber' in January, 1512, a unique experience for a boy of twelve.

Federico played a singular role in connection with the desperate state of his uncle, Alfonso, Duke of Ferrara. On Easter Sunday, April 11th, 1512, a bloody battle was fought at Ravenna between the Holy League, consisting of the Papal Corps and the Spaniards, and the French army of King Louis, led by Gaston de Foix, allied with the Duke of Ferrara. The French leader fell in the hour of victory, gained largely by the deadly efficiency of the French artillery. The papal captains surrendered. The Papal Legate, Fabrizio Colonna, bearing the cross of Rome, was taken prisoner. But months later the position was wholly reversed, the French were in flight and the desperate Duke of Ferrara was obliged to sue for peace to the Pope who had excommunicated him. Through the influence of Federico's father, the Marquis of Mantua, the Duke obtained a promised safe-conduct to Rome to make his subjection. So great was the rage of the Pope that on his arrival he placed him *incommunicado* in the palace of the Cardinal of Mantua, Federico's uncle. By the Pope's orders the boy was the only one allowed to go out to meet the Duke as he came, with his large retinue, within five miles of Rome. Later, the nominal prisoner was escorted to the Vatican, where, in a public Consistory, the Pope, dressed in full canonicals, seated upon his throne, awaited him. The Duke, dressed in black damask, had to kneel at the Pontiff's feet and make a most abject confession of his sins and errors. He was not spared the most bitter denunciation before he was absolved and dismissed with severe warnings as to future conduct.

A few days later young Federico, who was barely twelve, gave a banquet at the Vatican, by the Pope's special permission, to the Duke and his suite. The Duke afterwards viewed Pinturicchio's frescoes in the Borgia apartments, of special interest to him as the husband of Lucrezia Borgia, and then expressed a wish to see the ceiling of the Sistine Chapel, having heard much of Michelangelo's new frescoes. Young Federico thereupon summoned Michelangelo in the name of the Pope, and the Duke was conducted up to the vault by the artist, where he stayed and talked for a long time, enchanted by all he saw. He highly complimented Michelangelo, and obtained from him the promise of a picture. Meanwhile Federico had gone off with his guests to make a tour of the papal apartments and to view Raphael's frescoes in the *Stanze*. The Duke, having descended from the ceiling, declined the invitation to join the party, deeming it tactful to keep out of the Pope's chambers after his recent experience. The Duke held Federico in much affection, and when he died, twenty-two years later, he left his nephew, now become the Duke of Mantua, two of his best horses.

The boy's interest in art had shown itself early. He sat for his portrait to the greatest artists of the age, Francia, Raphael and Titian. In May, 1512, Isabella d'Este had written asking for her son's portrait to be painted by Raphael, then in the full flood of his genius. 'Since we have been obliged to give away the portrait of our son which was painted at Bologna, we wish to have another, especially as we hear he is still handsomer and more graceful than he was then.' Thus wrote the poor mother, centuries before the camera came to the solace of the separated. In January, 1513, her wish seemed about to be fulfilled. Raphael invited the young Prince to give him a sitting. His mother had sent him a special hat and military doublet for the portrait. The Mantuan agent sent the good news to Isabella:

'Yesterday Federico armed himself with Your Excellency's doublet, put on his plumed hat and cape and went to have his portrait painted by Messer Raphael Urbino, painter to His Holiness, who took a sketch of him in charcoal in this dress, which he will paint afterwards.'

A month later another correspondent reported to Isabella, grown anxious at some delay:

'As for Signor Federico's portrait, I ask Signor Raphael constantly how it is progressing. He tells me that he is working on it, and that I need have no fear, since he is very anxious to paint the portrait and serve your Excellency well.'

A few days later Isabella was dismayed by another report from her correspondent. It was cancelled. On February 19th Raphael made a bundle of the cape and doublet, and returned them to the Prince. 'He begs your Excellency to pardon him since, at the present time, it is impossible for him to give his mind to his work,' wrote the agent.[7]

[7] The sequel follows some eight years later. Federico is now Duke of Mantua. Baldassare Castiglione is in Rome charged by him with the mission of obtaining from Michelangelo a design for the deceased Marquis's tomb at Mantua. He succeeds in getting a design from Raphael, subsequently lost, but he has an even greater success. He writes in January, 1521, to the young Duke that his portrait, begun by Raphael in 1513, was finished by the artist, or some disciple,

What had distracted Raphael during the sittings? A love
affair, politics, dislike of the subject? It was none of these. He
felt his fortune was at stake, for Julius II, his friend and protector, became seriously ill, and within a few days was dead.
The news, so crushing to Raphael, caused rejoicing in Mantua, portrait or no portrait, for after almost three years as a
hostage Federico could be set free. As soon as the cardinals
had met in Conclave the Sacred College gave Federico permission to go. The family agent wrote to Mantua:

'The door was not quite closed so I could see through the opening how His Holiness bowed to the ground and tried to kiss their
hands, but they all embraced and kissed him.'

In joy, cheered by the populace of Rome, the little Prince's
cavalcade rode over the St. Angelo bridge, through the city,
out to the gate of the Piazza del Popolo, along the Via Flaminia, towards Mantua and home.

And the rest of the story? Briefly we may wander outside the
frame of the Roman picture. His life continued to be a
pageant, but the fine colours are tarnished with the usual
attributes of the lives of Renaissance princes, devout and debauched, cultured and criminal. His matrimonial affairs were
confused to a degree of comedy. When the boy was three
Cesare Borgia had proposed that a marriage should be arranged with his infant daughter. The proposal was considered, but the Marquis was wary, and when Cesare Borgia
descended like a wolf on the fold and seized the Duchy of
Urbino, property of the Marquis's brother-in-law, the proposal was dead, and all the tact of Baldassare Castiglione,
the soldier-courtier *sans réproche*, who handled the negotiations for the Marquis, was wasted. Federico was betrothed to
Maria Paloeologa in 1517. He broke it off and was betrothed
to his cousin, the Infanta Giulia of Aragon. He broke that off,

and is in the possession of Cardinal Colonna, who wishes to make the Duke a
present of it. The cherished portrait arrived in time to decorate his nuptial
chamber, and later there hung beside it Titian's portrait of Federico, painted
in 1530.

in order to marry the discarded Maria, now a great heiress.
But Maria died suddenly before the marriage was arranged,
and Federico immediately switched to her sister Margherita,
twenty years old beside his thirty. He married her, and she
gave him an heir, to add to three illegitimate children by a mistress, Isabella Boschetti. Titian wrote congratulating him.
'This news has filled me with unbounded joy so that I can
hardly contain myself.' Tasso composed an *Epithalamium*.
Ariosto turned from work on *Orlando Furioso* to write a
sonnet.

The marriage was successful despite the fact that Federico
was dominated by Isabella Boschetti. When her husband plot-
ted to poison her, Federico had him assassinated. On a state
visit to Venice he took his mistress with him, and so outraged
his mother that she refused to accompany him. But year by
year Federico continued his triumphant progress. When a
boy of fifteen he was an honoured guest of the young King of
France, Francis I, at Milan. He accompanied him to France,
staying through the spring and summer at the royal chateau.
He succeeded to the marquisate at eighteen, was appointed
Captain-General of the Papal Forces, captured Milan and
was created Duke of Mantua by the Emperor Charles V, who
visited his court. Like his mother he was a great patron of
art and letters. Ariosto was indebted to him for many favours.
One of these was permission to have paper brought from
Salo, through Mantuan territory, without paying duty. Later
Ariosto sent him an advance copy of *Orlando Furioso* 'as a
sign of a beginning of my devotion.' Artists also found a
friend in him. They were welcomed at a brilliant court
thronged with the most gifted men of the age.[8]

[8] 'It is impossible to look back upon the life of this prince without perceiving
that he did more than any other to foster the arts and keep up the dignity of
the artists of his time. He will always be remembered as the patron of Giulio
Romano, Titian, and a host of minor craftsmen. The galleries which he formed,
the palaces he adorned were second to none but those of Florence and Rome.
Nor is it to be credited that Titian would ever have gained the protection of
Charles V but for his countenance and introduction' (*Titian*, by Crowe and
Cavalcaselle).

The Pope's favourite, the radiant boy, the graceful youth who dazzled the French court and the Venetian Republic, the dashing soldier, the free lover, the art connoisseur, the builder of palaces, he was a commanding figure in a brilliant age. Then suddenly the pageant ended. Within a month of his fortieth year, even while he was busy with plans for his mother's tomb, he was struck down, leaving his little son Francesco to succeed him. To-day nothing remains of the church where he lay by his mother's side. In 1797 the French, after a grim siege, took Mantua. The church, with some three hundred Gonzaga monuments, was ruthlessly pillaged. The frescoes, paintings, sarcophagi, the entire interior were reduced to ashes and scattered by the winds. The shell of the old church was converted into a barracks, nothing remaining to tell of the glory of Isabella d'Este and her son Federico, Duke of Mantua.

III

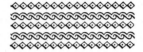

THE DICTATOR AND THE PRINCE

I

ACROSS the Piazza del Popolo, which has witnessed the journeyings of so many famous figures, between the two guardian churches, the Corso runs straight to that monstrous wall of glaring white marble, the monument to Victor Emanuel II. It commemorates an ironical victory. The King received the lion's share of praise at the expense of the two men who made Italy, Garibaldi and Cavour. By following the latter's advice he got a kingdom, which Garibaldi had destined for a republic, the warrior being compelled to acquiesce in the establishment of a monarchy by the superior political genius of Cavour. As for the monument, which is an ever-present incongruity damned by Italians and foreigners alike, there is only one thing to do with it: erase the peristyle and make a garden of its platform. Rising out of the Piazza Venezia, the monument now masks the Capitol, with the church of Santa Maria.

The Forum is our goal, but we shall be somewhat detained on the way, as always in Rome, a city of splendid interruptions. The Corso is a mile long and the finest street in Rome, but it is no wide, impressive thoroughfare. The pavements are narrow, the road is jammed with roaring traffic, for our Italian friends have tough ear-drums from infancy and measure *potenza* by noise. All along the Riviera they mark *Zona di silenzio* to attract tourists craving tranquillity. Not so here in Rome. For a short time Mussolini, in his ambition to discipline the Romans, forbade jaywalking and the blare of motor-horns. But again Rome is a *zona di pandemonio*.

The Corso is the first part of the great northern road made by Caius Flaminius in 187 B.C. which led to the Adriatic port of Rimini and thence on to Milan. The city section was once spanned by three triumphal arches. They have disappeared. It will be noticed that the houses and buildings are all well equipped with balconies, which is appropriate, for it was along this processional way of the triumphant Roman armies that the spectators rained down flowers upon the victors. The balconies on which they gathered were the invention of a Roman, the Tribune Moenius, and were called Moeniana after him. Together with the Roman road, the balcony spread all over the world.

The Corso, as its name implies, was a course, and this thoroughfare was so used by a Venetian Pope, Paul II, for horse races. Coming from the carnival city of Venice, he found Rome a sad place. He therefore instituted, towards the end of the fifteenth century, a horse race to be held during the annual Carnival. Perhaps he had a hunger for horse races, having lived in a city that possessed only four horses, bronze ones, in front of St. Mark's. The Roman Carnival is yet another instance of the adaptation of pagan to Christian institutions. The god Saturn gave his name to the wild festivity that became the Saturnalia. The columns of his temple still stand majestically in the Forum. To the festival of this god was added something of another, celebrating the little god of the shepherds, who drove away wolves and protected flocks. The season of festivity started with the Saturnalia, at the end of December (Christmas), and ended with the Lupercalia, when winter was over and all danger of wolves was gone (Lent). In the Christian usage the last ten days of the season were marked by celebrations, not exactly as the Romans celebrated, for we know that Mark Antony and the naked youths ran wildly through the streets hitting everyone with a leather thong, for purification (hence the Christian custom of flagellation), and, finally, symbolically offered the crown that Caesar thrice refused.

In the days of the Carnival, Rome was transformed. The windows were decorated and illuminated at night, the balconies were rich with hanging tapestries. There were grandstands overlooking the sanded course, and everywhere the throwing of flowers, the jostling of crowds, the storm of *moccoletti*, little paste pellets that stung the face, so that people wore masks for protection. No one dare venture into the street except in costume. The last night of the Carnival ended with a delirious mob extinguishing all lights and shouting 'Carnival is dead!'

In the year 1859 Carnival was seen by a celebrated man who came to Rome, later, to live near his mistress while he composed his music. He was seen one evening by a little American boy. He was Franz Liszt, dressed in a tight-fitting grey frock-coat and grey top hat. He was young, erect and something of a dandy, and, not being in costume nor in the soutane of an Abbe,[1] which he became later, he was nervous of being a mark for *moccoletti*-throwers. He looked right and left, rushed across the road and disappeared. A few minutes afterwards the same little boy saw a slender, good-looking youth, dressed in a black coat, smiling at the cheering crowd as he went by in an open carriage. It was the young Prince of Wales, Victoria's son, on tour with his tutor. In his honour, and to give Carnival the old-time fervour, masks were allowed by the Papal Governor. The little boy, who saw on that evening of Carnival the future Abbe Liszt and King Edward the Seventh, became famous as Marion Crawford, the novelist, who wrote *A Roman Singer*, *Saracinesca*, and many other popular novels of the day.

[1] Gregorovius, the historian, saw him in Rome, in 1865, a few days after he had become an Abbe. 'He was getting out of a hackney carriage, his black silk cassock fluttering ironically behind him. Mephistopheles disguised as an Abbe. Such is the end of Lovelace.'

Year after year the Carnival grew more and more rowdy with the swelling crowds of Rome. So for one last night the whole length of the Corso glimmered with lighted tapers (they burned waxen tapers in the Roman temple in honour of Saturn), until at midnight the church bells rang announcing Lent, and the lights went out and Carnival was dead forever.

At the far end of the Corso the Palazzo Venezia stands in the great square to which it gives its name, and where the Victor Emanuel II monument looks down the long Corso and shares with St. Peter's dome the skyline from most points of view. With the Palazzo Venezia we are in Venice rather than in Rome. This palace owes its origin to one of the outstanding popes. Pietro Barbo—Paul II—was a proud patrician of the great Venetian house. It is probable that he was already wealthy when he became a cardinal in 1440, at the age of twenty-seven, for he was a nephew of Eugenius IV, and popes' nephews were never poor, too many rich benefices came their way. He started life as a merchant of Venice. His immense fortune enabled him to become probably the greatest collector and antiquarian of the Renaissance. He pulled Rome to pieces, but it nevertheless owes more to him than possibly to any other pope, because of his collection of art treasures. Since he required a fitting place in which to keep and exhibit many of his acquisitions, he bought, in 1464, while still a cardinal, several acres of old property backing on to the Capitol. Clearing this, he built himself the palace, one of whose wings looked straight down the Via Flaminia, or the Corso, as it became known when he gave Rome its Carnival and instituted the races. This wing was removed in 1911, since it blocked the approach to the Victor Emanuel monument, and it was most cleverly reconstructed on the south-west corner. It had been menaced before by Napoleon in 1811, who wanted to continue the Corso to the Capitol, but the Romans, led by Canova, made such an outcry that he

abandoned his scheme. For another hundred years the Napoleon family occupied the palace that ends the Corso to-day,
so that his ghost probably feels satisfied.

The Palazzo Venezia shows the transition from the crenel-
lated fortress of the Middle Ages to the residential palace of
the Renaissance. The tower is still there, and wedged into
the palace is the church of San Marco, again Venetian in its
inspiration. It is the church of the Venetians in Rome. It was
Cardinal Barbo's intention to have two towers, with the
church in between, but death came and the design was never
fulfilled. This church was originally founded in the time of
Constantine, rebuilt in A.D. 833 and modernised in 1744 by
another Venetian, Cardinal Querini. It has twenty beautiful
columns of Sicilian jasper. The story is that the church was
founded in honour of St. Mark in A.D. 337, by Pope Marco,
who lies buried here. Did this attract Barbo to the site, a little
homesick for Venice and St. Mark's there? It is a beautiful
church, but, alas, I allowed myself to be decoyed by a
sacristan with a candle (they are all over Rome, waiting with
candles for victims), and down, down, down into the very
ancient crypt I went. 'Mind your head,' warned the sacristan,
and, stooping, we explored the early Christian underworld.
But I forgot the warning, and severely scraped my bare head
on the tufa ceiling. When with much candle-grease and an
aching back I emerged, blood was streaming down my face.
'Ah,' observed my friend, who had refused the pilgrimage,
'Rome is stained with the blood of the martyrs!'

Like Evelyn, who was here in the seventeenth century, and
believed his guide, who told him the palace was built by
Bramante, which it was not, I was enchanted by the great
building, since it spans almost five hundred years of history.
The last thirty have probably been the most exciting, for this
palace was Mussolini's headquarters until the hour of his
downfall. There on its long façade is the balcony where the
'sawdust Caesar' hurled his insults at democracy (and par-

ticularly the English variety) and harangued the mob with all the tricks of the superlative demagogue.

Paul II was quite ruthless in the matter of taking his building materials from the surviving edifices of ancient Rome. He plundered the Colosseum, the temple of Claudius, and even the tombs on the Via Flaminia for columns, marble slabs and anything his architects could use. He was almost as relentless as a collector; his mania stopped at nothing. Fabulously rich when he became Pope, no one dared oppose his will. His vandalism was more than balanced by his passionate love for antiquity and his care for beautiful things. The San Marco palace, as it was then called, became the richest museum in Europe. Not even Lorenzo the Magnificent could outvie this born collector. He gathered together scholars and antiquarians and financed their efforts. He re-established the University of Rome, he restored the arch of Titus, the arch of Septimius Severus. The riches of Rome not sufficing, he sent his agents all through Europe. They bought pictures, gems, jewelry, statuary, velvets and Byzantine cloths. They even invaded the churches, and no Madonnas either in mosaics, marble, wood or oil painting were safe if he coveted them. Literature, too, became his passion. He had a grandiose scheme for removing to his new palace the great library from the Abbey of Monte Cassino, but this proposal was not proceeded with. He had a passion for cameos, and the palace contained two hundred and twenty-seven. He heard of a beautiful one in Toulouse, and offered to build a bridge across the Garonne in exchange for it. An inventory of his artistic possessions would make the mind reel—forty-seven antique bronzes, three hundred intaglios, twenty-five Byzantine mosaic pictures, diamonds, pearls, emeralds, turquoises, amethysts mounted and inset by the thousand. He possessed four tiaras, one costing one hundred and twenty thousand gold ducats (a million dollars), another worth eighty thousand gold ducats. He dressed magnificently. Tall, with a good figure, and handsome, he proposed on his election to St. Peter's chair calling himself Formosus II (The Handsome), but this was too much for the cardinals, and he had to be content with the same name as the Apostle Paul.

The Palazzo Venezia became the Pope's official residence, and having set a fashion in building and collecting, the successive popes and cardinals built palaces and made collections, but Paul II's splendour was long unrivalled. As with the Castle of St. Angelo, though for a shorter period and in a lesser style, this palace reflects the history of Rome for more than four centuries. After the reign of Pius IV (1559-65) it was given to the Republic of Venice as the seat of its ambassador, Rome receiving in exchange the magnificent Palazzo Gritti on the Grand Canal as the residence of the Papal Nuncio. When Charles VIII of France made his swift descent through Italy in 1494 and Rome dared not resist him, he used the square as the camping-ground of his artillery. In the terrible sack in 1527 by the troops of the Constable of Bourbon, it was occupied by his Dutch pikemen. On the fall of Napoleon and the occupation of Italian territory by the Hapsburgs, the palace became the Austrian Embassy, and continued to be thus used until Italy's entry into the First Great War in 1916. The courtyard then presented an unusual sight. The famous four bronze horses from their pedestals in front of St. Mark's, the great Colleoni statue from opposite SS. Giovanni and Paolo in Venice and the Gattamelata statue from Padua were all housed here for safety. Rome thus possessed temporarily the seven most famous bronze horses in the world, five from Venice, one from Padua and the Roman horse carrying Marcus Aurelius. When the war ended and the five horses returned to Venice, and the Palazzo Venezia became a museum and the seat of the national government, the grateful Venetians made a charming gesture, and gave to Rome the copy of their traditional winged lion. It most fittingly replaced the eagle of the defeated Hapsburgs taken down from the corner of the palace nearest to the Corso. As offices for the Government the palace thus became the headquarters of Mussolini. It was a splendid setting, rich in tradition, and offered moreover that balcony rostrum above the great square in which thousands of Romans could gather for his belligerent orations and madly cheer the builder of an Empire who assured them that the Mediterranean was *Mare Nostrum*, despite the presence on its shores of the Spanish, French, Jugoslavs, Albanians, Greeks, Egyptians and English.

From this palace Mussolini re-vitalised Italy, disciplined it, put its house in order, made its prestige felt, flouted the democracies, violated the territories of Albania, Greece and Abyssinia, made a British Prime Minister flout his Foreign Secretary and run, umbrella in hand, to Rome. If Mussolini had stopped there and collected the spoils of peace from the bankruptcy of the Titans strangling each other, he might have been, in the annals of Time, one of Italy's greatest statesmen. But with France on her knees and England awaiting invasion, it seemed a safe thing to play the jackal.

Let us go inside and see the room where he ruined himself and wrecked his country. For the legend grows, and just as Napoleon came back to Paris, Mussolini may come back to Rome. Not a niche in the Pantheon, for that would affront the House of Savoy, nor a chapel in St. Peter's, for an agnostic and a loose-liver could not rest there, but a sepulchre by the palace where he ruled, facing the great artery of the Corso, might be considered a fitting place. Memories are short, and magnitude, of success or failure, is often everything. When we see Napoleon, who left a trail of blood and robbery across Europe, enshrined in the Invalides, it seems possible that the blacksmith's son may yet achieve an apotheosis, though he began with murder (Matteotti) and ended before a firing squad as a common thief caught in flight with nearly a million pounds of his country's money, and jewelry from the House of Savoy.

We enter through a beautiful porch by Giuliano da Maiano, above which we see the arms of Paul II. A wide staircase brings us to the floor of the state rooms. They are well set out, partly as a museum. The pictures are carefully selected, the *objets d'art* are sparingly but impressively displayed. Again and again one halts by the windows to enjoy the superb vistas of Rome; often it is like looking down the telescope of History.

The palace has a large quadrangular inner courtyard, with arcades on one corner. It was never completed, but it is nevertheless a thing of beauty. In another corner rises a tower of the fifteenth century with a graceful Gothic note. The walls carry some lovely pieces of majolica ware with the coat-of-arms of the Pope. In the centre there is a garden, refreshingly green, with palm-trees and a seventeenth-century fountain that keeps the Venetian character by representing the legend of Venice as the bride of the Sea borne up by mossy Tritons, with cavorting dolphins. The high walls of the surrounding palace shut off all sound of the city, and only the murmur of falling water is heard in this oasis. Under the arcades is the quietest and loveliest little post-office in Rome, decorated with panels presenting the Goddesses of Letters and Telegrams.

The rooms that command the chief attention are those once used by Paul II, and finally by Mussolini. A suite of small reception rooms leads to three magnificent *salons*, the Mappamondo, the Consistoro and the Regia. The first of these commands our attention. Towards one end of this vast *salon* there is a large window that gives access to the small balcony overlooking the Piazza. By stepping out of this *salon*, which served for his workroom, Mussolini was in immediate view of the multitude below him, and it must have seemed as he stood there, his words reported to the ends of the earth, that he was addressing not only the modern world but also the ancient. In this room behind him Roderigo Borgia, Pope Alexander VI, had entertained the invader, Charles VIII, whose formidable cannon were drawn up in the Piazza. Immediately on the Duce's right rose the gigantic monument to the king who had fulfilled Garibaldi's dream of a united

Italy. Just visible was the column of the Emperor Trajan, and in the far distance, beyond the splendid Avenue of the Empire he had opened up along the side of the Forum, could be seen the huge mole of the Colosseum. There are few views in the world that embrace so much history and ancient grandeur. Mussolini was addressing not only the Romans but the scene of two thousand years of history, from a time when Rome was the mistress of the world to this hour when again her ambition was boundless. One need not wonder at the high ambition of any Roman, confronted with such a history.

The great *salon* in whose corner Mussolini had his desk, originally on the left of the fireplace, and later removed to the right side, by the door, in order to get the daylight from the windows, had been restored to its former condition. The Austrians, finding the room too large, had divided it into two parts. The original ceiling, put in by Cardinal Barbo, a work of magnificent wood-carving and painted plaster, carries the motif of the Lion of St. Mark. It is workmanship dating back to 1490, and is in a marvellous state of preservation. In the panels are architectural perspectives, delicately done, the work of Andrea Mantegna, called to Rome by the Pope. The marble door-jambs are richly carved with garlands of fruit, workmanship of the same period. But it is the tessellated floor which deserves careful attention for the story it tells. The design covering the vast space has been tampered with and modernised. Three new designs have been inserted, and they sing the glory of the era of Fascism. Raphael, on order, inserted the Pope's portrait into some of his frescoes in the Vatican. These mosaic artists, whether from command or flattery, have worked the head of Mussolini into the central mosaic. There are other designs, including those of the signs of the Zodiac, and if the visitor carefully examines the Archer he will recognise again the bull-head of the Duce. Two square panels at each end of the central one show the fasces and the eagle, with inscriptions. I was told that these mosaics were done while Mussolini was using the room as his office, and that the work was constantly delayed by the Dictator's sudden return at unexpected hours, whereupon all the workmen were hurriedly moved out.

By the place where the Duce's desk stood are the wall-plugs for his telephones. One could not help speculating on the conversations and eventful decisions that had been carried by these telephones on his desk to the Foreign Office and the Embassies of Europe. One can almost hear the high-pitched voice of Hitler goading his reluctant ally into some new move. But it is a smaller room—the Sala del Pappagallo, so called because in it Pope Paul kept his favourite parrot—that recalls momentous scenes. It was here that Mussolini had a last stormy scene with Goering, who reproached him with Italy's failure to support Germany in North Africa. Later, in the last hour of the grim drama of Italy's collapse, it was here that the final meeting of the Fascist Grand Council was held. After a long and stormy debate Mussolini stamped out, repudiated, to offer his resignation to the King, and to find himself a prisoner. From that hour his desk in the Sala del Mappamondo, where he had made such fateful decisions, knew him no more. Not far off, in distance and time, was his squalid end before the erratic rifles of some ruffians in a lane in Donga, and the revolting orgy of a Milanese mob that desecrated his corpse and that of his mistress.

II

On the other side of the Piazza there once rose the great palace of Prince Torlonia, the banker. It disappeared when the square was widened in 1902. It had been rebuilt from a former palace of the famous medieval family of Frangipani. The Torlonia family is an example of the rapid growth of some ennobled houses of Italy. Its founder was Giovanni Torlonia, a mercer, born in 1754. He was agent at the Holy See for Prince Furstenberg, who had created him a noble of the Empire, in 1794. He became money-lender and banker

to Pius VI and Pius VII. The latter created him Marquis Torlonia, later Prince Torlonia. He became Duke of Bracciano.
The dukedom and the estate originally belonged to the
Orsini, then to the Odescalchi, by whom it was sold in 1802.
They afterwards bought it back. The title went with the purchase of the estate, as in the case of Prince Lucien Bonaparte,
who in 1814 became thereby Prince Canino. His son, Charles
Lucien, nephew of the Emperor Napoleon, being pressed for
money, sold the estate to Prince Torlonia in 1847, for the
sum of nine thousand crowns, and threw in the title for an
extra fifty crowns. The puppet kingdoms of Italy created
princes, dukes, marquises and counts with the greatest gaiety.
The Papacy also distributed titles, and does today.[2] Its only
remaining competitor appears to be England.

The new Prince Torlonia strengthened his position still
further by marrying his elder son into the house of Duke
Sforza-Cesarini. Of this marriage one son married Princess
Chigi, another Princess Ruspoli. Giovanni's second son, Alessandro, married into the ancient Colonna family, than which
there was nothing higher, and his daughter Anna Maria
married Giulio Borghese. Thus in two generations the Torlonias established themselves by ability, money and favour
of the Popes in the great feudal families of Rome.

Prince Torlonia believed in real estate as well as in cash.
In addition to two palaces and five villas, it was said he
owned twenty-six estates and almost half of the Campagna.
His bank flourished. It was used by a multitude of travelling
English at the opening of the nineteenth century. Brilliant
young Mr. Thomas Babington Macaulay, in his diary for
1838, wrote: 'Went to Torlonia's to get money for my journey.' Then, as now, Italian banks were likely to be old pal-

[2] One day in Palm Beach I found myself dining in the company of a handsome old American gentleman who presented me with his card. It bore a
coronet and under it the name 'The Marquis Frederick Macdermott.' It was a
papal title, somehow acquired. Opposite to me sat Prince Odescalchi (among
whose ancestors was Pope Innocent XI, Benedetto Odescalchi, 1611), possessor
of one of the oldest Roman titles, who winked naughtily as I pocketed the card.

aces with painted ceilings, as in Shelley's Rome lodging, the Palazzo Verospi, occupied now by the Banca Credito Italiano.

'What a curious effect it was to see a bank in a palace, among orange trees, colonnades, marble statues, and all the signs of the most refined luxury,' observed Macaulay, after a call at Torlonia's. 'It carries me back to the days of the merchant princes of Florence, when philosophers, poets and painters crowded to the house of Cosimo de' Medici. I drew one hundred pounds worth of scudi, and had to lug it through the streets in a huge canvas bag, muttering with strong feeling Pope's "Blest paper credit".'

Prince Torlonia's palace at the end of the Corso was magnificent, as became the Roman Rothschild. Its four sides, enclosing a great courtyard, had galleries filled with sculpture, tapestries and works of art. A Frenchman with a degree of venom remarked, 'It would be impossible to describe the marbles, pictures and gorgeous furniture, all in the worst degree of taste, which fill the corridors and *salons*. As they are not able to make beautiful apartments they content themselves with making them gaudy. It is in this palace that the Jew, Torlonia, receives the first aristocracy of Europe, who are eager to attend his routs.'

Torlonia was not a Jew. Alessandro, the second prince, married to a Colonna, was a man of considerable culture. He was among the leading patrons of art, and purchased the Villa Albani with all its treasures of ancient sculpture and monuments. His father had acquired the Apollo Theatre, and opened it with Rossini's new work *Mathilda di Shabran* in 1821. Showing a similar interest in music, Prince Alessandro bought the ancient Argentina and Alibert theatres. He had a passion for horses, buying them from the most famous studs in England, and his liveries and equipages, when he drove out, were the finest in Rome.

The old Prince Torlonia was a shrewd judge of nature, and correctly read the characters of his sons. Stendhal was frequently his guest between 1810 and 1828, and narrates a conversation he had with the Prince one evening at a reception in September, 1827. He had just opened his palace in the Piazza Venezia, and told Stendhal how he had obtained the vast mirrors so much admired by his guests. He went to Paris dressed to look like a shabby old Jew and told the shopkeepers he had been sent from Rome by Torlonia the banker, notorious for his avarice, to buy mirrors for him at a cut-rate price. 'In that way I obtained them with a five per cent discount,' said the old Prince, chuckling. He pointed to his sons. 'Marino loves art, but he will never make anything. I shall leave him three million crowns and two duchies. Alessandro is of very different stuff. He knows the value of money, so he shall have my bank. One day you will see him richer than any single prince, than all the Roman princes put together; and if he has the prudence of his father he may make his son Pope.'

Man proposes, God in His time disposes. Young Torlonia married one of the most beautiful and high-born women in Rome. But they had no sons, and the Princess died insane after giving birth to a second daughter, stillborn.

The second Prince Torlonia bought another palace for the sole purpose of using it for his entertainments. For his father's opinion was justified. The banker-prince turned all he touched to gold. Pious, he had the confidence of the Vatican and all the great papal families. He could hardly number his castles, estates, villages and farms. In his Villa Albani, whose treasures had occupied so much of Winckelmann's life, there stood the famous 'Antinous Crowned with Lotus Leaves,' and the long galleries held priceless treasures.

The visitor to the Vatican to-day, after passing the Castle of St. Angelo, no longer has to thread his way through an agglomeration of slummy houses before he gains the great square and colonnade of St. Peter's. Mussolini swept all this away, and created the wide Via della Conciliazione. Unhappily this clearance, opening up a worthy approach to St.

Peter's, resulted in the loss of the house built by Bramante for Raphael, in which his studio was intact, and where he died.

The visitor will see on his right a very fine palace, with the Torlonia coat-of-arms over its doorway. This is the Palazzo Giraud, bought by Torlonia for his splendid entertainments. One must look at it for another reason and speculate upon the momentous events, affecting English history, that took place within it. It was built in 1496 by Montecavallo, and was finished by Bramante. It is considered one of the finest examples of Renaissance architecture in Rome. The material, alas, was mostly taken from the Basilica Emilia. Here lived its first owner, Cardinal Adriano da Corneto, who was also Bishop of Bath and Wells and, as Papal Nuncio, a trusted adviser of Henry VII.[3] The palace was the scene of a mysterious and tragic supper-party on August 17th, 1503. The Cardinal entertained at supper Pope Alexander VI and his son, Cesare Borgia. At this party the Pope was taken ill, and died the next day. Cesare Borgia almost died. Rumour at once supplied a story that Borgia had sent in advance some wine for the party, instructing the butler to serve it during the banquet, the intention being to poison their host and confiscate his estates. The Pope, being thirsty on arrival, called for some wine. His son Cesare came in next and also drank. They were both poisoned.

Any death near Cesare Borgia was almost certain to be attributed to him, but three facts suggest his innocence on this occasion. He drank the wine himself and nearly died; the Pope after death turned black and putrescent, whereas arsenic, the basis of many poisons, preserves the body; the

---

[3] He was a benefactor of Bath Abbey, where his arms are displayed in the choir vault. He took with him to England his relation, Polydore Vergil, who was given the living of Church Langton, Leics. Vergil, a lifelong friend of Erasmus, was encouraged by Henry VII to write the first History of England. He was born in Urbino in 1470, and probably knew young Raphael there. He returned from England in 1550, and died that year.

Pope's secretary, who gave precise details of Alexander's last illness, makes no mention of the supper-party as a cause of poisoning. This, of course, may have been caution, fearing Borgia.

When Cardinal Corneto fell into disfavour with Leo X he left Rome and presented the palace to Henry VII, from whom it passed into the possession of Henry VIII, and was the seat of his ambassador to the Vatican. When the tremendous quarrel broke out between the Pope and Henry, over his divorce from Catherine of Aragon, involving the ruin of Cardinal Wolsey, and the cruel suppression of abbeys and monasteries under Thomas Cromwell, it was in this palace that the British Ambassador was charged with the delivery of thunderous messages from the irate King to the Pope. The documents that arrived here from England, and were read, transcribed and conveyed to the Pope, resulted in the break of the English Church with Rome, in consequence of which most Englishmen to-day are Protestants and not Roman Catholics. With that break the Embassy was closed.

The palace had been sumptuously decorated by Wolsey. Its vast halls, high, painted ceilings, its terrace and loggia overlooking the River Tiber, its great marble staircase, up which a coach and six could have been driven—all this regal splendour was added to by Torlonia. He created an enormous ballroom by opening up two floors, and built at one end a golden temple to hold the orchestra. Fifty chandeliers of Venetian glass lit the room. Thackeray went there as a guest, and gained copy for *Vanity Fair*. Becky Sharp, conducted by Major Loder, attended a reception and marvelled at it all:

'They turned their steps towards a boudoir of rose-coloured velvet at the end of the long range of rooms, where in the midst stood a statue of Venus, a thousand times repeated by the reflection of Venetian mirrors on the walls. In this room the Prince had prepared a choice supper for his most honoured guests.'

Let us go to a Torlonia ball on a night of Carnival in 1821. Nearly two thousand guests have been invited. The women are wearing high combs, with ringlets falling on each side of their faces. They blaze with diamond necklaces. Their gowns are sleeveless and puffed at the shoulders. Their bosoms are half-exposed, their waists are contracted by gold belts. Full skirts reach to their ankles, showing feet in openwork silk stockings and shoes tied over the instep. They wear heavy earrings, some of cameos, a gold fillet round their brows, and they carry enormous fans. Dupré and Massoni, of Paris, have dressed them in the gaudiest colours. But the men are not outshone. Their coats of maroon or blue, cut away in the front, have large gilt buttons, their tight knee-breeches are of cream, yellow or brown cloth, their waist-coats are of piqué, silk or velvet, embroidered with gold. Their shirts are pleated and frilled, and they wear large white neckties twice wound round their high collars, with frills hanging down. Their wrists are covered with lace ruffles. The youthful Count D'Orsay, whose horsemanship in the park astonishes even the young Roman bloods, takes the eye as he enters, wearing peach-satin knee-breeches and green velour shoes. At the head of the great staircase the Princess Torlonia, flashing with diamonds, receives her guests. And now something happens that sets Rome by the ears for a month. The Countess of Perugia brings with her, uninvited, her cousin, the beautiful Marchesa Florienzi, a bride who has just arrived in Rome for a visit. She presents her to the Princess, who withholds her hand, and, turning to the Countess, says haughtily, 'These may be the customs of Perugia, Madam, but they certainly are not of Rome!'

Under this crushing remark the poor little bride retreats in tears to a corner of the ballroom, whereupon an elegant young man seeks to console her. While he assures her the Princess's rebuke was not directed to her, the son of the house comes up to the young man and asks if His Royal Highness

will honour them by opening the ball. Thereupon the Crown
Prince of Bavaria leads the beautiful but distressed Marchesa
on to the floor and opens the ball. All through the evening she
monopolises his attention, and so triumphs.

That was the beginning, not the end of the story, for Louis,
as King of Bavaria, installed her, four years later, in Munich,
where he reigned until the scandal of his conduct with the
dancer, Lola Montez, compelled his abdication in 1848, when
he retreated to Paris, dying there twenty years later, aged
eighty-two.

Prince Alessandro Torlonia lived to a great age. Born in
1800, he lived till 1886. 'I walk with the century,' he said
once, sadly. Every day in Rome they saw the old banker
propped up in his smart landau, open in all weathers. His
coachman had instructions to drive for two hours where he
would, but he must always stop at one church, where the old
prince, a devout Catholic, went in to pray. Then he resumed
his drive back to the Palazzo Torlonia by the Corso. One day,
while carried up the great stairs in a chair, he sank, and
breathed his last on a spartan iron bed. With no son to follow him, he knew the vanity and loneliness of riches. Not a
brick of the palace in the Piazza Venezia now remains.

But the tradition of lavish hospitality is maintained in the
Torlonia line. When the vivacious young Princess Margaret of
England made her first visit to Italy, another Prince Alessandro Torlonia gave a reception at the family palace situated on a
corner of the Via dei Condotti and the Via Bocca di Leone.
On the evening of May 7th, 1949, more than three hundred
guests thronged the splendid *salons* of the *palazzo* where the
young Prince and his wife, the Infanta Beatrice, daughter of
King Alfonso of Spain, received the pretty young Princess
and their guests. A grand staircase led to reception-rooms
whose lustre chandeliers shone beneath gilt-coffered and
painted ceilings, on rich tapestries and Renaissance works of
art. Down in the courtyard, seen from the inner windows,

was the statue of Apollo in a floodlit alcove. Beneath a belvedere ablaze with flowers, over a moss-green grotto surmounted by an heraldic stone eagle, cascades of water splashed into a fern-rimmed basin, making cool music in the quiet night. The ghosts from forgotten pageants seemed to walk again in the palace of the Torlonias.

IV

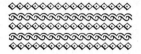

THE HOUSE OF DORIA

I

A LITTLE way down the Corso, coming from the Piazza Venezia, on the left-hand side, there is an open gateway with a low grille which permits the passer-by to gain an alluring glimpse of a courtyard with a garden of palm-trees and an arcade of Doric columns. This is the Palazzo Doria, originally built in 1435 for the cardinals who took their title from the church at the corner of the palace. It later passed to Cardinal Santoro, and this unhappy man was forced to part with it to Pope Julius II, who admired it so much that he acquired it for his nephew, the Duke of Urbino. The dispossessed Cardinal died of grief from this loss. Bramante added to the ornamentation of the palace, which in turn served as a Spanish Embassy for Charles V and Philip II, and passed successively to the Aldobrandini, Pamphili and Doria families. It has three imposing doors on the Corso, though its State entrance is on the other side of the vast block. For a time it was the seat of the French Government and of the general who, on Napoleon's orders, arrested Pius VII on the night of July 16th, 1809, and carried him into captivity. Here, in one of the largest palaces in Rome, Napoleon's representative gave splendid entertainments.

The Doria palace presents to the busy Corso a façade of decorated windows, of Ionic and Corinthian columns, of coats-of-arms, with the Pamphili dove carrying the sprig of

olive, and a general ornamentation that expresses the extravagance of the last phase of baroque art. But little of this is seen,
so narrow is the street, so heavy the dust of centuries. One
would scarcely suspect that behind that long, dark façade is
one of the great private art collections of the world, or that
under the palace, deep in the foundations, lies ancient Rome
in the form of the covered porticoes of the Septa Julia built
by Julius Caesar for the people to record their votes in, and
used in the Second World War as an air-raid shelter.

One expects a palace to be large, hence the adjective
'palatial.' There is no question about the vastness of the
Palazzo Doria; it is almost two-thirds the size of St. Peter's,
or a little less in the area it occupies than that covered by the
Colosseum. It once held more than eight hundred persons,
family, relatives and retainers, in the manner in which
Roman palaces were once hotels for all branches of the family tree. To-day few of these palaces are inhabited by descendants of the original owners, and in cases where the present resident bears the founder's name only a small part of the
original palace is occupied.

The ground floors of these vast houses, dark and tunnel-
like, have become the workshops of innumerable craftsmen,
jewellers, engravers, carpenters, electricians, printers, cabinet-makers, etc., who carry on a skilled tradition from father
to son. They work in these dark arches and rooms lit by a
single unshaded electric bulb dangling on a cord. How they
retain their health and the eager, joyous spirit of their craft
I have never understood. Yet one cannot enter these humble
little shops without a feeling that the long tradition of craftsmanship has descended from the days when Benvenuto Cellini
and his fellows brought glory to the Italian Renaissance. Alas,
the line is dying out. More and more it becomes difficult
for the old craftsman to find an apprentice. But let us not
mourn too early the triumph of mass production and the decay of beautiful workmanship. Rome is still honeycombed
with these modest artists, poorly remunerated men, carrying

on a great tradition. I found nowhere a derelict workshop or a vacant pigeon-hole in the ground floors of the huge palaces. The decay of some of these palaces has resulted in their slumification. The fallen plaster, the broken windows, the chipped columns and busts in the derelict courtyards, the air of ancient splendour, frayed by the reckless hand of Time, are often all that remain in witness of a dynasty whose name once rang like a trumpet across the dead centuries. The ground floor is now a dank slum where somehow the pale Roman, in one room with a visible bed, with a hencoop and no water-tap, ekes out his existence, while from the upper floors, from the former *piano nobile*, with its vast painted ceiling still intact, from the loggia from whence the ghostly strains of a guitar are almost audible, from the *mezzanine* whose oval window once framed the bright inquisitiveness of a ruffled page-boy, from the high pergola terrace whose balustrade still presents an armless Venus or a noseless Apollo, there hangs, colourfully fluttering, not the *gonfaloni* and the *bandiere* of a noble occupant, but the no less vivid washing of a score of families.

The Doria Palace has suffered no such change as this. It is all beautifully kept. Part of its ground floor on the Corso has been converted into high-class shops, and all around the vast block one finds numerous callings and businesses in various arches or recesses of the great palace. The whole edifice is engulfed in history. The palace is flanked by the Palazzo Bonaparte. Here after the collapse of the *gran ladrone*, as the Italians called him, heavy sufferers from his depredations, Napoleon's mother, Madame Letizia, entrenched herself, with her cardinal brother and members of the family. Madame Mère, as she became known to the world, was a woman of tremendous personality. Austere, capable, she gathered in her family from the storm, and sat firmly in regal dignity while an outraged Europe sought vengeance on her brood. She died here in 1836, and the mercenary porter of the palace allowed the curious crowd to witness her last moments through the crevices of a screen, for the sum of one *scudo*.

II

On the north corner of the Doria palace is the church of Santa Maria in Via Lata. Whatever we are called upon to believe in Rome, where legend, historic fact and crude superstition are often indistinguishably mixed, one may assent to the claim that the crypt of this old church covers the site of the house where Paul resided for two years and wrote therein his Epistles. He was a prisoner awaiting trial, and at times chained to his gaoler, but some latitude was accorded him as one who could proudly claim Roman citizenship. From this dwelling he was taken to the palace and judgment hall of the Caesars on the Palatine, and we can, even to-day, stand in that ruin of the basilica, the Imperial Tribune, its hall divided into nave and aisles, with an apse for the throne, where the prisoner confronted his Roman judges.

This Hall of Justice was lined with precious marbles from Egypt and Libya. Here sat twenty councillors, with Caesar in their midst. Nero himself sat here in judgment, the ruler of the world, and a criminal of deeper hue than any confronting him. It was before this tribunal that St. Paul was brought from his gaoler's house. The trial was a protracted one. The prosecution had to produce its witnesses, for the Roman law demanded that the prisoner should be confronted in person by his accusers. The case was complicated by the fact that the charges originated in Judaea, and the depositions had to be forwarded from there. St. Paul was accused of desecrating the Temple, of molesting the Jews in their worship, and of breaking the public peace by agitation and the dissemination of a strange doctrine. The real crime, however, in the eyes of the Roman authorities was that Paul had been a public nuisance as an agitator to a degree that made him guilty of *majestas* treason against the sovereign power of the Roman people, a capital crime.

The case of Paul was not hopeless. The accused was not a nonentity nor a man without a background. He had been born in Tarsus, in Cilicia, a city famed for the art of trans- forming goat's hair into tent-cloth, a skill acquired by Paul. It was also the seat of a university teaching philosophy, science and letters, and it was in a province within the Roman Empire, so that Paul, a Hebrew sprung of Hebrews, of the strict sect of Pharisees, was a Roman citizen. Since this part of the Roman Empire lay in the eastern province once dominated by Alexander of Macedon, it was Hellenised. Its cultured citizens, as those of Egypt, Judaea and Syria, spoke Greek. Hence the Greek, Latin and Hebrew inscription on the Cross, the writing of the Septuagint and the New Testa- ment in Greek, and also Paul's ability, when standing on the Areopagus at Athens, to address his sceptical audience in its native tongue.

He was a prisoner of some social standing also. At Caesarea he had exercised his privilege as a Roman to be sent for trial to Rome, being distrustful of the bribery of the local courts by the Jews accusing him. He travelled with a convoy of con- victs, most of them doomed to perish in some gladiatorial show, but he was not treated as a convict. He had once been poor, and had practised the profession of tent-maker, prob- ably following repudiation by his well-to-do family. But now he obviously had money, since he was travelling with two 'slaves,' for in this manner Luke and Aristarchus accom- panied him. He was also capable, it seemed, of financing his protracted trial. It may be there had been a family recon- ciliation or, in the course of time, he had inherited family property. Be that as it may, he was a man of culture and some substance. Above all, when he reached Rome he could exer- cise the proud right of donning the toga, denied to all but the true *civis Romanus*.

On arrival in Rome, Paul was treated with much leniency. He was permitted to hire a house and to dwell there at his convenience under the guard of a soldier. The symbol of im-

prisonment was a light chain with which he was attached to
his warder. His friends were free to come and go. He was
visited by Mark. He regarded himself as 'an ambassador in
chains,' and it was from this house, within ten minutes' walk
of the Capitol and the Forum, that he indited his beautiful
letter to Philemon, the master of the runaway slave, Onesi-
mus, who had come to him in Rome, to the Colossians, and to
the Asian churches. There sounds in these epistles a confident
note. He will be acquitted, he will carry on his mission. Possibly he felt the charge against him was not well-founded
under Roman law. At this time it was no offence to be a
Christian.[1]

There is much prejudice and misconception concerning the
attitude of Rome towards the early Christians. Encouraged
by Nero, who wanted a scapegoat for the burning of the City,
and by subsequent emperors seeking a means to divert public
feelings from their own misdemeanours, the persecution of
Christians became general, but this was not due to their faith.
The Christians were persecuted by the Romans not because
they refused to believe in Jupiter and Venus, but because
they refused to let anyone else believe in them. In their zeal,
in their claim to be of the elect, they became intolerant. They
assailed the Roman faith and thereby weakened the whole
fabric of society as it was then established. They were the
Communists of the era, and in the eyes of the conservative

---

[1] In the subterranean church under the present one the visitor is shown the
well, alleged to have been created by St. Paul's prayers in order to baptise
converts, and the pillar complete with chain to which he is said to have been
bound. There is no lack of pillars and chains all over Rome as relics of Christian
martyrs. The well was obviously the house supply, the church was once on the
street level and adjoined the Septa Julia, used by Caesar for voting-booths,
which also ran under the adjacent Palazzo Doria. St. Paul appears to have
kept open house with a centurion, Martialis, for guard, who is further identified
as the child to whom Jesus once said, 'Suffer little children to come unto Me',
who carried the basket of bread and fishes in the wilderness, and served at the
Last Supper. These relics and embroideries are found to be somewhat em-
barrassing in a more enlightened age and are being quietly disposed of. It is
not altogether impossible that this was the site of one of Paul's Roman lodgings.
He must have lived somewhere for two years of captivity, and this house
undoubtedly existed in his day.

Romans they were closely associated with the criminal underworld, with the rabble and with the rebellious slaves. Nero presented them to the public not as adherents of a new religion, but as social missionaries subverting the State.

When Paul first came to trial Nero had not yet sought to inflame public opinion against them as a mask for his own outrages. During the trial he burned Rome, but he had not yet proceeded to burn Christians; that was to come later.

At the time of Paul's lodgement in the house on whose site in the Corso successive churches have arisen since the eighth century, he was confident of his rights in the law. His confidence was not misplaced, though we can wonder at the acquittal, for when the witnesses from Judaea, Ephesus, Corinth and the vindictive Sanhedrin of Jerusalem had been heard there was the baleful influence of Nero's wife, Poppaea, a proselyte, to contend with, and doubtless Paul's enemies from Palestine had not failed to solicit her support. It was the custom for each of the judges to state his opinion in writing, and these collected judgments were sent to the Emperor for him to accept or ignore. Let it be credited to a wicked man's memory that Nero acquitted Paul on his first trial. After long captivity he walked out of his gaoler's house to renew his mission with undiminished zeal.

When Paul's second trial was held he was doomed because Roman law had shifted its ground; it had become an offence merely to be a Christian. When Nero became Emperor in A.D. 54, religious beliefs were treated with singular freedom, due in part to the spirit of Nero's tutor, the philosopher Seneca, who in many ways was not far removed from the liberal spirit of Paul. Seneca, disgraced, retired in A.D. 62. Within two years the attitude of the State had changed. Seneca's spirit had departed from the administration. The pupil, a debauched tyrant, relapsed into matricide and homicide. The aesthetic young Nero became physically as well as morally repulsive, with his blotched skin, fat neck, protuberant belly, thin shanks, shortsightedness, bad odour and yellow hair.

It is reasonable to speculate whether Paul and Seneca ever met. It was possible, though it was improbable. They were both in Rome, both of some philosophical renown, the city was not large, the population of free educated men was comparatively small. Certainly we know that Paul was free to welcome visitors to his house, and foreseeing the length of his trial he wrote to Timothy and Mark summoning them to him. At the second trial all this was changed. There was now an established hatred against the Christians. The Emperor had a short way with dissenters. Public opinion was inflamed, and apprehensive of this rapidly multiplying sect. Paul was doomed by the mere fact of testifying to his faith. His confinement now became rigorous, 'he fared ill as far as bonds, like a criminal,' and Onesiphorus had much difficulty in gaining access to him. Paul had now lost hope of acquittal. From the dreadful Mamertine Prison under the Capitol, where it is believed he was finally held with St. Peter, he sent to the Christian Church his moving farewell: 'For I am now ready to be offered, and the time of my departure is at hand. I have fought a good fight: I have finished my course, I have kept the faith.' Paul was sixty-eight when he wrote these lines in A.D. 67, after thirty-five years of travelling and incessant missionary zeal. Outside the walls of Rome he found a martyr's crown.

III

We are on our way to the Doria palace, and we have been detained on its corner by St. Paul's lodging. Such delays often happen to one in Rome. On how many a bright morning have we set forth to view some particular object only to find ourselves diverted by some other irresistible attraction. An old woman in a shop where we call for a paper, the sound of a fountain, some memorial inscription on a wall, an enchanting architectural group, a statue, an arch, a garden, a church hung with ceremonial draperies for a funeral, a wedding or a cardinal's visit—all these can deflect our purpose. For this is

Rome, the idler's paradise, the gossip's bottomless well and the inexhaustible treasure-house for all to whom history, art, architecture, religion and life make appeal. 'For a visit to Rome at least fifteen days are necessary,' says Baedeker, no time-waster. But we know, in the brief span of our mortal days, that ten lives would not suffice to slake our curiosity or tire our interest. Any sojourn in Rome is an excursion in unforeseen delights and ravishing surprises. Our human destiny is continually mocked, for we are made aware how frail a leaf we are in the storm of circumstance, how feeble a candle we carry down the corridor of Time.

The grille gate opens under the portico of the Doria palace and we ascend a marble staircase to find the butler waiting to usher us into the Great Hall. At once we know we are in a museum which happens to be an Italian prince's home. A week could be spent trying to comprehend all that our eyes casually fall upon. We utter a prayer that the advent of our host will be delayed. This is no impolite or unkind wish; it springs from the undeniable fact that great art can be appreciated only by the individual mind, that galleries are best seen without one's garrulous friend to interrupt speculation and delight. Our host, of course, will be able to tell us much about these treasures, though a lifelong repetition might well have wearied his kindness. We take a swift survey: a massive sixteenth-century fireplace, two ancient altars, four superbly carved sarcophagi and, in the centre, a vigorously executed centaur in coloured marble, brought originally from Pompey's villa at Albano. Tapestries hang on the four walls, the painted ceiling is remote. Columns of porphyry, antique busts, bas-reliefs—ancient Rome lies about one. We are following a frieze of bacchantes round a vase when Prince Doria and his wife enter. Our questions begin, and presently his curator, a shy Roman professor, joins us. We learn, and we can well believe, passing from *salon* to *salon*, along galleries that surround four sides of an interior court, that one can take a day's walk over these floors. A domestic speculation at once arises concerning dusting alone, whereupon the Princess answers the query with the cheerful assurance of her sturdy Scottish character, for she hails from the land behind Hadrian's Wall. She tells us that, strange to say, the palace is better cared for by five servants than ever it was in the vanished days of fifty. 'They passed on the job to one another,' says my hostess with a laugh.

In her bright face and manner nothing shows of the grim anxieties of long years, when the house of Doria was harassed and hunted by Fascists and Germans. In the era of Fascism Prince Doria would not suffer himself to be intimidated by what he regarded as the tyrannical domination of illegitimate power centred in the hands of an able but ill-balanced dictator. One of a very few Italians whose example more widely followed would have spared Italy a terrible experience, he consistently opposed the encroaching domination of the Fascist rulers and became a marked man. His courage was matched by that of his wife. The Abyssinian War and Sanctions brought Italy to fever heat. When the Duce appealed to the matrons of Rome to deposit their wedding-rings on the altar of their country, as a gesture of patriotism, there was a general response. Not to respond was perilous in the state of inflamed public opinion. The rings were given, though the Roman jewellers worked overtime to supply dummies for those who clung to their rings from reasons of sentiment. What would the Princess Doria do? asked the colony of British women married to Italians. She replied that they must do what they thought right, and what she thought was right she would do when the time came. Thus she could not be accused of subversion.

When the day came for the Roman women to sacrifice their rings at a ceremony spectacularly staged before the Victor Emanuel monument, in the presence of the Duce and all official Rome, the Queen of Italy invited the Princess Doria to accompany her. The Princess declined the honour. There was no ring deposited by her. There was also, despite the

command to the city, no flag hung out from the Palazzo
Doria. The enraged Fascists marched on the palace, and
heavy boots resounded, and revolver-butts banged peremptorily on the great closed doors, while the mob howled.
They were opened by a confused domestic, and the crowd
surged up the marble staircase to find itself confronted by a
small, sturdy woman wearing a ring. 'She must be a visitor,'
they said, and loudly demanded to see the Prince. A posse of
booted simulacra of Mussolini, with all his arrogance and
none of his genius, stamped through the long galleries until
they found him quietly working in his office. They made
their demand that the Doria flag should be hung out to
honour the Day of the Ring. The Prince resolutely ignored
their presence and proved implacable. Then one of the booted
swarm rushed to a balcony, opened a window and put out a
flag. It was one of their own, and the crowd below cheered;
but the flag of the Dorias, that had once waved proudly on
galleons that defeated the Turks at Lepanto, made no salute
to mob dictation.

The Fascists had one childish triumph. The wedding-ring
is the *anello di fede*, the pledge of faith. A street on the south
side of the Doria Palace, leading from the Corso, was named
the Vicolo Doria. The Fascists tore down the name-tablet and
replaced it with one calling it the Vicolo Fede. To-day the
old name is back again.

Princess Doria's *anello di fede* is something much more
than a pledge of faith. It marked the beginning of a romance.
When Prince Doria as a young man was on a shooting ex-
pedition in Scotland he suffered a serious accident. Throughout a long illness he was devotedly nursed by the daughter of
a Scottish physician, with whom he fell deeply in love. It was
only after repeated proposals that he succeeded in bringing
her to Italy as his bride. Since then many trials have sealed a
life-long devotion to each other.

When Italy entered the war, in 1940, the Prince was
arrested one day, while in church, by the Fascist police. His

wife insisted on accompanying him. The Prince, a steady opponent of a regime that he was certain would lead to disaster, was proscribed and sent into exile for a year, in the old Imperial fashion. He left Rome attended by his devoted wife and daughter. Later, when Rome sat under the thrall of the German occupation, the Prince, a marked man, became a figure of suspicion, but this time it was as the enemy of Italy's enemy. Resolute again through many trials, he survived to serve his country, and in particular his city of Rome, of which he was the first mayor on its liberation.

There is a photograph of the Prince which his wife proudly shows, though there might well be other photographs revealing the equal courage of his wife and daughter under trial. One night during those war years there was a hammering on the door by the German Gestapo. They marched in, heavily armed and booted, and arrogantly began a systematic search for the Prince, with the object of carrying him off to some unknown destination. He left his bed and took swift refuge in the Muniment room. The palace is so large that a thorough search is almost an impossibility to those who do not know its geography, but the Nazis made the attempt.

In the long galleries there are some particularly splendid chairs of Genoese velvet. They have old Spanish leather covers. The Nazis kicked under the skirts of these covers, splitting them, to ensure no one was hiding beneath. Their search for the Prince was unsuccessful; they left the palace, but it was certain that another attempt would be made and that the place would be carefully watched. Late that night a shabby old man, in a long black coat and with a false beard, shuffled out of a side door, walked down over the Tiber bridge and went into hiding in a small house in the crowded working-class district of Trastevere, where he remained for some months. A reward of a million lire was offered to anyone who could give information leading to the Prince's arrest. One day the police came to the house and asked the old man who lived in it if the Prince was hiding there. The old man laughed derisively at the absurd idea that Prince Doria should be living in his poor little house, and the police departed. Tough Romans of the Trastevere breed were not to be bought by the enemy, whatever the price.

Knowing well that they might be seized as hostages, the Princess Doria and her daughter also planned their escape. The young Donna Orietta, carrying only a small handbag, having completely disguised herself by dyeing her fair hair and eyebrows black and wearing dark glasses, slipped out of the palace. Waiting until it seemed clear that her husband had made a successful escape, the Princess Doria, the last of the family, went into hiding. For a time not one of the three had word of each other, since contacts were perilous.

About a year later, when the day of liberation came, the Prince and his family returned to the palace. Their great Villa Doria-Pamphili, up on the Janiculum, had been occupied by the German S.S. They stripped it of its valuable contents, and what they failed to take away in forty lorries they carried up to the roof and threw down, in order to smash it beyond use or value. To-day nothing in the appearance or manner of the Princess betrays the anxieties of those long years when they were hounded by Fascists and hunted by Nazis, except that her hair turned grey. This story of faith and courage makes a not unworthy chapter to add to the remarkable history of the house of Doria.

When Pope Innocent X stretched out his hand to effect an alliance with the mighty Dorias of Genoa, despots and high admirals of the city-Republic for four hundred years before the Pamphili climbed to power, it was so much a matter of state policy that a council of lawyers was called to make the arrangement. Great sailors and warriors, the Dorias were, in turn, the tyrants and the idols of Genoa, Venice's deadly rival for the dominion of the seas. In A.D. 1298, Lamba Doria vanquished the Venetian navy at Curzola. Pagano Doria again humbled the mighty republic off Constantinople in 1352, and two years later destroyed its navy at Sapienza. With Andrea

Doria, hero of a hundred sea-fights, admiral of the Pope's navy, ally of Francis I, and fierce opponent of the proud Gonzalvo da Cordova, High Admiral of puissant Charles V, we come to the chief founder of the glory of the house of Doria. It is his superb portrait we shall see in the private apartments of the palace, by Sebastiano del Piombo. Andrea's heir presumptive was his nephew, Gianettino, whose portrait by Bronzino is also near those of Andrea and of Velasquez' Innocent X. The young warrior has one hand on his hip, the other on his sword, and the neat, dark head and firm face are Bronzino at his best. Gianettino fought the Turks and the Barbary pirates, and his valour at the siege of Algiers in 1541 contributed largely to the saving of the Imperial troops. As the heir to his uncle's great position he had many enemies, and he was assassinated by an arquebusier six years later.

His younger son, Pagano, took service with Spain. He was captured through treason and decapitated outside Tunis in 1574. Gianettino's elder son was the great Admiral Andrea Doria, soldier and politician, who was with Don John of Austria at the historic battle of Lepanto, which threw the Turks back to their shores. He commanded the galleys of the Genoese navy. The spoils of that famous sea-fight, the arms, armour and banners hang on the walls of the palace to-day.

IV

To describe an art gallery is often more wearisome than to walk in one, but a few pictures in a great collection shall arrest our steps, and occasionally we may sit on some magnificent chairs upholstered in settecento velvet, brought from Genoa. Naturally there are some poor paintings in a gallery of this size; the fashion and taste of four centuries are fallible, and even the best critics cannot agree. Here is Claude Lorraine's famous painting *The Mill*, but hark to Ruskin, master of a lucid prose style, in which he often wrote much nonsense. He had violent dislikes, as Whistler learned, and just

as violent enthusiasms, as Turner experienced. He wrote a
massive work *The Stones of Venice*, so heavy and laborious
that it makes you feel as if you had been stoned by Venice.
When one turns from his pontifical study to the dove-grey,
lagoon-lit city, one wonders how Ruskin could have missed
the spirit of the place and have made a didactic sermon out
of what is a lyric in marble.[2]

Ruskin charges *The Mill* with a sharp lance:

'This is a fair example of what is commonly called an "ideal"
landscape: i. e. a group of the artist's studies from nature indi-
vidually spoiled, selected with such opposition of character as may
ensure their neutralising each other's effect, and united with sufficient naturalness and violence of association to ensure their producing a general sensation of the impossible.'

The fact remains that *The Mill* is a great composition. Rus-
kin's criticism could be equally well applied to Giorgione's
The Tempest. And if probability and naturalness are to be
essential qualities of art, what becomes of Ruskin's beloved
Turner? His Venetian gondolas never touch the lagoons.
They are hydroplanes, taking off.

Past the Holbeins, past the Bellinis, the Caraccis, the Bron-
zinos, the del Sartos, the Raphaels, the Titians, the Guido
Renis, we halt briefly by a commanding marble bust of a de-
termined-looking veiled lady. She is Olympia Maidalchini
Pamphili, the sister-in-law of Pope Innocent X. These galleries were sometimes turned into temporary dormitories for
British soldiers on leave in Rome. They dubbed this formidable lady 'The Matron.' She could indeed well stand in any
hospital as the *beau ideal* of a firm matron.

In the wing of the gallery facing the Corso there is a portrait of Joan of Aragon, beautiful both for its subject and its
execution. The first thought is that only one hand could have

---

[2] What one feels about *The Stones of Venice* others feel about his *Mornings
in Florence*. 'They are very irritating and the affectation of simplicity is most
offensive. It seems a pity when he knows so much about art and can write so
well, that he should be so silly: he wants a good shaking' (*Two Englishwomen
in Rome*, by the Misses Lucas).

painted it. Leonardo da Vinci's. For a long time it was credited to him, but now it is believed to be the Flemish copy of an original by Giulio Romano, now in the Louvre. There are those who firmly maintain it is da Vinci's work. He would not be shamed by it. Near the portrait of Joan of Aragon there is a drawing that conveys some idea of the splendour of eighteenth-century hospitality. One would have thought that a palace with so many *salons*, galleries and a large ballroom would have met all the requirements of social festivities, but on April 2nd, 1769, when a great ball was given in honour of the Emperor Joseph II and the Archduke Leopold of Austria, the open courtyard was converted into a pavilion. A canopy was hung between the four walls, a floor was laid and a special gallery was built for an orchestra of fifty musicians. There were fountains, decorated alcoves, buffets—everything requisite for the entertainment of a thousand guests. The finely-drawn plan of the decorator, Nicoletti, is itself a work of art. All Rome was there to meet the Emperor and the Archduke, in an era of swords, satins and perukes, of cardinals preceded up the grand staircase with footmen carrying ceremonial candles, their prerogative of arrival and departure observed to this day.

I paused in this long gallery to look out of one of its many windows commanding the Corso. I scanned the buildings on the opposite side, wondering just where was that poor lodging taken by a youth of genius in 1741, whose small allowance had been cut off by an irate father in Venice. For there, despite his penury, dwelt Giovanni Battista Piranesi. He had just published, at twenty, his first four etchings of the ruins of Rome. Probably the first knowledge of the splendour of Rome derived by most of us came from the series of romantic etchings which have carried his fame down through the centuries and have greatly influenced British and American architecture and furniture.

I thought also of the angry crowd that in 1840 had looked up at these windows, muttering imprecations against a son of the house, while the body of a beautiful young woman, openly carried on a bier, passed to its last resting-place. The story of Vittoria Savorelli is the simple and affecting one of a lovesick girl who died of a broken heart. In this hard-bitten age girls do not die of broken hearts. They are more inclined to go out to a night club and pick up another swain. But once upon a time there were real Ophelias who died from the ill-treatment of their Hamlets. They moped and they swooned. To-day they bang a tennis-ball with the best of the boys and wear shorter shorts.

The Savorelli were of an ancient line, and when Vittoria was born in 1813 the family had just inherited the large possessions of the Marchese Muti-Papazurri, including the palace in the Piazza S.S. Apostoli inhabited by the last of the Stuarts. Beautiful and accomplished, Vittoria first saw young Don Domenico, the second son of Prince Doria, at a ball in 1836. He was just twenty-one, she was twenty-three. He was a gay youth. His mother was dead, his father spent his time in hearing Masses while the sons ran wild. Domenico lacked the good looks of his eldest brother Filippo, the inheritor of the title. He had burnt his face with gunpowder, but this did not impair his attraction for the fair sex. He rode and danced well, was elegant in his attire and polished in his manners. He appeared to fall in love with Vittoria at first sight, a thing not pleasing to the mothers of Rome, who regarded him as one of the best catches of the day. The news soon spread across Rome, one of whose chief occupations was gossip, that the young couple were in love. On a certain morning a gentleman friendly with the Dorias called upon the Savorellis, and, as was the fashion of these days, brought a proposal for Vittoria's hand from Don Domenico. The two families being in accord, the young lovers now openly met. Don Domenico had had to overcome a strong objection to the engagement from his uncle, the Cardinal, but it was subsequently arranged, and the dowry was fixed and found to be generous. Domenico now became a frequent visitor to the Palazzo Savorelli. Alas, early in the new year an epidemic of cholera smote the city. The Savorellis took refuge at Castle Gandolfo, and Vittoria was separated from her adored Domenico. Ecstatic letters passed between them. He had nicknamed her Tolla, and he signed himself 'Your eternal and affectionate Dom. D.' The months of separation grew, 'You can imagine and you ought certainly to know what is in the heart of a lover,' he wrote, 'but you can hardly guess the rapture with which I receive your letters; as proof of this I may tell you that I have ordered a casket of polished walnut wood from Castellani,[3] in which I mean to keep them. It unlocks with a golden key, which I shall have fastened to my ring and one day, if Heaven so wills it, we will read them all over together, and rejoice in company over such evidences of our mutual affection.'

That is in the great tradition of romantic letter-writing, not unworthy of the land that gave the world Romeo and Juliet, and far removed from the non-ecstatic, though possibly not less genuine staccato missives of to-day.

These young lovers separated by the plague are impatient to see each other again. The delay is agonising, and at last, in October, 1837, they are once more united. But tragedy dogged them. The Cardinal uncle was struck down, then Domenico's father, Prince Doria, died in February, 1838, and Domenico had to go into retirement with his brother Prince Filippo at the family villa at Albano. There was another spate of affectionate letters, and then came a shock for poor Vittoria. Domenico's brother was going to England, first to visit the Earl of Shrewsbury, and secondly to attend Queen Victoria's coronation. It was essential Domenico should accompany his brother. He bemoaned his hard fate, and gave his fiancée an engagement ring and a miniature of himself. Before the altar in the beautiful private chapel of the Palazzo Doria he prostrated himself and took God to witness that he was Vittoria's affianced husband. Then he tore himself away

---

[3] The Cartier of the day, with a shop full of jewels near the Fontana di Trevi.

from the distracted girl. She had a presentiment she would
never see him again.

As a lover he was not neglectful. His progress was marked
by informative and affectionate letters from Leghorn, Genoa,
Marseilles and London. Meanwhile, in conformity with a
common custom of the day, Vittoria had gone 'into retreat'
at the Convent of Sant' Antonia. She was thus spared much
venomous gossip concerning the delayed marriage. Letters
passed between the lovers, but he was constantly moving,
and some of them were lost in transit. Vittoria began to chide
him, her pen unable to hide the pangs of jealousy beginning
to torture her. Why had he changed his attire? why had he
allowed a moustache to grow? why had he altered the cut of
his hair? He accepted her reproaches cheerfully, he wrote her
ardent and long descriptions of his experiences in far away
England:

London, June 30th, 1838.

'My dear Tolla,

'I seem to be another man since I at last received your letter. . . .
You will have been longer than usual without hearing from me
but you must forgive me as this blessed coronation has not left
me time to eat, and we were obliged to take provisions with us in
order not to die of hunger. You will understand this better when
I tell you that I was in uniform from five in the morning until
three in the afternoon. Of the function itself I can only say that I
was completely dazzled by its splendours and magnificence. There
were about five hundred peers and their wives, all arrayed in robes
of crimson velvet trimmed with ermine; and at the moment when
the crown was placed on the sovereign's head, each of the peer-
esses put on her coronet. That moment is indescribable. The cries
of "Long live the Queen!" inside and outside the church, the boom-
ing of cannon and the crowning of all these ladies, combined to
form a marvellous spectacle.

'In the evening all the city was illuminated and I was delighted
with the sight. Can you guess why? Because everywhere around
me I saw the name to me most dear—that of Vittoria.'

With such a letter, so nicely turned, any lovesick maiden

would have felt assured. There were other letters, steadily maintained. After London, Domenico went on, alone, to Paris, where, unknown to her, he was met by Count Malatesta. The name, recalling Dante, had a menacing ring even for a girl not named Francesca. His mission threatened her happiness. He had been sent by Domenico's uncle in Rome to induce him to break off the engagement. The young man refused, but two weeks later, in Brussels, the envoy had evidently succeeded. Domenico wrote coolly to Vittoria and her father saying that, since his family strongly opposed the match, he must obey. He hoped she would forgive him and forget him. Count Savorelli, stunned, held back the letters for a time and pleaded with the young man, reminding him that his honour was involved. It was unavailing, and the unhappy Vittoria was shown the letters.

Doctors deny the physical phenomenon called 'a broken heart,' but people die of it nevertheless. Vittoria had received a mortal blow. All her forebodings were now confirmed. And how strong they had been! Two months before this treacherous desertion she had written to a friend, 'Sometimes I am almost reduced to despair; I imagine myself abandoned, dishonoured and the talk of all the city, and without the aid of the Lord I believe I should have already taken away the life He has given me. I even got so far as to provide myself with poison, and I am horrified now to think of it.'

This was the wail of a neurotic young woman, but it was an age when a neurosis was forced upon the unfortunate female who could not, except by marriage to however miserable an object, emancipate herself from lifelong spinsterdom, with its cold corner, back bedroom, begrudged allowance, or the care of somebody else's children. Such was the fate of most middle-class spinsters. The higher born, in Catholic countries, resorted to the nun's veil.

The deserted Vittoria pined away behind the dreary walls of St. Antonia. She clung to her lover's portrait, she consecrated his ring to the Virgin. Her mother was sick, she had only the nuns for company. Delirium and convulsions seized her. Dying, she wrote a last letter to Domenico, and a few days later, in pencil on the back of his portrait, she feebly wrote some final words of forgiveness. Then she died. Her age was just twenty-five.

Throughout Rome a storm of indignation arose. The pamphleteers got busy. Her biography and what purported to be the lovers' letters were sold by hucksters. Waves of abuse broke over the walls of the Palazzo Doria. The faithless Domenico was safely away. He was in Venice when the news of Vittoria's death reached him. He waited a whole year before venturing to return to Rome, and when he came his reception was so icy that he fled. He went to Genoa, and there remained for twenty years with only the briefest visits to Rome. Ten years after his fiancee's death he married a Genoese lady, and died in 1873, scarcely remembered in Rome.

The burial of the unhappy Vittoria became a public event. All Rome went to the funeral. Gregory XVI's vicar was approached by the Savorelli family for permission to revert to the ancient custom of *morto scoperto*. Thus it was that the dead girl was laid upon an open bier, dressed in a white satin robe, her hands clasping a crucifix, her luxuriant locks tumbling on the pillow, her brow wreathed with roses. A great veil of white muslin draped her body, leaving her face in view.

The funeral procession began at seven-thirty in the evening. It was attended by all the confraternities, chanting, with banners. The bier, covered with a pall of white velvet and gold tissue, was borne on the shoulders of eight acolytes. The black-and-white-cowled fraternities, rows of priests, monks, friars, bearing lighted torches and chanting as they walked, preceded the bier. The red light of the torches played over the dead girl's ivory face. A guard of soldiers escorted the procession and stemmed the emotional crowds. All along the route flowers fell from crowded balconies. The procession

started from the convent where Vittoria died. The direct route
to the church of S.S. Apostoli was a short one, but this was
deliberately changed. By a dramatic gesture, a circuitous
route was adopted with the purpose of taking the cortege
along the Corso so that it should pass by the many-windowed
façade of the Palazzo Doria. And as it slowly passed, the
voices of the chanting monks were drowned in the imprecations of the crowd, directed at the home of Don Domenico.

The memory of that sad procession lived long among those
who saw it. Edmond About wrote a romance called *Tolla*.[4]
The historian Silvagni was then a child of seven, living in a
palace overlooking the Forum of Trajan. On the evening of
October 18th, 1838, he saw a stir in the piazza, and then at
about eight o'clock the flower-strewn body of Vittoria Savorelli passed below as the long procession, chanting, filed
through the piazza, the bier lit only by the light of the
torches.

v

I turned from the window overlooking the Corso and
passed into a smaller room decorated with mirrors. It contained three busts, one of Prince Filippo Doria, brother of
Domenico; one of Lady Mary Talbot, his wife, and one of
her sister, Lady Gwendolen, the saintly wife of Prince Marcantonio Borghese, who died in 1840.

When young Prince Filippo Doria returned from England
he had found an English wife, Lady Mary, daughter of the
Earl of Shrewsbury, and sister of Lady Gwendolen, who, in
1835, had married Prince Marcantonio Borghese. One May
evening in 1839 Prince Doria gave a fancy dress ball for his
young bride. It was an era of splendid fetes. At that time the

---

[4] Henry James recorded in his Life of W. W. Story that he had read *Tolla*
in his extreme youth—'Edmond About's first and truly beautiful novel, a
masterpiece of the pathetic, as we used at least to think it. . . . I remember how
during the first walk I ever took in Rome Tolla, though even then of respectable
antiquity, seemed so recent and fresh to me that I was half the time occupied
in wondering which of the palaces stood for the Palais Feraldi—in which of
them the exquisite Tolla had lived, loved, wasted, died.'

pace in Rome was set by Prince Torlonia, whose wealth enabled him to provide lavish entertainments. On this occasion the Dorias were determined not to suffer by comparison. The eight hundred guests were all in historic costume. At the foot of the staircase stood the young nobles of Rome, all in military costume denoting the famous Romans of the Imperial era from which their houses claimed descent. At the top of the staircase Prince Doria and his bride received their guests. Tall and handsome, his costume was a copy of that worn by Alexander Farnese in the Titian portrait hanging in the long gallery. The Princess was dressed as Margherita of Austria. Napoleon's Republican brother, Lucien Bonaparte, exiled from France because he never approved of the Corsican's plan for world conquest and prophesied his downfall, came dressed as a sultan. He was at this time Prince of Canino. Around him were the Roman princes and princesses, the Torlonias as Byzantine Greeks, a Rospigliosi as Don John of Austria, his princess as Lucrezia Borgia, two Borghese princes as Castor and Pollux, the Duchess Sermoneta as Bianca Capello. Here in the long series of *salons*, blazing with candelabra multiplied in the great gilded mirrors, through state rooms with their tapestries depicting the battle of Lepanto and the deeds of Philip le Bel, amid the music of four stringed orchestras and the splashing of fountains in the courtyards, the large company gathered for the ball.

Two rows of retainers in the Doria livery lined the grand staircase, holding aloft flaming torches, as the guests, glittering with jewels and decorations, greeted their host and hostess. In *salons* beyond the ballroom supper was served on the household plate by powdered lackeys in scarlet and gold, with white satin knee-breeches and buckled shoes. All Rome was there, and in a *salon*, before the dancing began, whereupon they would leave, the cardinals and monsignors, in purple and crimson, held court, seated by walls enriched with the works of Leonardo da Vinci, Titian, Rubens, Holbein, del Sarto and Raphael.

On one figure we may look briefly, as the pageant passes. It is the Princess Gwendolen Borghese, sister of the bride. Little more than three years earlier she had married Prince Borghese, who had succeeded to the titles and wealth of his uncle, Prince Camillo, husband of Pauline Bonaparte, who had died without a legitimate heir. How different was the new chatelaine of the *palazzo* and the Villa Borghese from her frivolous and vain predecessor! Already in Rome, within three short years, she was a beloved figure among the poor, for whom her care was unwearying. She had known Rome since she was a small girl, and had lost her heart to it. Beautiful, with a head of rich chestnut hair and a smile of singular sweetness, she was known to the people by her visitation of the hospitals and the sick wherever they lay.

Young Prince Borghese was accounted a fortunate fellow when he took to himself this girl bride of England. What she gave of her wealth none knew, but she was not content with the mere giving. From her great palace she would go obscurely on foot into the poorest districts, not always considered safe. She was appalled by the terrible contrast between the flaunted wealth and the dire poverty that arraigned this city of the Holy Church. The palaces rose over terrible slums, as nowhere else in the civilised world. The coaches of princes and cardinals rolled past alleys where the hungry and crippled inhabitants died of recurrent plagues. When, in 1837, a frightful visitation of cholera sent all the leading families and citizens scurrying out of Rome, and death took its terrible toll, the Princess Borghese remained in the city and went about fearlessly on her errands of mercy. The terror passed, and on an October day in 1840, following their usual custom, she and her husband gave a public fete at the Villa Borghese. She talked to the mothers and children, played games with them and had a smile and a word for the poor Romans who filled the terraces and gardens of that ilex-haunted pleasance in which the selfish and petulant Princess Pauline had once held court.

Three days after the fete the Princess complained of a sore throat. The doctors who examined the beautiful young matron had an alarming verdict. They told the distracted Prince that he must prepare for the worst and send for a priest. 'Do what seemeth best with Thy servant, O Lord,' she said, when praying with him. Her four infant children, the eldest only four, were brought to her. In the evening she died, aged twenty-three. The news stunned Rome. Within the next few days the unhappy Prince faced the loss of three of his four children, who followed their mother to the grave.

On the evening that Rome received the news of the Princess Borghese's death a great multitude stood in silence before the Palazzo Borghese. The next day she lay in state, and for three whole days the sorrowing public filed by the flower-laden catafalque in the hall of the palace. On a Friday evening the cortege started on its way to the Borghese chapel in Santa Maria Maggiore. It seemed as if all Rome had turned out to pay reverence to the beloved Princess. A vast concourse of the poor followed the hearse, while flowers fell from windows and balconies.

When the service in the church was concluded a chamberlain came out, according to ancient custom, and announced to the Borghese coachman, waiting with the family carriage, that his mistress no longer needed his services. Solemnly breaking his staff of office, the coachman drove the empty carriage homewards, whereupon a weeping multitude knelt before the church and prayed for the soul of the Princess.

Naturally the dead woman became a source of legends. It is one of the joys of Rome that the ecclesiastical Grimms can tell the most fantastic fairy-tales without provoking a cynical smile. You believe as little or as much as you please. The invention is often charming and ingenious. One summer's evening, narrates W. W. Story, an old woman was praying and weeping in a corner of the Borghese chapel. A lady beside her, clothed in black, seeing her distress, spoke to her, and learned that because of her acute poverty and loneliness the old woman was in the deepest despair. Thereupon the dark lady took off a ring with a large stone, saying 'Be of good comfort; you shall be taken care of—"Silver and gold have I none, but such as I have I give unto you." ' Give the ring to the poor old woman, she then disappeared. The next day when the recipient took the ring to a jeweller to sell it he detained her, called in the police and gave her in charge, certain that she had stolen the ring, for he recognised it as belonging to the Borghese family.

The Prince was informed, and on seeing the ring nearly fainted. It belonged to his wife, and had been buried with her in the Borghese chapel! A theft from the tomb was impossible. He visited the old woman in prison and heard her story. The only solution was that the donor was the Princess Borghese herself. The old woman was thereupon released, and the Prince arranged for her to be cared for.

VI

Our tour of the galleries is finished and lunch is ready. We pass into the private apartments. In one of these hang four magnificent tapestries of the Battle of Lepanto, in which a Doria commanded the Genoese fleet under Don John of Austria. Our host moves a panel and a staircase to a secret chamber behind the fireplace is revealed. It is in another room that we reach the climax of our tour. This is the family's intimate room. The palace belongs to the world. Here and in a few personal rooms the Dorias are at home. The apartment in which we drink our aperitif seems lined with history. Here we see a painting showing the great admiral, Andrea Doria, with Christopher Columbus. It was long attributed to Raphael, but is now ascribed to Sebastiano del Piombo. It is worthy of the reputation of either master. The end wall holds the prize of this magnificent collection, Velasquez's wonderful portrait of Pope Innocent X, Giovanni Battista Pamphili, declared by Sir Joshua Reynolds to be the finest picture in Rome.

POPE INNOCENT X by *Velasquez*

VILLA BORGHESE

In the seventeenth century every cultured Spaniard dreamed of a visit to Italy. It was said one was fortunate to be born in France because of its nobility, to live in Italy because of its culture, and to die in Spain because of its faith. At last the dream of Velasquez came true: he obtained Philip IV's permission to leave Madrid and go to Rome. He set off in high spirits, and travelled via Venice, Ferrara and Bologna, well furnished with letters of introduction. He reached Rome in 1630, in the sixth year of the reign of Urban VIII, the Pope who forbade snuff, condemned Galileo and plundered the Pantheon. Velasquez was thirty years of age, and already famous. Cardinal Barberini, the Pope's nephew, secured him rooms in the Vatican, but he found them too much out of the way. One day, visiting the lovely Villa Medici with its gardens on the Pincio, a fine view of Rome below, and the vast pine-studded and ilex-haunted park behind, Velasquez approached its owner, the Medici Duke, and gained permission to reside there. For two months he was in paradise until that scourge of Rome, fever, drove him to a healthier neighbourhood. Three years later the arraigned Galileo was confined in this same villa.

The city was astir with events in what was regarded as the Golden Age. Urban VIII was busy with new fortifications of the Castle of St. Angelo. The walled passage of escape from St. Peter's was cleared, and under the library lay a well-equipped arsenal. It may be that Velasquez saw the bronze roof of the Pantheon being stripped to make cannon for the Castle and the Baldacchino for St. Peter's, though it was then without those twin towers, added later, 'the asses' ears of Bernini,' as the Romans call them, that would disfigure the building for some two centuries. There was an unending pageant of cardinals, envoys, soldiers, Roman nobles and visiting foreign notabilities. We know what Velasquez looked like at this time, for Rubens told us that the young man painted a self-portrait, still in Rome, 'in the manner of Titian and not inferior to that great artist's heads.' We see

an elegant young man with trim up-pointed moustachios
and small pointed beard. His setting in the Villa Medici was
superb, for it was decorated with famous antiques, the Venus,
the group of Wrestlers, the Mercury fountain by Gian da
Bologna and the renowned Niobe group at the end of the
alley, under a pillared canopy. Beyond this pleasance lay
the new marvel of the Villa Borghese, Evelyn's 'Elysium of
Delight.'

Velasquez made two sketches of his retreat. In one we see
the high arch of the columned loggia, a garden, and, beyond
the balustrade, the statue of the reclining Ariadne, then
called the Cleopatra, all backed by the dark cypresses and
ilexes of the Borghese Gardens.

Here in Rome the artist worked and enjoyed himself. *The
Forge of Vulcan* was of this period. Possibly Michelangelo's
nudes in the Sistine Chapel suggested these studies of the
human form, but the brawny blacksmiths seem to have come
from the Asturian uplands rather than from Italy; they are
Spaniards, with their overhanging locks.

After a short stay in Naples, Velasquez sailed for home,
and reached Madrid early in 1631. He was delighted to find
the King had not sat to any other painter, and was gratified
because 'His Majesty was much pleased at his return.'

He who has once been to Rome is seldom content until he
has returned there. The Fountain of Trevi was not made until
a hundred years after Velasquez's visit, so that he could not
follow the popular custom of throwing a coin into its waters
to ensure his return. Eighteen years were to pass at the court
of Philip IV before Velasquez could satisfy his wish. In the
meantime Spain had ceased to be a great Power, wrecked by
a disastrous war. In Rome Urban VIII had died, and the
fallen idol, Gian Lorenzo Bernini, the man who made Rome
baroque, had been brought back to favour by Innocent X,
who found him irresistible. 'One must not look at his designs
unless one is prepared to adopt them,' he said.

Velasquez's second trip was primarily for business, to buy

pictures and sculpture for the Royal Galleries. He left Madrid in November, 1648, and went first to Venice, now the picture mart of the world. But others were there before him, and the works of Bellini, Titian, Veronese and Tintoretto were having a boom market. Velasquez reached Rome in 1650, the year of the Universal Jubilee. It was a stirring time. The Campidoglio Museum, after Michelangelo's design, had just been opened. The new Pope's family, dominated by Olympia Maidalchini, its wealth augmented by the Pope's nephew's marriage to the richest heiress in Rome, planned the glorification of its name.

Bernini, for whom Urban VIII, when Cardinal Barberini, had actually held the looking-glass by whose aid the handsome young sculptor had modelled himself as David, was back in favour and busy with the fountain in the Piazza Navona, which just missed the stupendous by reason of the fact that Innocent X, in a mood of meanness, cut down the plans. The Pamphili family wanted glory, but they did not want to pay for it. Innocent X expressed his dislike of painters, who, he said, did nothing but annoy and deceive him. It is ironical that he should have been the subject of one of the greatest paintings in the world and have been surrounded by great artists. Raphael and Michelangelo were gone. Salvator Rosa and Bernini reigned. It was the sunset of art, but luridly glorious. Rosa's house on the Pincio was the meeting-place of the princes, prelates, ambassadors, artists, poets and musicians. He strutted, and had a fine conceit of himself, quite certain that he was the pinnacle of art for all ages. Velasquez looked on the scene with a cool eye. He preferred the Venetian school, and did not subscribe to the 'Sanziomania' that had arisen since the death of Raphael Sanzio d'Urbino.

Velasquez must have been gratified by his commission to paint the Pope. Innocent X was now in his seventy-seventh year. Robust, saturnine, tenacious and unwearying in his public duties, his mania was the amassing of wealth, filched from the papal revenues, in order to endow a dynasty. In this he was assisted by his rapacious, fierce sister-in-law, Olympia Maidalchini. His end was ignominious. Olympia, dubbed 'the Papessa,' took all she could lay her hands on. It was said that in the last ten days when the old Pope lay dying she amassed half a million crowns by the sale of benefices in his name. He died in the only shirt he possessed, covered by a rough blanket. As the breath left his body Olympia dragged from underneath the bed two coffers of money he had tried to hide. His servant stole even the brass candlestick with the poor taper burning beside his deathbed and substituted a wooden one. His body was carried from the Quirinal to St. Peter's on a bier so short that his feet hung over the end. His relations refused to pay for his funeral, Olympia declaring she was only a poor widow. The body went into a storeroom, full of rats, used by the Vatican stonemasons, and one workman, stirred by pity, bought the sole candle that burned by it. Finally a wooden coffin was found and a monsignor paid five scudi to have the corpse taken away. It was slung between two mules and taken in darkness to the church of St. Agnes. Olympia, with the accumulated spoils of the Pontificate, endowed her son Camillo, who acquired the beautiful Palazzo Doria in which we now find Velasquez's portrait of the Pope, her brother-in-law. Prince Camillo built the Villa Doria-Pamphili, the largest in Rome, on the site of thirty-four ancient tombs.

Donna Olympia died soon after the Pope. She had had to battle against a multitude of enemies. She organised with her wealth an independent party, known as the Flying Squadron, to block any election of a pope dangerous to her interests. For three months she kept the cardinals imprisoned in conclave until, in despair, they abandoned their own candidates and agreed on a harmless and honest man, Fabio Chigi of Siena, Pope Alexander VII. It was a blow to Olympia. She sought an audience of the Pope and was refused. 'Donna Olympia has had too much conversation with Popes and she must understand that things henceforth will be very different,' he said. She was ordered to quit Rome within three days, to render up an account of the monies she had annexed, and to return all the jewels and valuables carried off by her from the Vatican. It was a paralysing blow. Over her hung the threat of imprisonment and the loss of a colossal fortune, but the pestilence then sweeping over Italy proved her ally. She died of the plague in her villa at Viterbo. In addition to large estates and a great treasury of gold and precious stones, two millions of crowns were found in her coffers. The whole of this passed to her son, Prince Camillo, who had resigned a cardinal's hat to marry a widowed heiress. Thus two vast fortunes passed into the Pamphili line.

There is no need to read anything into the face of Innocent X. Velasquez has it all there—'*Un Papa buono per le donne*' (a Pope good for the ladies), said Cardinal Barberini, caustically. The portrait has great directness.[5] Velasquez had to work quickly. The economy of genius is stamped on the canvas. The colour is unsurpassable, the hands, the light in the eyes, the rubicund complexion, build up a portrait that is pitiless but not unjust. 'Our Velasquez,' wrote Palomino, 'came to Italy, not however to learn but to teach, for the portrait of Pope Innocent X was the amazement of Rome, all copied it as a study, and looked on it as a marvel.' And so we look on it to-day. Velasquez made sure of his immortality in a double sense. The letter in the Pope's hand carries the artist's signature.

Before Velasquez left Rome the Pope presented him with a gold chain and medallion, engraved with his likeness, a distinction remembered on the painter's tomb. When the Pope sent his chamberlain to pay for the portrait, Velasquez, a Spaniard of unfailing pride, remarked that the King, his master, always paid him with his own hand. The Pope

[5] The irascible J. M. Whistler left Rome after three days, exclaiming—'Ruins don't count! This is only a stucco-town! I am going!' The one object that gave him pleasure was the Velasquez portrait in the Doria gallery.

accepted the rebuke, and paid him personally. Then, having bought some of the art treasures for which he had a royal commission, and having secured two renowned fresco-painters for work in the palace at Madrid, Velasquez set sail from Genoa for home.

V

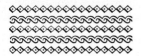

PRINCESS PAULINE BORGHESE

I

AGAIN and again one's curiosity is provoked by some scene or object in Rome, and the answer to the question that often arises is not always immediately forthcoming.

'What is the Banco di Santo Spirito—the Bank of the Holy Ghost?' I asked a Roman friend one day.

'It is a bank.'

'Of course; but what kind of a bank? Can you draw a cheque on it?' I asked.

'Certainly—it has quite a number of branches in Rome.'

'But why the Bank of the Holy Ghost? It sounds a little blasphemous to me, and that heads all the sins in the confessional box.'

'Does it?' asked my Roman friend, a good Catholic. 'Surely murder is the greatest of all sins?'

'Oh, no. The list runs—Blasphemy, superstition, homicide, abortion, *oppressio infantis*, *peccatum sodomiticum*, *etiam cumulatiore sexus persona*, *copula carnalis cum persona infideli*, *stuprum violentum virgini illatum*, *incestis*. . . .'

'Are you an unfrocked priest?' demanded my friend, a suspicious look in his dark eyes.

'I am always in search of knowledge,' I answered.

He confessed he could not tell me how the bank got its singular name. No one seemed to know. No book provided the explanation, and finally I went direct to the Banco di

Santo Spirito and asked a clerk behind the desk. He brought
a superior, who politely asked me why I wanted to know.

'Because I don't like to remain ignorant,' I replied.

'If you will leave me your name and address, I will send
you the explanation,' he said.

'You don't know it?' I asked, as gently as possible.

'No—not exactly,' he replied, almost contritely.

But before he kindly wrote to me, I had satisfied my curiosity. One morning I found myself in the Via del Banco di
Santo Spirito. I had found this street, as is so often the case in
Rome, while searching for something else. I made two dis-
coveries at the same time. The Via del Banco di Santo Spirito,
a street that leads directly to the bridge and the Castle of St.
Angelo, was a centre of merchants and bankers in the Middle Ages. It was from his workshop here that Benvenuto Cellini, insulted through the window by the goldsmith Pompeo,
rushed out and stabbed him to death. Cellini was rather
proud of his dexterity with the dagger. There is another re-
minder of this talented braggart and assassin, who lives,
vividly if odiously, in his famous *Autobiography*. The papal
mint stood at the corner of this street, and in it Cellini worked
on his medallions. It was originally built by Bramante, in
1503, for Pope Julius II. About a hundred years later Paul V
converted it, for papal transactions, into the Banco di Santo
Spirito, which took its name from the fact that its deposits
were guaranteed by the estate belonging to the Hospital of
Santo Spirito, along the Tiber bank.

In a most extraordinary manner an Englishman has an
interest in this Banco di Santo Spirito, even though he has
no deposit in it. The full name of the hospital is Santo Spirito
in Sassia, so named in commemoration of its founder, Ina,
King of the West Saxons. He had succeeded Cædwalla, the
young prince who journeyed from England to Rome in A.D.
683, and died there, a week after his baptism by Pope Sergius
on Easter Eve, so that he was buried in his baptismal robes.
Ina came to Rome with his Queen Ethelburga in A.D. 720,

after a reign of thirty years. It was he who built St. Mary in Sassia, later called Santo Spirito, as a hospice and school for his countrymen. He devoted his fortune to the hospice, took a vow of poverty, and died there eight years later. His hospice came into the care of the Hospitaliers of San Spirito, an order founded in 1198. It became derelict in the thirteenth century, when a transference was sanctioned by King John of England, who ceded the property, together with a monetary gift, to the hospital. Many bequests came to this great hospital with its one thousand seven hundred beds, its medical library and foundling department. Thus from the pious gift of an Anglo-Saxon king a great hospital has grown whose rich estates guaranteed the deposits of the Banco di San Spirito created by Paul V, Camillo Borghese.

It happened on the day that I made this discovery that I was destined to encounter the work of Camillo Borghese in a different form. In the afternoon I was due at a reception given by a British official resident in Rome. His address would have graced any visiting-card and opened historical vistas, for he lived in a suite in the Palazzo Borghese. So thither I went, with a dozen names familiar in history ringing in my head. There was the great Camillo himself, who purchased and finished the vast Palazzo Borghese, second only to the Palazzo Doria in size and grandeur. No pope ever devised a more magnificent seat for the establishment of a dynasty, with its great art gallery, its cloistered courtyard facing the two-storied arcade of ninety-six granite columns. Here in regal magnificence lived the wealthiest and most powerful family in Rome during the papacy of Paul V. His nephews were loaded down with wealth derived from the Holy See, by methods as dishonest as they were iniquitous. Cardinal Scipione Borghese had an income of 150,000 *scudi*; Marcantonio Borghese had principalities, palaces, villas and great treasures of jewelry and furniture. Eighty estates in the Campagna were acquired from the Roman nobles, tempted by high prices. All over the Ecclesiastical States the grasping

Borghese hand was felt, and orders and confiscations, backed by Papal Bulls, reduced whole communities to a condition of vassaldom.

All visitors to Rome know the Via Vittorio Veneto, which leads up to the Pincian Gate and the Villa Borghese. Its hotels, its cosmopolitan crowds thronging the pavements, make it the great rendezvous of the foreign and native boule-vardiers. What were once the grounds and parks of great villas are now crowned with hotels, offices, and cafés spread out in the sunshine. It is to-day one of the richest and busiest areas of Rome. All this tract of land, its villas and parks, came into possession of Paul V by confiscation of the estates of the Cenci family when its members were beheaded for the murder of the infamous Francesco Cenci. It was one of the wealthiest families in Rome, and Paul V took a heavy toll of its possessions. His nephew, Cardinal Scipione Borghese, built the great Rospigliosi palace. We owe much of our pleasure to him to this day. He was a tremendous restorer of the churches, and spent a large part of his fortune rebuilding them, so that his name on their façades is ever before our eyes. The park which takes the name of the Villa Borghese and contains the Casino, or Villa, with its superb art gallery, was his work, in co-operation with his uncle. It adjoins the Pincio, and to walk in it is to experience one ravishing delight after another, with its lake, its long avenue of dark ilexes leading to vistas of temples and statues, its tall cypresses, its parasol pines. At every turn there is a composition of meadow and wood, with masses of dramatic trees against the brilliant blue sky. Here surely is the haunt of all those figures that flit through the classic mythology— Pan, Apollo, Aphrodite, the satyrs, the fauns, the nymphs, the wild maenads, and down by the still lake the naiads whose cool beauty enamoured strayed Hylas. Well might John Evelyn, wandering in its shades, in 1644, call it 'a real Elysium of delight, a Paradise.'

But we are straying again, seduced by the beckoning hand

of History. We have come to the curving portico of the
Palazzo Borghese. Which staircase do we take, for there are
four, and which wing, which floor, for this is a palace that
housed all the branches of a large family spread over two
or three generations? Two obvious guests gave me a clue. A
lift had been ingeniously placed in the well of a circular
staircase. I scorned this anachronism in the palace of the
Borghese and ascended by the shallow steps. Round and round
and round one went; finally a pair of rich walnut doors
confronted one, and by them I gained access to my host's
suite. Damask, and gold-and-green-painted walls, high ceilings with rubicund gods and goddesses soaring above, an
exquisite little library off the panelled reception rooms—
everything was perfectly composed in a seigneurial vista.
This was one suite in perhaps forty, tucked away in one
corner of one floor of the great palace. I tried to evoke the
scenes it had witnessed, the voices that had echoed from its
walls, the long procession through three hundred years of its
inhabitants: princes and princesses, cavaliers and cardinals.
And here we were balancing glasses of sherry, truncating one
another's gabbled sentences, adroitly gliding from the bore
to the beauty in the murmuring swarm that left no room for
the ghost of a social prelate, though a living one, imported,
more addicted to the haunts of rich tourists than to the gloom
of silent churches, a veritable Monsignor Pappagallo, recalled Wordsworth's lines upon a parrot:

> Arch, volatile, a sportive bird
> By social glee inspired;
> Ambitious to be seen or heard
> And pleased to be admired.

Could it be possible that in this suite, through these *salons*
and the countless rooms of this vast palace, the light foot and
the petulant head of Princess Pauline Borghese had passed,
reflected briefly in these old mirrors? For she had lived here
once, the favourite sister of an upstart emperor, and by virtue

of Napoleon's power and her own beauty had drawn about
her a court of gallants.

Let us leave this crowded *salon* of a palace down in the
city and, mounting up towards the Trinità dei Monti and the
Villa Medici, make our way towards the Pincio and through
the park of Villa Borghese, or, as they prefer to call it now,
Villa Umberto. We pass the arena where the riders on horseback go round and round. The name of the place is a tongue-
twister for an Anglo-Saxon, but once you have got it you are
proud of it.

'Shall we go to the Galoppatoio?' I would ask, for the sheer
pleasure of the name, a gallop in itself.

So past the Galoppatoio we will take an avenue of dark
ilex and wander by pavilions, fountains and statues until at
last, against the sky, we see the twin towers of the vast
Casino, as they call this villa built by Cardinal Scipione
Borghese.

And here, as it seems, I am on familiar ground. How
strange that in Rome I am suddenly transported forty years
back to a terrace on a hill overlooking the Thames. It is a
natural thing that young poets should dream of the Italian
scene. It seemed to me then that slender cypresses dark
against the vivid blue, terraces of silvery olives, the russet-
golden walls of a villa with a pergola, the sound of falling
fountains, and nightingales singing in the warm night existed somewhere and would be found in a happier day. I
recall how, a very small child, taken into the drawing-room
of a country vicarage, I saw hanging by the fireplace a
water-colour painting that was the very essence of poetry,
though at that age I was spelling out of a book. It was a
water-colour of a bright villa, sun-drenched, on a hillside,
with flower-filled urns on a long terrace, and blue-shuttered
windows. And all I can retrieve from those lost years is a
voice saying, 'Yes, that is my brother's villa at Fiesole.'
Another score of years and the whole picture seems to take
shape before me as I stand in a garden on a terrace above

the Thames. The sun shone, the sky was blue, and around me spread the glory of the Cliveden woods, above Maiden-head. The setting of balustraded terrace, benches, urns and statues spoke to me of Italy again, still unvisited and deeply desired. It was not so wild a fancy, I learned much later, for this beautiful English terrace had been transported from the Villa Borghese to Cliveden Court. And here, now, before the Casino, a copy of that terrace has replaced the original.

Cardinal Scipione Borghese was only thirty when he began the construction of this great villa to house the art collection he was forming. Prince Marcantonio Borghese (IV) rebuilt it in 1782 and added further treasures.

The height and vastness of the hall as we enter are over-whelming, so also are the crowded frescoes. How many artists worked here, and for how much, and for how long? one is inclined to ask. In the first room on the right, under the painted vaulted ceiling, dominating the centre, we are con-fronted with Canova's world-famous statue of Pauline Bor-ghese—the *Victorious Venus in Repose*. With much reason Canova regarded it as one of his most successful works. Its technique leaves one speechless. True, there are those who do not like it. 'Beautiful bad taste,' said Keats, though whether it was the shamelessness of the nude princess or the sculptor's creation he criticised we do not know.

The Princess, half-draped, might have posed as a famous courtesan, which she was, though marriage made her a legiti-mate practitioner. Her irresistible charm is immortalised in marble, and if for her age the pose was immodest, we no longer care, for it is the whole truth and nothing but the naked truth concerning this woman. It is easy to credit the story that her husband, Prince Camillo Borghese, was so outraged by this exhibition of his wife's figure that, while never jealous of a wife who did not know the meaning of fidelity, he was jealous of the statue and kept it locked away from the vulgar gaze. Whatever the verdict on the lady, there can be only one verdict concerning her beauty in the perfect classical tradition in which Canova has immortalised her.[1] She is safe forever against the withering touch of Time, enthroned here in her husband's great villa, deep in the ilex groves beyond Rome's walls. We are told Pauline was a minx, that she had a procession of lovers, that she flouted her husband, that she was outrageously extravagant, vain and imperious. All this is probably correct. She possessed a dazzling pink-and-white complexion. Her beautiful little head was crowned by a mass of black curls, she had a faultless Greek profile, and was a perfectly formed woman of great vivacity. She was Napoleon's favourite sister, and when crowns fell, and the Empire melted away, she alone was faithful. She sacrificed her jewelry to finance his campaigns and clamoured to go into exile with him. This much can be said for her.

It was natural that the statue of Camillo's wife, bearer of one of the proudest names in Rome, a half-naked study of a woman on a sofa, should outrage the whole Borghese clan. It was a deliberate flouting of all the conventions. She had untameable roguery. She disliked Rome, despite the possession of half a dozen palaces and villas through which she restlessly moved with her cavalcade. There was no moment in her life when the immediate wish was not paramount. She was a born *cocotte*. Created a princess, she lived like a courtesan, and yet of all the tribe of pinchbeck kings and queens and princesses, moved over the European chessboard by a ruthless player, she is the most warmly human and vivid, with a touch of the Napoleonic fire. As a child, driven with her family into exile, she had lived with them on public assistance in Marseilles. At sixteen she was madly in love with a sinister middle-aged *roué*, stained with the blood of his vicitims sent to the guillotine. Napoleon rescued her from

[1] It was not quite flawless. Her Achilles Heel was her ears, if one may use the metaphor. They had no rims. For this reason in all her portraits the ears were covered with a bandeau or hairdressing. Canova with great artistry portrays her with a hand over the ear facing the viewer. In the case of the other he pulled the hair down over it.

her folly. She flirted wildly with his officers at Montebello, in those first hours of his expanding glory. Dinners, balls, theatricals, the pageant of a minor Court, set her on the path of dalliance. 'She was,' wrote a friend of Napoleon's, 'a singular combination of the most perfect physical beauty and the queerest moral sense.'

Napoleon, well aware of his sister's instability, hurriedly married her to one of his staff, young General Leclerc, who was intoxicated with her. She was frantic when she found herself shipped with her husband to uncivilised Santo Domingo, where Leclerc was given the task of crushing the negro liberator, Toussaint L'Overture, in order to re-establish slavery in France's rich colony. The campaign was disastrous. Yellow fever swept the French forces, twenty-five thousand soldiers were dead in a month. Pauline showed spirit and kept her head. 'I am Napoleon's sister, I am afraid of nothing,' she said, as she held receptions and dances amid the dying. In October, 1802, Leclerc died. Pauline cut off her hair, put it in his coffin, and a week later sailed with her infant son and her embalmed husband for France. She was a widow at twenty-two, and back in her beloved Paris. Napoleon was First Consul. Life was just beginning.

She had now endless money, a large house in Paris, an establishment, an estate from her husband, and a very liberal grant from Napoleon. She set up a court at the Hotel Charost. It became imperative to find her a second husband. The Vice-President of the new Italian Republic was selected. He declined the perilous honour. At that moment Fate brought the scion of a great Roman house to Paris. Owner of eighty estates, a palace in Florence, a palace in Rome, a villa outside the gates which housed the famous Borghese collection, young — being only twenty-eight — handsome, with dark curly hair and a good figure, Prince Camillo Borghese had everything but the one thing essential. He was a nit-wit. In the eyes of Pauline this was an asset. It made her task so much the easier. By this marriage she entered one of the great Roman houses. The famous Borghese jewels became hers. After the marriage the sister-in-law she detested, the Empress Josephine, gave a brilliant reception for her. Flattered as a divine beauty, an Imperial princess, the conquest of lovers was now her chief occupation.

A guard of honour greeted the young couple in Rome when they drove to the Palazzo Borghese. The Dowager Princess welcomed her, the Cardinal Consalvi, the Pope's Secretary of State, brought greetings from Pius V. The Pope received her in his private apartment. The great Borghese palace was lighted from floor to roof. Eight hundred guests sat down to dinner, sixteen hundred came to the ball. All Rome was at the feet of the enchanting Princess. She in turn was delighted with Rome—for a few weeks. Her husband was a poor lover, and that for Pauline was a crime. The Dowager Princess began to raise her eyebrows. Extravagance, irresponsibility, contempt for conventions, and worse, became discernible. There was that dreadful business of Canova's statue—a Princess Borghese bare-breasted to the public! Napoleon scolded his sister in a letter. She was not to break with her husband. 'If you quarrel with him the fault will be yours, and then you will lose your happiness and my affection,' he threatened.

To keep an eye on his unbalanced sister, Napoleon despatched his sturdy mother, Madame Mère, who never lost her head. But it was not long before the wayward daughter escaped from her. Pleading illness, she went to Bagni di Lucca, where she received news of the death of her little boy, left behind in Frascati. Within two weeks she was out of mourning and in a whirl of festivities. She went to Paris and was a train-bearer at Napoleon's coronation. He was harassed by all his sisters clamouring for higher rank, a bigger establishment, a larger income. When Piedmont was converted into a Department of the Hautes-Alpes, Prince Camillo was appointed Governor-General, and proceeded to Turin to set up a court. The young pair had already collected one principality. Princess Pauline was created Princess and Duchess of Guastalla, but, the income apart, the title was almost a joke, Guastalla itself being a village of six thousand souls. Later she traded it in to the new Kingdom of Italy for six million francs. Prince Camillo's new position was a serious one. His principality was filched from the kingdom of Sardinia. He inherited the residences of the King of Sardinia, together with a household of court chamberlains, equerries, aides-des-camps and ladies-in-waiting. All that is now remembered of this petty court is that several members of the local Cavour family obtained appointments in the household and enjoyed the friendship of the newly appointed Governor. A son being born to this family, Prince Camillo and Princess Pauline stood as godparents, the latter holding the infant at the font. The child was destined later, as Count Camillo Benso di Cavour, to be the great statesman of liberated Italy. There was much gossip concerning the paternity of the child.

II

It was not long before Princess Pauline tired of her principality, and returned to her beloved Paris, and a succession of lovers. She was enamoured of her chamberlain, M. de Forbin. *Si, ti amo di piu, caro idolo mio*, she wrote to him from Greoux, and was not content until her dear idol had gone to join her there. Within a year the romance had ended. She reduced her lovers to abject slaves. At a picnic she commanded one of her court to lie on his stomach that she might sit on his back, and another to lie on his back that she might rest her feet on his stomach. She had contracted singular habits in Santo Domingo, such as commanding her lady-in-waiting to lie on the floor and bare her bosom that she might warm her feet. She had herself carried in a flimsy wrap to and from her milk-bath in the arms of a huge negro named Paul. When someone seemed shocked by this familiarity, thinking it might be because the negro was single, she rang the bell for a kitchen-maid, and there and then commanded the two servants to get married. In vain the poor girl protested against becoming the wife of a coal-black negro. They were married. The girl went back to the kitchen, the favourite Paul continued to carry his mistress to the bath. Two other negroes carried her around in a palanquin, while she was accompanied by pages in grotesque attire. One boy, stripped naked, and painted gold, had the task of spraying her with scent as she sat before her cheval mirror, holding court. She exacted the strictest etiquette as a royal princess, though she flouted every rule herself. She wore out her staff with her capriciousness. Prince Camillo, ignored and abandoned, consoled himself with other ladies.

The fate of her lovers was often as strange and tragic as a tale from an Eastern court. There was the fascinating Colonel Jules de Canouville, a swaggering Adonis on Berther's staff. Princess Pauline's eyes fell on him, and Paris rang with a fresh liaison. The Emperor Napoleon, having received a magnificent Russian sable-lined pelisse from Czar Alexander, presented it to his sister. A few days later at a review he beheld it again, on the stalwart shoulders of young Canouville. Within twenty-four hours he was sent out of France. He was killed later at the Battle of Borodino, and one of Napoleon's aides reported to the Princess that he had found upon Canouville's breast a portrait, covered in blood, that would have compromised the original. 'I alone saw it and destroyed it.'

Nevertheless, there were remarkable qualities in this frivolous, hysterical, over-sexed creature. She was full of spirit and charm. Her compelling beauty was always worthily framed, for both in dress and the management of her household she had unfailing taste and discernment. She had fire also. When her brother was on his way to Elba and called at her villa in Provence, she refused to embrace him until he had divested himself of the odious uniform of an Austrian general in which he had sought disguise from the hostile mob. In 1813, when Wellington had worn him down and his star was set-

PRINCESS BORGHESE
(front and back, by *Canova*)

PRINCESS PAOLINA (BONAPARTE) BORGHESE
(Detail by *Canova*)

ting, he began to have money difficulties. Pauline at once sold jewels to the value of three hundred thousand francs and sent them to him. Journeying to her villa, she heard Napoleon had abdicated and was on his way to exile at Elba.

'I want to see him and comfort him,' she said, 'and if he allows me to accompany him I shall never leave him. If he refuses I will then go to Naples to stay with the King. I have not loved the Emperor as a ruling monarch. I have loved him as my brother and will remain loyal to him to his death.'

What she wrote then on the eve of abdication she carried out. She accompanied him to Frejus, the port of embarkation, and only her health prevented her from sailing with him to Elba. She would come later, she told him; and kept her word. Meanwhile, the two brothers he had made kings, the uncle he had made cardinal, and all the brood of princelings and dukes he had created, were scurrying to safety.

Within five days of the tragic scene at Frejus, the Princess Pauline was in the arms of a new lover, Durchand. She made the journey to Elba, and a young English captain, who went on board her ship, with a welcoming delegation from Napoleon's staff, found her posing most effectively in a hammock, ravishingly attired. From Elba she went to Naples, to visit King Murat and Queen Caroline. But she was worried and restless. She was receiving an income of three hundred thousand francs from the Bourbon Government, but nothing seemed certain now. She began to sell her properties. It was ironical that she sold her Paris house to the Duke of Wellington to serve as a British Embassy. It was just in time, for the Bourbons took possession of all the Bonaparte properties. Prince Borghese, alarmed at the way things were going, began to claim back pictures and furniture lent under the marriage jointure.

Then came the thunder-clap of Napoleon's escape from Elba. Pauline was on the island at the time and, learning of his intention, immediately gave him her diamond necklace, worth five hundred thousand francs, for his needs. She faced the irate British Governor, who denounced Napoleon for breaking his parole. The Hundred Days had begun. Pauline went to Viareggio, to her sister's chateau. She sent for a priest from Lucca to say Mass, and shortly afterwards found herself a prisoner, for the Governor of Lucca, on Austrian orders, put her under guard. She staged an illness, alarmed the doctors, who were unanimous that any attempt to take her to Austria would be fatal and suggested a cure at Bagni di Lucca. But it was touch and go. One of the doctors, Pacini, was young and handsome. The Austrian authorities, suspecting malingering, sent their own specialist, a greybread of seventy. Before his arrival young Pacini and the Princess rehearsed the 'symptoms.' The scheme succeeded. Instead of making the dreaded journey to Austria, with all its threatening import, the Princess left for Bagni di Lucca, young Pacini and her household in attendance. In Lucca itself she was received like a reigning royalty, the charming little town all unaware that in the near future it was to see the long and happy reign of the Princess Louise de Bourbon, while in nearby Parma another Princess Louise, a Hapsburg, Napoleon's wife, would reign happily and marry her one-eyed chamberlain.

Meanwhile Princess Pauline was busy. She obtained the permission of the Holy Father, and of the Austrian authorities, to make her home in Rome. Thus, after many vicissitudes, she came back to the scene of her first glory. On the day that she arrived, Napoleon, a prisoner on board a British man-of-war, entered the harbour of St. Helena. When amid the carnage at Waterloo some of Blücher's staff had come upon the Emperor's famous carriage, which served both as office and bedroom, they found in a secret drawer the Princess Pauline's jewel-case holding the diamonds she had given her brother at Elba.

Back in Rome there was a gathering of the Bonaparte clan. Madame Mère was established there, at first in the Palazzo Falconieri. Under its roof also were Pauline's brothers, Lucien, Louis and Jerome, together with uncle Cardinal

Fesch. Pauline remembered that in the marriage contract she was entitled to half the great Palazzo Borghese, the use of the Casino, and an allowance of two hundred thousand francs. She made a claim to these, which was wholly repudiated by Prince Borghese, now settled happily with an *amie* in his Florentine palace. The Pope was appealed to. The Prince was not favourably viewed at the Vatican, where the European roundabout had brought some astonishing changes in the Pope's attitude. True, he had been taken prisoner by Napoleon, forcibly evicted from Rome, and threatened by him for refusing to annul the marriage with Josephine.[2]

All that humiliation was now forgiven, and in a magnanimous mood the Pope, in 1817, was endeavouring to influence the Prince Regent of England to make some amelioration of Napoleon's exile, without effect. Pius VII wrote to Cardinal Consalvi, his Secretary of State:

'We must remember that, after God, it is principally to Napoleon we owe the re-establishment of religion in the great kingdom of France. The pious and courageous initiative taken by him in 1801 (the Concordat) has caused us to forget and forgive the wrongs we so long endured.'

The whirligig of Time now brought its revenge. When the Pope during his exile had arrived at Turin, Prince Borghese, then Governor-General of Piedmont, refused permission to the aged Pontiff to rest there awhile. Five years later he had to write to Consalvi begging the Pope's permission to come and settle in Rome. He humiliated himself in vain, for although he obtained permission, he was given so chilly a reception that he retreated to his palace at Florence and spent the rest of his days there. The Vatican had not forgotten his

[2] Napoleon's envoy, General Radet, scaled the wall of the Quirinale and at three in the morning broke into the Pope's bedroom. He made the old Pontiff dress and follow him, accompanied by his minister, Cardinal Pacca, out to a waiting carriage where, in silence and darkness, he was carried off a prisoner. As the carriage came to Florence the Pope asked Pacca if he had any money. 'No, I was dragged out of my room and had no time to take anything.' The two prisoners searched their pockets, finding only a few pence. 'See,' exclaimed the old Pope, with a sad smile, 'all that remains of my kingdom!'

early revolutionary fervour when Napoleon was in the
ascendant. It now ordered him to open the Princess's suite at
the Palazzo Borghese, whereupon Pauline wrote to him sug-
gesting the resumption of marital relations. The Prince
firmly refused, happy in Florence with the Duchess della
Rovere. Pauline in the past few years had been trying in vain
to induce him to re-enter the bear-pit. All this displeased the
Vatican. It ordered him to give her quarters in the Palazzo
Borghese, in the Casino, in the villa at Frascati, and to make
her an allowance of seventy thousand francs.

While the cardinals and the lawyers settled her dispute
with the Prince she installed herself at the Casino Sciarra,
later Villa Bonaparte, near the Porta Pia, for she had tired
of the Borghese palace, and the Casino in the Villa Borghese
was not convenient, she declared, though in an amiable
mood she had written to her husband: 'I sometimes go
through the park of the Villa Borghese from my villa to the
Casino. I think your villa the most beautiful in Rome, and all
foreigners of taste say the same thing.'

She was soon the dominant woman of Rome, with her face,
her figure, her dress and resplendent equipages. She received
regally and established something like a court. Her appearance in public always created the stir she delighted in. Every
afternoon she went out driving. Her glittering carriage was
drawn by four horses, with two postillion outriders in scarlet
and gold, and two negro pages standing behind. It was probably this dashing equipage that the dying Keats and his
friends saw one day on the Pincio, her bright eyes quick to
notice the young men. Even the English aristocracy was soon
dancing attendance upon her. From Rome, on December
10th, 1816, Elizabeth, Duchess of Devonshire, more inter-
ested in archæology than in *salons*, wrote to her son:

'Mr. Playfair, Mr. Elmsley, Mr. Sotheby are among the clever
men of science and literature at Rome, and Mr. Brougham and
Lord Henry are the cleverest men of the set here. Almost all alike
flock to the Princess Borghese, and the grave Lord Lansdowne,

the silent Lord Jersey, the politician Mr. Brougham, all go and play *aux petits jeux* with Paulina. Forfeits condemned Lord Jersey to recite: he got off by promising to waltz. Lord Cowper was to *soupirer pour une dame* and so on. She shows her fine plate with the eagle, etc. I admire the Pope's firmness in letting them all of that family remain at Rome but I think that the English should put a little reason in their eagerness to go to her. Were it Josephine, who did thousands of benevolent generous acts; Maria Louisa, who was twice a sacrifice to politicks; Madame Lucien, who is an excellent mother and wife, I think the attentions would be natural and commendable but this person has only been cited for extreme extravagance in prosperity, extreme gallantry, and a good deal of beauty.'

'This person' was indeed viewed suspiciously by the cautious. The Austrian Count thought the attention she attracted was excessive, her income too large. Their Secret Service was reporting also on Madame Mère, now quietly established in her palace on the Corso, attended by her brother, Cardinal Fesch:

'If Cardinal Consalvi (for the Pope) finds himself in want of money recourse is had either to the Duke of Torlonia, a man of the lowest origin, who, thanks to the French, has grown suddenly rich, or to Madame Letizia (Napoleon's mother). The first makes a great interest out of these subsidies, the second also lends to much profit. A hundred thousand scudi were provided by Madame for the furnishing of the apartments occupied by our Sovereign in 1819, and were afterwards repaid.'

Prince Metternich took alarm and warned the British Government. The Princess never ceased her attempts to ameliorate her brother's exile. For six years she pleaded with the British through one source or another, seeking permission to join him on St. Helena. It was all in vain. When news of Napoleon's illness reached her in Rome she bombarded Lord Liverpool, the British Prime Minister, with appeals. Would he not let her have a ship in which to sail? 'If you refuse me it will be a sentence of death to him.' There was no response.

Then, on a hot July day in 1821, the crushing news came that Napoleon was dead at St. Helena. The Princess, distraught, took to her bed. 'I am in despair,' she wrote to her sister-in-law. 'Life has no longer any attraction for me, and all is at an end.'

She meant it and felt it, while she wrote this, but the leopard cannot change its spots. It was odd that her new lover's name should be Pacini, the same as that of the young doctor from Lucca. She had summoned him to her box at the opera, where a composition of his had been enthusiastically received. He was young, dark and handsome. From that moment she had him constantly by her side. He played the piano at her soirees, he sat beside her when she drove out. She cared nothing for the gossip she provoked. The news of Napoleon's death caused her to turn to her Nino still more. When she went off on an autumn tour she took him with her. Soon he began to tire. He wrote excuses. The Princess Pauline had a quite new experience, and it was shattering. It was he, and not she, who broke off the affair. He had a career to pursue, or so he thought, but in Trieste another pair of eyes had taken him captive. 'I am wounded to the heart,' she wrote, 'as I am not accustomed to such treatment.'

She now turned to tormenting Prince Camillo. She wanted more money. She charged him with desertion. Then suddenly she frightened him by a new line of attack. 'Here in my loneliness I have been thinking things over, and I see that my heart yearns for you and that your affection is the only thing that matters.' She followed up her letter by obtaining a Papal edict commanding him to rejoin his wife. Thus she delivered a double blow. She wrecked his happiness with his duchess in Florence. She made him again an object of derision in their home, the Palazzo Borghese. Triumphant, she launched out in great receptions, balls and dinners. Her looks had gone, she was thin and sallow, exhausted yet restless. In June, 1825, she was conscious that she was failing.

She disposed of her jewels, she made her Will. It forgot no one, it was generous and detailed. Not a tradesman, even, was missed. Her library went to Lord Holland. A medallion went to the Duke of Devonshire. To her nephew, the son of her brother Jerome's repudiated American wife, she left twenty thousand francs, and two million francs to her sister Caroline, whose husband, Prince Murat, had been executed in Naples. To Camillo she bequeathed her villa at Lucca, 'in appreciation of his sincere and faithful attention' during her illness. For at the end poor Prince Camillo was in tears. 'Forgive all the trouble I have caused you,' she pleaded. And when the priest approached to administer Extreme Unction, she said faintly, 'My life, alas, has been completely worldly.'

She realised the truth at last, but at the very end the two dominant passions of her life asserted themselves in the death rattle. 'My mirror . . . Napoleon!' she gasped.

She was buried in Santa Maria Maggiore, in the grandiose Borghese Chapel. She was joined there fifteen years later, by another Princess Borghese, her antithesis, the saintly Lady Gwendolen, whose passing moved all Rome to tears.

III

When to-day one ascends the staircase of the Palazzo Borghese, or walks in the galleries of the villa wherein are displayed some of the great art treasures of the world, there arises in one's mind a brief speculation on the fate of this wealthy family. What was the end of the story? It was an end completely ruinous, such as came to a large number of the great Roman families whose glory was sunk in a wild speculation in real estate and building. When Augustus Hare published his guide-book in 1906, he wrote a bitter preface on the destruction of Rome by the Government of United Italy, accusing it of having caused more spoliation of its ancient and natural beauties in the years 1807–1905 than that caused by all the invasions of the Goths and Vandals. He bitterly denounced the Roman aristocracy, a charge endorsed by Lanciani, the great Roman archaeologist. 'If the Government, the Municipality and, it must be confessed, the Roman aristocracy had been united together since 1870, with the sole object of annihilating the attractions and interest of Rome, they could not have done it more thoroughly,' wrote Hare. To his lament we can add Lanciani's sorrowful words:

'The blame must be cast especially on the members of the Roman aristocracy. We have seen three of them sell the very gardens which surrounded their city mansions, allowing these mansions to be contaminated by the contact of ignoble tenement houses. We have seen every one of the patrician villas—the Patrizi, the Sciarra, the Massimo, the Lucernari, the Mirafiori, the Wolkonsky, the Giustiniani, the Torlonia, the Campana, the San Faustino—destroyed, their casinos dismantled and their beautiful old trees burnt into charcoal.'

Horrified by the new building craze in 1886–88, *The Times* of London repeatedly protested in its leaders against the terrible new jerry-built tenements, 'aesthetically and economically a disgrace to Rome, which could have been the most beautiful city in the world. . . . What the municipality has done is to make it impossible without the intervention of a great earthquake that it ever should be anything but the most absurd of all cheap imitations of Paris.'

D'Annunzio added his denunciation:

'There passed over Rome a blighting blizzard of barbarism, menacing all the greatness and loveliness which were without equals in the memory of the world. Even the laurels and rose-trees of the Villa Sciarra, for so many nights of so many summers hymned by their nightingales, fell destroyed, or remained in their desecration behind the gates of little gardens parcelled out to the little cockney-boxes of tradesmen.'

To-day the visitor to Rome is drawn to the Via Vittorio Veneto by the cafés and the cluster of hotels and tourist agen-

cies. It is a fine, broad avenue mounting to the Porta Pinciana. But if he could see at what a price this ordinary
twentieth-century boulevard has been achieved, the loss of
the gardens, woods, glens, waterfalls and incomparable vistas
over Rome it has entailed, he would suffer a terrible shock.

One rainy morning, after visiting the exquisite Temple of
Vesta by the Tiber, I took shelter in the Roman Museum, a
singularly undistinctive name in a city that has dozens of
museums. It was closed, but, having mounted a wide staircase
in vain, a gentleman emerged who took pity on me. He
proved to be the curator, and with that ample courtesy so frequently encountered throughout Italy, he spent an hour of
his time conducting me through the galleries. Seldom have I
suffered such acute depression. It is a bold act of the authorities to maintain this museum, largely devoted to evidence of
their own vandalism. It contains a very comprehensive collection of water-colours and oil-paintings made by artists
early in the nineteenth-century. You realise, seeing these, the
terrible loss Rome has suffered in her picturesque buildings
and squares. There is, for instance, a water-colour of the old
Piazza Barberini, with its fountain, façades, palaces, old
houses, booths and flower-stalls. Contrast this with the Piazza
of to-day. The old fountain is there, Bernini's lovely bronze
Triton blowing water out of a conch, but where is the site of
the Temple of Flora, one of the most painted features of
Rome? It has vanished, the pavement has been raised and
straightened. The old houses opposite are gone, and a great
modern hotel blocks the sky with its commonplace façade,
looking as if it had been transported direct from Chicago or
Detroit. The base of the old fountain has been half-buried,
and where the noble paired oxen used to surround it, with
their colourful wagons, we now see scrubby taxis standing
in rank. What once was a quiet scene of patient oxen, dozing
waggoners and softly falling water, is now a roaring vortex
of murderous traffic. There has been added a new horror to
make Rome the noisiest city in the world—the abominable

motor-cycle, which contributes to the Italian lust for the maximum speed with the greatest possible noise.

Let us not lose our heads from easy indignation. Every generation destroys and builds something for another generation to destroy in turn. Nowhere else in the world is the problem of destruction and preservation so difficult as in Rome. Which age shall have a prior claim, the faint Etruscan, the era of the Empire, the Middle Ages with its squalor, the Renaissance with its splendour, or modern Rome with its hygiene? Every age has a school challenging the others. Nothing can excuse the vandalism that destroyed the villas and gardens in the late nineteenth century. An influx of over two hundred thousand immigrants after the union of Italy brought grave problems of housing and hygiene. Five-storied houses, looking like barracks, reared their frightful facades, blocking lovely vistas. The Rome of a golden hue, of domes and dense foliage, with the lovely background of the Sabine and Alban Hills, was blotted out, and glaring masses of plaster-daubed barracks now obstruct the eye. Italian speculation in these building schemes ran riot. The old families flung their estates, their homes and their glory to the winds in a wild gamble for aggrandisement. There was a moment when even the Villa Borghese was threatened, but a court decree saved it. The general devastation changed the Roman climate. The average summer temperature rose two degrees, the winter temperature fell three. To-day Rome of the eighteenth century has been engulfed by a sprawling giant that has burst through the city walls and extended huge concrete limbs into the surrounding meadows and hills.

The city presents an astonishing graph of the rise and fall of the Roman people. In the days of the glory under the Caesars she grew to over two million inhabitants, in the Middle Ages she shrank to eighty thousand, in the time of Pope Sixtus IV she had one hundred thousand, in 1809 she had one hundred and fifty thousand, in 1890 two hundred thousand, in 1900 she grew again to a million, in 1930 to a million and a quarter, in 1950 to nearly two millions. In the matter of sheer destruction of the ruins of ancient Rome the period of the Renaissance is the most guilty. It showed a brutal indifference to the ancient monuments, though it enslaved itself to the classical tradition, and the popes, politicians, bankers and merchants raised magnificent churches, palaces, castles, villas and fountains, giving us the golden age, but these builders of the Renaissance plundered and obliterated ancient Rome. Well might the pasquinade run—*Quod non fecerunt barbari, fecerunt Barberini.* ('What the barbarians have not done the Barberini have done.') But would we willingly forgo the splendour of Renaissance Rome for more temples, forums and statuary of classical Rome? It will always be a debatable point. The builders of modern Rome destroyed the banks of the Tiber, with its picturesque houses. They pulled down the old bridges and tore away the bastions of the Castle of St. Angelo, but could modern Rome have tolerated the stench arising from the Tiber, then the main sewer, liable at any time to flood the lower part of the city, with all the attendant evils? Much of the old picturesqueness was a product of filth. The crowded slums bred a race handicapped by darkness and disease.

The building boom was inevitable when Rome became the capital of Italy and entered a new era. Unhappily the temptation to gain by this building craze infected and destroyed many of the great families. Among them, falling more ruinously than any other, was the Borghese family. Prince Camillo Borghese, husband of Pauline Bonaparte, despite his brother-in-law's depredations, left his fortune, his villas, estates and a large part of his art collection intact. He had lost some of this last, by French looting in 1797, but the biggest loss occurred in 1807. Frightened by the imminent landing of the English Navy, Prince Camillo was induced by Napoleon to sell his art collection at the Villa Borghese for the Emperor's Imperial Collection. Thus it happened that when Canova, on Napoleon's downfall, negotiated a restoration of

Italian works of art, the Borghese sale precluded the return of some two hundred statues, the finest in the collection. Camillo's nephew, Prince Marcantonio (V), enhanced the gallery with new acquisitions, but tragedy came on the succession of his son, Prince Paolo. He was utterly ruined in building speculations. He was compelled to dispose of the Palazzo Borghese, and the library, manuscripts, and archives passed to the Vatican Library in 1891. The pictures were removed, pending sale, to the Villa Borghese, but the Italian Government refused to permit Prince Borghese to sell them abroad. In 1901 it acquired them for the sum of one hundred and forty thousand *lire*, not the present price of a dozen frames or the value of one of the five hundred works of art. The Villa Borghese and the estate were acquired for three million lire. These with the art collection then became the property of the city of Rome.

Prince Marcantonio proved to be a man of much thrift and business ability. A millionaire, one of the great nobles of Rome, he lived simply and kept his accounts, managed his household and ruled his vast domain with an eagle eye. But tragedy marked him for its own. When he lost his first wife, Lady Gwendolen, and three children, all within a few weeks, he married a La Rochefoucauld, by whom he had seven sons. In the manner of those days he compelled them all, single and married alike, to dwell under the roof of the Palazzo Borghese, a tax upon the capacity of even that tremendous building. He was iron in his rule. Faithful to the Papacy, he would not accord any recognition to the usurper of Rome's temporal power, Victor Emanuel, dwelling in the old palace of the popes, the Quirinale. When the Prince threatened to close the grounds of the Villa Borghese to the public he was challenged by the Mayor, Duke Torlonia, who said the grant under the Borghese Pope had been made on condition that the people of Rome had access to the park. The nature of this grant, moreover, had been engraved on an old tablet let into the walls. This, Prince Borghese denied. A search was made,

the tablet was found and the Prince lost his lawsuit. Because
of this the Roman public enjoy the park to-day; otherwise it
might have been built over.

On his death Prince Marcantonio left an increased fortune,
the result of his long frugality and shrewd business instinct.
It was all in vain. His son Prince Paolo lost it all, ruined after
nearly four hundred years of princely splendour by speculation in 'modern buildings.'

The crash of the building boom brought down many of
the noble houses. Those observant ladies, the Misses Lucas,
were living in Rome at the time, and wrote in the diary for
1891:

'Everyone in Rome is smashing up. Prince Borghese lost money
in building, tried to retrieve himself by speculations, and came to
grief. They have left Rome.The Borghese Palace is to let and the
pictures removed to the Villa. I do not know how many of them
have been sold. . . . Prince Sciarra has also come to grief. It is
said that his creditors made him give up his carriage and took
even that from his possession.'

Sic transit. All over Rome the vanished glory of the
Borghese is now proclaimed only by the inscriptions on the
façades of churches and buildings. The vast wealth of Cardinal Scipione Borghese, a jovial *bon viveur*, was lavishly
expended on the restoration of churches. The great art collection in the villa owes much to him. His uncle, Pope Paul
V, who finished St. Peter's, wrote his own advertisement
across its wide facade: 'In . Honorem . Principis . Apost .
Paulus V . Burghesius . Romanus . Pont . . Max . . A .
MDCXII . Pont VII.'[3]

He planned an elaborate memorial chapel in S. Maria
Maggiore. The Temple of Minerva was plundered of columns
and alabaster to decorate it. A magnificent altar of lapis

---

[3] It provoked a pasquinade:
> *Angulus est Petri, Pauli frons tota. Quid inde?*
> *Non Petri, Paulo stat fabricata domus.*

(The corner stone is Peter's, the whole façade is Paul's. What then? Not for
Peter, for Paul is the house built.)

lazuli has over it a picture attributed to St. Luke, who is alleged to have taken to oil-painting in his old age. If anyone should doubt it, a papal Bull attached to the wall admonishes the scoffer. The tomb itself glorifies 'a truly herculean figure, with a grandly developed head, while in his neck pride, violence and sensuality seem united,' according to Gregorovius. This was the Pope who excommunicated defiant Venice and ordered the assassination of Paolo Sarpi. Venice and the courageous Sarpi defeated him, checking his assertion of absolute power.

VI

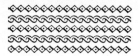

RAPHAEL: A PHASE

I

LET us return to the Villa Borghese. It is a sunny May morning, and as we go up the Via Vittorio Veneto the visitors to Rome, and that large population which seems to have nothing to do but drink coffee—fourteen cups of 'Expresso' a day, one Roman confessed to me—*'Sono molto nervoso!'*—are sitting out across the pavements and under the trees. We pass the flower-stall, a free glory by the Pincian Gate, and walk by our beloved 'Galappatoio,' the riding-ring, where three pretty girls in yellow velvet jodhpurs, accompanied by a groom, go cantering by. We turn right. Here one of the most enchanting vistas of Rome greets us. A flutter of coloured washing draws our attention to a little building on a hill, with a background of tall pines. The washing of Italy is everlasting and kaleidoscopic in colour. It decorates the storeys of tall houses, it flutters by the columns of a broken temple, or shines in some grim alley of the poor. Nowhere else in the world is it so gay, so much a companion of the sun, so bright a witness to all the needs of domestic life. And now here it was again, fluttering brightly above a raised balcony over which ran a vine, and where pots of geraniums and cyclamen added to the festive riot.

I discovered this washing belonged to the resident caretaker of a little chapel into whose side his house seemed to have grown. The little place was the *Chiesetta di Raffaelle,*

formerly that bosky retreat where Raphael is said to have
taken his love in the heat of a summer's day. It is now a
charming little chapel set on an eminence above the black
ilex and the pines, with a columned portico. Something was
happening there, I observed. A few taxis waited on the gravel
before the portico. My curiosity was soon satisfied. Out into
the sunshine and through a small group of relations came the
bride on her young husband's arm. Children they were, the
boy dark, sleek and slim, like a baby dolphin; the girl, her
white veil crowned with a chaplet of orange blossoms, long-
lashed and lustrous-eyed. Briefly they paused for the old-
fashioned photographer gesticulating from under a black
cloth. Soon they were free, and drove off, young and happy,
into their future.

It is the art gallery that calls us, not horseback riders or
brides and grooms, or young lovers kissing each other on a
stone bench beneath a laughing faun, or a little, long-legged
boy, a Donatello cherub to look at, but a little devil in reality,
with a catapult and four wretched birds dangling on a string,
that in turn would delay us on this bright morning when the
sun pours down the long avenues leading to the great villa. It
is an artist I am going to see at the Villa Borghese, a young
Roman one. Raphael was not born in Rome, but it was here
he triumphed, and died all too early, though not before having touched the pinnacle of fame. He tarried in his youth in
Florence, at a time when two giants were contending for the
palm, Leonardo da Vinci and Michelangelo. In the heated
discussion over the rival cartoons, *The Battle of the Standard*
and the *Bathers in the Arno*, young Raphael had for com-
panions Michelangelo, his senior by eight years, whose colossal statue of David had just been erected before the Palazzo
Vecchio, Sansovino and Filippino Lippi. When Pope Julius II
invited Raphael to Rome to decorate a suite of apartments in
the Vatican he departed south the more easily because Leonardo da Vinci had left Florence, and Michelangelo was

already in Rome, labouring on that everlasting tomb for the Pope. Raphael was twenty-six when he went into Rome by the Porta del Popolo in 1509. The little boy, left an orphan at eleven, in the mountain town of Urbino, presided over by Duke Guidobaldo da Montefeltro, had passed, first, to the care of his father's brother, Don Bartolomeo, and then to his uncle Simone, a notary who sent him, at the age of seventeen, to Perugia to study under the renowned Perugino. Now, his fame having spread from Florence, Rome lay open to conquest. He could not know that in little more than eleven years, dying on his birthday, he would be mourned by all Italy and a grief-stricken Pope. Has ever a brighter immortality been gained in a briefer period?

It is not in the Borghese Gallery that we find him at his greatest. Two of the pictures are by a boy of under twenty. But even the *Portrait of a Man* painted at nineteen, under the influence of his master Perugino, has the spiritualised quality which is so often the mark of his work. There is a picture painted by him at twenty-four, for the mother of the young Grifone Baglioni, of the ruling family of Perugia, who was killed in a street fight in one of that sinister city's many feuds. The bereaved mother was called to her dying son and heard him as he breathed his last forgive his enemies. She chose as a memorial for a church in Perugia *The Bearing of Christ to the Sepulchre*, in which another mother mourned over her Son, and she asked young Raphael to paint it. A hundred years later Paul V bought the painting for the Borghese collection. Napoleon annexed it, and it went with much other artistic loot to Paris in 1797, but it came back to Rome on his downfall. It is full of fire and feeling, though derivative, for it is believed that the cartoon for it was drawn in Florence under the suggestions of da Vinci and Michelangelo. He found difficulties almost beyond his talent, and he changed the composition several times, transforming the position of the figures and changing it from a study of repose into one of dramatic action. The colour is superb, and it has poetic touches such as the dandelion in flower by the bottom step of the sepulchre.

A great trio was at work in Rome in the opening years of the sixteenth century. Bramante was building the new St. Peter's, Michelangelo was painting the ceiling of the Sistine Chapel, and Raphael was decorating the apartment of a pope who drove them all on with his dynamic personality. Bullying, pleading, he was an inexorable taskmaster. Had the warrior-Pope failed in everything else—and he had troubles enough: the menacing French to the north, the troublesome Henry VIII in England—he still would have gained immortality for his reign through any one of these three men of genius he employed. Raphael's portrait of the Pope explains his personality. The old Julius in a red robe, seated in his chair, is no senile pope.

The young 'interior decorator' began his work in the Vatican apartments known as the *Stanze* at the age of twenty-six, on trial. He was not without competitors—Perugino and Sodoma had been at work—but when Julius saw what Raphael could do he had the rooms stripped in order to give the whole task to this youngster, who put the old and new masters in the shade.

There is one picture in the Borghese Gallery, attributed to Raphael, that presents a problem and opens the book of his private life, in all its passion and frailty. It is a portrait called *The Fornarina*, and purports to be a painting by Raphael of his mistress, a baker's daughter, as alleged. It shows a young woman, her black hair in a gold-and-blue turban, with unveiled breasts. It is a study of seductive beauty with a Jewish lushness. The expression is sweet, the dark eyes are alluring, and a man's love has gone into the creation of the whole work, which is at once a tribute to and a boast of possession. And, as if to put the matter beyond any doubt, the name of the painter-possessor, Raphael Urbinas, has been revealed on the gold-and-blue bracelet on her left arm.

Is this the woman young Raphael openly loved until the day of his death, and is it, as the catalogue confidently asserts, the work of his brush? Some say 'Yes.' Others say 'No.' One would like to think it is his, though another portrait, called *La Donna Velata* (the Veiled Lady) with its veiled head and girl's face, more tender and more innocent, in the Pitti Gallery at Florence, is claimed to be that of the mistress he loved and to have been painted by him. It bears a close resemblance to the Virgin of his *Madonna di S. Sisto*, and obviously the same model sat for both. It is certainly by Raphael, but this young woman cannot have been the model for *The Fornarina*. Which was his mistress, then?

The art critics do not help us; indeed, they flatly contradict each other. Before we examine their opinions let us make a short pilgrimage to the place where Raphael lived and worked and where he met, and it is believed had living with him, the girl he loved, to the humiliation of the girl to whom he was betrothed. On the subject of Raphael's loves the biographers have fought for four centuries, and the battle is not yet over. There are the Blacks and the Whites: those who assert that Raphael was a typical young man of the period, a libertine in a den of iniquity, who shortened his life by his excesses. Others will not hear of any blemish in the genius whose art, in its sacred aspects, has never been surpassed; they speak of him as a saint almost worthy of canonisation. There are those who avoid any extreme attitude either way, knowing the flesh is weak and the spirit often only fitfully capable of ascendancy. Lanciani, the Roman historian and archaeologist, a safe guide in most matters, has a simple explanation in which the two extreme views find some common ground. Raphael was a shy, sensitive youth for whom promiscuity was not so easy as for most in those loose times. He was, nevertheless, quietly passionate, and when he had succeeded in finding a companion who satisfied his needs he completely surrendered himself to her charms, and would not let himself be hurried into marriage. Thus it was that he clung to his

beautiful model, the baker's daughter known as the Fornarina, satisfying alike to his senses and his art. It seems probable that he had other adventures. Young, handsome and
renowned, he cannot have lacked admirers, and that the
heat of youth momentarily overcame even his passion for
work is revealed on a sketch of two bishops for his *Disputa*.
His mind wandered from his work, and on the sketch he
scribbled a love sonnet:

> Now O tongue, loosen the bonds of speech
> To tell of that delightful snare
> Which love has set for me, to my great trouble.

It is natural, as a result of the enormous output of paintings depicting the Madonna, the Holy Child and the Saints,
to conclude that their painters were all devout men and believed in the scenes and stories they illustrated. Actually,
some of them were not; they had more relish for the Hellen-
ism of the fifteenth century than for the abounding miracles
and objects venerated by Christians. Perugino had no faith
in an after life and the immortality of the soul. Raphael was
his pupil, and, like his colleagues, he was as ready to paint
the amours of Cupid and Psyche for a bathroom or a private
dining-room as to paint a Madonna for the churches and
monasteries that, with their great wealth, commanded the
services of painters. Thus men of genius, such as Leonardo da
Vinci and Michelangelo, who would be regarded to-day as of
doubtful morals, could furnish on demand a surpassingly devout *Last Supper* or *Pieta*. The argument, therefore, that
Raphael could not have had a mistress because of the spirit-
uality of his sacred pictures cannot be accepted in face of the
evidence that he, as many of his age, was a product of an in-
divisible union of paganism and Christianity: of the Renaissance painters it is often difficult to determine whether they
believed all of the one, something of either, or nothing of
both.

Raphael showed to his fiancée, Maria Bibbiena, a cardi-

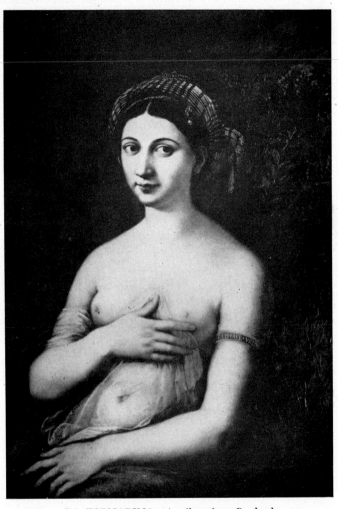

LA FORNARINA—Attributed to *Raphael*
(Borghese Gallery, Rome)

THE VEILED LADY—LA DONNA VELATA, by *Raphael*
(Pitti Gallery, Florence)

nal's niece of high social position, a conventional and frigid attitude that ultimately killed her. For there is no doubt that poor Maria, long humiliated by her postponed marriage, died of a broken heart. And should this seem an exaggeration, there is Raphael's own contrition on his deathbed and his tardy acknowledgment of Maria in the inscription he ordered to be engraved in the Pantheon:

'We, Baldassare Turini da Pescia and Gian Battista Branconi dall' Aquila, testmentary executors and recipients of the last wishes of Raphael, have raised this memorial to his affianced wife, Maria daughter of Antonio of Bibbiena, whom death deprived of a happy marriage.'

When Raphael came to Rome he found in Cardinal Bibbiena a most influential friend. This clever statesman became his special patron. He obtained for his young friend commissions for the cartoons of the tapestries which took Raphael nineteen months to draw, and which were sent to Arras for weaving. The completed tapestries created a sensation when they were hung for the first time in the Sistine Chapel on December 26th, 1519, only three months before his death.[1] They were not only hung on the chapel walls but used for decorations on festival days. Goethe, visiting the Vatican on Corpus Christi Day, 1782, saw them put to such a use:

'They transformed colonnades and open spaces into handsome halls and corridors; and while they placed before us the power of the most gifted of men they gave us at the same time the happier examples of art and handicraft, each in its highest perfection, meeting for mutual completion.'

Cardinal Bibbiena commissioned private work also. The spirit of the Renaissance was Greek in its derivation. Its inspiration was drawn from the humanists who at the capital

[1] Raphael received only 434 ducats in payment for his ten cartoons. Seven of these are now in the South Kensington Museum, London, having been purchased in Flanders for Charles I, in 1630, by Rubens, who recognised their worth.

of the Byzantine Empire had preserved the Hellenic tradition. Thus art as well as literature drank deeply of the classical springs. How otherwise would it have been possible for the Raphael of the Madonnas, the Holy Child, the Saints, to have painted for the Cardinal's bathroom in the Vatican decorations of such complete paganism? The free-love antics of gods and goddesses were scarcely subjects for the bathroom of a cardinal vowed to celibacy. When they were exhibited, contemporary Rome was not shocked, but was in a state of ecstasy over this essay in triumphant paganism.

The Cardinal, a cherished friend of the Pope, had seen in the brilliant young Raphael a suitable husband for his niece, Maria. Their formal engagement took place in July, 1514, but Raphael showed no sign of fulfilling the contract. It is possible there was another reason besides his infatuation with the mistress whose face he transferred to his Madonnas for church altars. The Pope had hinted to his favourite artist that a cardinal's hat might one day reward him. Marriage would have proved an insurmountable obstacle to any such ambition. Yet it would be wrong to infer, despite the sorry figure Raphael cuts in this matter of a mistress and a fiancée, that he was cold or calculating. He was an attractive, industrious, sweet-tempered young man, and well-balanced, despite his tremendous endowment of genius. When he died there was universal sorrow not only for the passing of a very great artist, but also for the loss of an engaging companion with warm loyalties.

On his father's early death an uncle had taken care of Raphael through boyhood and youth, and to the end their relationship was affectionate and confidential. There is a letter Raphael wrote from Rome, in 1514, to his uncle, Simone Ciarla, living in his native Urbino. It is the letter of a young man who knows he has made good and is rightly proud of his rapid success and his position at the Vatican. 'He never went to court,' Vasari tells us, 'but he had a company of fifty painters—good and valiant painters all of them—who escorted him from the moment when he left his dwelling; indeed he lived not as a painter but as a prince.' His uncle Simone, Cardinal Bibbiena and others, were all busy with plans for the marriage of this most eligible bachelor of thirty-one. Raphael writes to his uncle on the subject, and his letter is an excellent picture of the man, the career he was making, and the times in which he lived. How charmingly it opens, yet how firm it is in the assertion of his independence!

'Beloved in place of a father!

'I have received your letter, which is a very precious proof to me that you are not angry with me, as indeed you have no cause to be, considering how tiresome it is to write when nothing of importance occurs. Now, when I have matters of importance I reply to you, to tell you circumstantially everything which I can impart.

'In the first place, as regards taking a wife, I reply to you that in respect of her, whom erewhile you were for giving me, I am quite at ease, and thank God continually that I have taken neither her nor another, and in that I have been more prudent than you, who wished to give her to me. I am sure that you, too, have now recognised that I should not be in the position where I now am; up to the present time I find I am in a position of holding property at Rome worth three thousand gold ducats, and an income of fifty gold ducats monthly, since His Holiness, my Master, has given me a salary of three hundred gold ducats for directing the building of St. Peter's, and this salary is never to fail as long as I live, and I am sure to obtain still more, and, further, I am paid for my work according to my own estimate, and I have begun to paint another chamber for His Holiness, which will come to one thousand two hundred gold ducats, so that I do credit, dearest uncle, to you and all my relatives and my native place.

'But for all that I carry you always in my inmost heart, and when I hear your name it seems to me as if I heard the name of a father; and do not complain of my not writing to you; I should rather have reason to complain of you, since you have a pen in your hand all day long and you let six months pass between one letter and the next, but with all that, you will not make me chide you, as you do me without just cause.

'I have wandered from the subject of marriage, but to return to it, I reply to you: you know that Cardinal Bibbiena wishes to give me a relative of his own, and I have promised him, with the permission of my clerical uncle, and with yours, to do everything which His Reverend Grace desires of me; I cannot break my word, we are on closer terms than ever, and I shall soon inform you about everything. Have patience till this good affair is decided, and then, if I do not this, I will do what you want.

'And if Francesco Buffa has parties to propose, let him know that I have too; I find at Rome a pretty little woman, of very good reputation, according to what I have heard, both herself and also her family, who will bring me three thousand gold ducats as a marriage portion; and I live in my own house at Rome, worth twice more here than elsewhere, of that you may be sure.

'As regards staying at Rome I shall never be able to stay anywhere else again, out of love for the building of St. Peter's, for I am in Bramante's place. What spot on earth is more dignified than Rome, what enterprise more dignified than St. Peter's? It is the first temple in the world, and the greatest piece of building that has ever been seen. It will come to more than a million in gold—and know that the Pope has resolved to spend sixty thousand ducats yearly on the building, and he thinks of nothing else. He has given me an assistant, a very learned monk, more than eighty years of age. The Pope sees that he cannot live much longer, so His Holiness has resolved to give him to me as an assistant, since he is a man of great reputation and wisdom, in order that I may learn any fine secret in architecture which he possesses and that I may become quite perfect in this art. His name is Fra Giocondo, and every day the Pope has us summoned and speaks a little while with us about this building.

'I beg you to go to the Duke and Duchess and tell them this, for I know that it will be a pleasure for them to hear that one of their subjects is doing himself credit, and commend me to their Graces. And I commend myself to you continually. Greet all my friends and relatives, and especially Ridolfo, who has shown me so much kindness and affection.

'The 1st July, 1514. Your Raphael, painter, at Rome.'

If this letter came through the post and lay on our breakfast table to-day, bringing thus modestly the news of a nephew's success in a great capital, it would seem to us as human as it must have done to Uncle Simone. The boy had indeed gone ahead. Famous as a painter, the familiar of a pope and a cardinal, and suddenly an architect promoted to the building of the greatest church in the world, and recommended for the part by the famous Bramante.

And where, we may ask, was the mighty Michelangelo, of such established renown as an architect? The sculptor had been absent in Florence, working on the monumental tomb of Julius II, when the news of that Pope's death reached him. He had produced there the *Slaves* and had begun the *Moses* for it. When Leo X ascended the throne his court ridiculed the morose master. Raphael was in the ascendant. Twenty-seven years later Michelangelo was to fill the post formerly held by Raphael. He was then seventy-two, harassed and disillusioned. He did not want the post, but he accepted it as a mission from God.

The proposal by Cardinal Bibbiena, mentioned in Raphael's letter to his uncle, was carried as far as a formal betrothal. It was announced in the same year. But that was as far as it ever went. The marriage was indefinitely postponed from year to year. Poor Maria, aware of the low-born mistress-model sitting in his studio and lying in his bed, died in time of wounded pride. In the contest with the Fornarina, ambition, social respectability and considerable beauty—for she was a *bella et dignitosa fanciulla*—had lost to simple passion.

II

What manner of person, then, was this mysterious young woman loved by Raphael? She never wholly comes out of the mist; her name, her portraits and her background are challenged by many. Yet the few facts, augmented with the passage of years, build up a fairly acceptable story even when legend is discarded.

In the Via Santa Dorothea, in the Trastevere district, there
was a small house with a kitchen garden. Into this garden,
whose wall was low, Margherita went, perhaps to gather
vegetables, perhaps to hang out the washing to dry in the sun.
Impressionable young men saw her over the garden wall, and
a legend relates how Raphael often passed through the Porta
Santo Spirito 'between love and work.' There is still the house
on the corner of the Via Santa Dorothea, with a window
under an arch, which was occupied by a bakery called 'il
Forno dal Fornarina.' The garden has been built over. But
no record of any kind has been found to confirm any occupant here with her name, in the sixteenth century; the house
adjoins the grounds of the Villa Farnesina where Raphael
worked for his wealthy patron Chigi.

We are on much surer ground when we come to the Via
Parione. In the vestibule of the old palace of the Sassi family
on the corner there is a tablet which runs: 'Tradition says
that the one who became so dear to Raphael, and whom he
raised to fame, lived in this house.' Some facts seem to confirm the tradition. A census taken in 1518 states that in a
house belonging to the Sassi lived a baker from Siena, named
Francesco Luti. We shall see how this links up with other
facts unearthed in 1897. The various houses where Margherita is supposed to have lived fit into the picture of a girl
moving to dwellings near Raphael's work. Thus when he is
decorating the villa for Chigi, the banker, she is near, in the
Via Santa Dorothea. When he is at work on *The Transfiguration*, in which she appears, as also, it is believed, in his
Madonna di San Sisto, she is near, in the Vicolo del Mer-
angolo.

For nine years she seems to have been near Raphael or
with him, and he finds in her face, and not in that of his
neglected fiancée, the inspiration of his Madonnas. It does not
seem likely she could have been a coarse or vulgar young
woman. There is a picture in the Uffizi Gallery at Florence
that is also alleged to be a portrait of the Fornarina. She is

very much the type of the courtesan of those days. By no
effort can she be transformed into the *Madonna di San Sisto*.
It is now recognised that the painting is the work of Sebastiano del Piombo, and its subject is believed to be Beatrice da
Ferrara, one of the fashionable courtesans of the day renowned for her mental powers and known to Cardinal
Bembo, Raphael's friend. The expression is hard and the pose
assertive.

This leaves two portraits contending for authenticity.
These are *The Fornarina* we see in the Borghese Gallery, and
the *Donna Velata* in the Pitti Gallery at Florence. It is the
latter, a beautiful girl whose face might well be the model
for Raphael's Madonnas, that seems most likely to have been
his choice. She is a simple creature, modestly dressed in a
rich gown, with a veil draped over her head, and a necklace
of medallions. Her eyes are lustrous, her mouth tender. The
portrait reveals the artist's affection for his subject. 'We are at
last before the real object of Raphael's love,' declares Lanciani. But two distinguished German critics dismiss it.
Knackfuss will not allow that this *Donna Velata* is by
Raphael, or is a portrait of his mistress, or anyone resembling
the Sistine Madonna. He goes on to demolish *The Fornarina*
of the Borghese Gallery, joining company here with Lanciani,
who finds it a type of vulgar courtesan. Against this testi-
mony we have that of Vasari, who speaks repeatedly of the
existence of a portrait of a baker's daughter; and also we have
the evidence of Pope Alexander VII, who declared that the
only genuine portrait of the *meretricula* (prostitute) as he
called her was the one which bore the name 'Raphael Urbinas' in gold letters on the blue band encircling her arm,
now in the Borghese Gallery. But Alexander VII was not
born until 1599, seventy-nine years after Raphael's death. He
could not possibly have known the Fornarina.

Here we must leave the matter, observing that the *Donna
Velata* and *The Fornarina* have no possible resemblance to
each other; and it is hard to extract a Madonna from the

latter and easy from the former. As for the authenticity of either work, we must remember that most of the great artists had assistants working for them, and that some of these assistants were so skilled, as in the case of Giulio Romano, that often the *maestro* himself failed to distinguish his own work from the copy.

Raphael's appointment as director of the building of the new St. Peter's enormously increased his work. He was constantly refusing the pleadings of princes to favour them with a painting. He was terribly pressed and began to lose his natural gaiety. The excavation of ancient ruins, the planning of a full survey of ancient Rome—these labours were piled on the top of a prodigious output, unequalled in quantity and quality by any other artist in history. Behind him stood a powerful and insatiable patron, the Pope; around him the world clamoured for his work; about him moved an adoring court of assistants and pupils. At the peak of the art history of the world, in an age that produced Da Vinci, Giorgione, Michelangelo, Titian, to name the foremost of a brilliant galaxy, he revealed a great virtuosity. Sacred works, portraits, cartoons, architectural works, sculpture, a great scheme for the restoration of ancient Rome and the excavation of its monuments—all this came in the space of his thirty-seven years.

In an age marked by ferocious cruelty, foul murders, treachery, robbery, lechery, arson, he had covered the walls of the Vatican with works of unsurpassable beauty. In dozens of churches the Madonna and the Holy Child gazed from their altars in a sublimity of divine radiance no other artist had ever approached. When he was attacked by the fever so prevalent in Rome he had no stamina to resist it. A bleeding hastened his collapse, and in the last few days he set his house in order. As the news of his death spread through Rome on the night of Good Friday, April 6th, 1520, an unutterable sorrow gripped all classes, from the Pope in tears, to the young apprentices in his workship. 'I cannot believe myself in Rome now that poor Raphael is no longer here,' cried Count Castiglione, the soldier and courtier, a close friend.

For three days Raphael lay in state in his own house near St. Peter's. His last work, *The Transfiguration*, was hung above his body, and was carried in the great procession that followed him to his tomb. He had selected a sepulchre in the Pantheon, under the altar of a chapel he had endowed with the income from 124 Via dei Coronari, a small property of his which still exists. He was buried near Maria Bibbiena. His bronze coffin lies under the stone arch of the altar.

And Margherita? She was beside his deathbed in those last hours in his studio near St. Peter's. When a messenger came from the Pope carrying a last blessing for one *in articulo mortis* she was forbidden to remain. Raphael does not seem to have had the resolution to make his companion of nine years his lawful wife. Possibly the administering priest had exhorted him to repent a sinful life and atone by having Maria Bibbiena declared his affianced wife. In his Will he remembered Margherita, leaving '*all amata sua si desse modo di poter vivere onestamente*'—to his love sufficient means to live honestly, a wish not fulfilled.

Driven from his deathbed, she had no part in his funeral, although her face had contributed much to his immortal works, and despite the fact that *tuttavia le perferi fino all' ultimo respiro la Fornarina*, to his last breath he always preferred *The Fornarina*, as his biographer said. When she attempted to follow the bier into the Pantheon she was violently driven away, beside herself with grief. It was said that melancholia overcame her and, seeking the aid of Cardinal Bibbiena, she was placed in an institution for fallen women. Then for three hundred and seventy-seven years oblivion covered her, so that many said *The Fornarina* was an empty legend of Raphael's life and the portrait a fake in art. But in 1897 a searcher, Antonio Valeri, found a clue. He discovered her name on a sheet torn from a ledger of the Congregation of Sant' Appollonia. This was an institution which had long

ceased to exist. In the fifteenth century it offered a refuge to
fallen and repentant women. The branch of this institution
into which Raphael's mistress was received, as no longer fit
for society, although her face shone above many altars as the
Madonna holding the Holy Child at her breast, was an extremely strict one. Behind its doors its inmates were dead to
the world. Here on August 18th, 1520, Margherita disappeared from life. But the entry of admission not only tells us
her fate, it establishes her reality and confirms her name. In
kindness they allowed that a mistress of nine years might be
called a widow. The entry ran: 'To-day, August 18, 1520,
Margherita, daughter of the late Francesco Luti da Siena, a
widow, was received into our institution.'

So that under whichever portrait may be considered au-
thentic, the one in the Uffizi Gallery or the one in the
Borghese Gallery, we may add to the title *The Fornarina*, the
beloved mistress of Raphael, the name of Margherita Luti.

Raphael had chosen as his last resting-place the Pantheon,
the best-preserved ancient monument in Rome. For one hundred and fifty years an annual Mass was said there for the
repose of his soul. When the income from the house he had
willed for this purpose was exhausted, and the Masses ceased,
the tomb still attracted attention because of a number of
miracles alleged to have been performed by the Madonna
over his sepulchre, which Raphael had commissioned. But
neither Masses nor miracles prevented an act of monstrous
vandalism perpetrated upon his corpse. For years the Academy of St. Luke claimed that it possessed the skull of Raphael.
A rival body made a similar claim. To settle the dispute between the two academies, Vasari having said in his description of the interment that the body was intact, the
sarcophagus was opened in 1832 and the skeleton of the
artist was taken out and exhibited to crowds of sightseers. It
was then demonstrated that neither academy possessed the
artist's skull, the remains being found intact, exactly as
Vasari had described. His skull was fine in form, with thirty-

three perfect teeth and one just appearing.[2] The skeleton measured five feet seven inches, and indicated the slender form of a young man of thirty-seven. It was placed in a glass case and exhibited for five whole weeks, and after this monstrous desecration it was enclosed in a new leaden coffin and re-interred with great solemnities in the bronze sarcophagus. On its front is engraven the distich written by Cardinal Bembo:

> *Ille hic est Raphael, timuit, quo sospiti, vinci*
> *Rerum magna parens, et, moriente, mori.*

This inscription Pope shamelessly stole for his epitaph on so second-rate a painter as Sir Godfrey Kneller, translating it:

> Living, great Nature feared he might outvie
> Her works, and, dying, fears herself to die.

[2] Goethe when in Rome in 1788 was duped. 'I have seen the collection of the Academy of San Luca, wherein is Raphael's skull. This relic appears to me indubitable. An excellent bone-structure wherein a beautiful soul might freely dwell. The Duke (of Weimar) wants a cast of it, which I shall probably be able to procure.'

VII

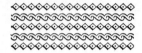

GALILEO AND MILTON

I

THE literature of Rome has been augmented by its many distinguished visitors. For more than a thousand years it has been enriched by the diaries and writings of all those who have made the pilgrimage, so that we see the great city through many eyes, in many phases, and the record is often the work of a man of genius. It is singular that Montaigne's diary of his visit is so little known, overshadowed, it would seem, by his famous Essays. On November 30th, 1580, M. de Montaigne passed through the Porta del Popolo and took his lodgings at the *Orso* (*The Bear*). This inn is still in business, on its corner by the Tiber embankment. It retains its old loggia, which has been closed in and converted into a modern restaurant. Here stayed Dante, ambassador from Florence in 1301. Rabelais, Montaigne, and, later, Goethe have slept under its roof. Like *The Lion* nearby, it was the property of Donna Vanozza, mistress of Pope Alexander VI and mother of his children, Lucrezia and Cesare Borgia. The Pope from time to time gave her exemption from vexatious taxes on wines and comestibles. When Donna Vanozza died in 1518, in a devout old age, she owned four inns, *The Lion*, *The Cow*, *The Eagle* and *The Bear*.

Montaigne was annoyed to find such great numbers of Frenchmen in Rome, so that everyone addressed him in his own tongue, but he was delighted by its many rich men, coaches and horses, beyond all he had seen elsewhere. He went almost at once, on the suggestion of his ambassador, to kiss the Pope's foot. He twice knelt, advanced sideways, and finally arrived on both knees in front of the Pope. The French Ambassador turned back the Holy Father's robe from his right foot, shod in a red shoe with a white cross on it, which Montaigne kissed.[1] He was astonished to hear the Pope address him with a Bologna accent, 'the idiom of this city being the worst in Italy,' but found him to be a fine old man of nearly eighty. 'By nature he is kind, caring little about affairs of state, a great builder.' He was devoted to his illegitimate son by a servant in his brother's house.

Montaigne was a great sightseer. He saw a bandit cast off a gibbet and his body cut into four pieces. He saw the execution of two brothers who had slain their master:

'Their flesh was torn with pincers and their hands cut off, and after this mutilation they put over the wounds the bodies of capons which they killed and cut open just before. This execution took place on a scaffold where the criminals were first knocked down with heavy wooden clubs and then their throats were cut.'

On January 30th, 1581, he witnessed 'the most ancient ceremony that still subsists amongst men, to wit, the circumcision of the Jews and gave most attentive and profitable attention thereto.'

Courtesans were a well-established institution in Rome. If they died unmarried their bodies were buried in a ditch outside the walls and their property was seized by the Church. While living they enjoyed the hospitality and protection of the popes and cardinals, who kept them often in considerable state. Those in the highest class had *salons*, as in ancient Greece. Imperia was a 'queen of beauty' in the time of Julius II. The banker Chigi, Il Magnifico, erected an elaborate tomb for her in St. Gregorio Magno. The inscription runs:—

[1] Foot-kissing is a well-established ritual still in vogue in Rome. On St. Peter's Day the bronze statue of the Apostle is decked out in jewelled vestments and triple tiara while thousands advance in file down the nave of St. Peter's to kiss the well-polished bronze toe.

'Imperia, Roman courtesan, who, worthy of the great name, was gifted with incomparable beauty, lived twenty-six years, twelve days; died August 15th, 1511.'

When the famous Tortona walked abroad, Lanciani tells us, 'four footmen, two pages, one maid, and several admirers formed her escort.' In 1490 there were six thousand courtesans in a city of sixty thousand; in 1549 there were four hundred and eighty-four *cortigiane oneste*, registered, with thousands of the lower grades. Pope Adrian VI issued an edict putting them out of business. 'Alas,' lamented a pilgrim in 1525, 'what a sad Jubilee we expect to have since Rome has been deprived of its best attraction.' The edict does not seem to have had effect, for in the year that Montaigne visited Rome there were nineteen thousand. He remarked how they sat at their windows:

'. . . with such refinement of trickery that I often wondered at the address they display in attracting men's eyes. Often I have got down from my horse and induced some of these ladies to admit me, and have wondered how they contrived to make themselves appear so much handsomer than they really were. They have the art of letting a beholder distinguish them by whatever traits of theirs is most seemly; they will let you see only the upper part of the face, or the lower, or the side, veiling and unveiling according to the particular style of countenance, so that an ugly woman is never to be seen at a window. Each one takes her position there for the purpose of saluting and bowing to her acquaintance, who, as they go by, throw up many a glance. Another privilege granted to any gallant who may have paid one crown or more for passing the night in a house of this character, is that he is allowed to salute his inamorata in public the next day. . . .

'There are always sermons to be listened to at all seasons, or disputes in theology; or, again, diversion may be found with some courtesan or other but in this case I found one disadvantage, to wit, that these ladies charge as extortionately for the privilege of simple conversation (which was what I sought, desiring to hear them talk, and take part in their play of wit) as for the supreme

favour, and are just as niggard thereof. All these revelations kept
me effectually from melancholy, which is the death of me, and of
irritability with which I was troubled neither without doors nor
within. Thus I found Rome a very pleasant place of sojourn.'

On Low Sunday Montaigne went to the church of St.
Maria sopra Minerva, and was rewarded by the spectacle of
the Pope arriving in procession to bestow alms on a number
of selected maidens.

'On this day besides his equipage, the Pope had twenty-five
horses led before him, decked and covered with cloth of gold, and
most richly caparisoned, and ten or twelve mules covered with
crimson velvet, all these being led by lackeys on foot. Then came
the Pope's litter, also covered with crimson velvet. The Pope himself rode on his mule, and before him went four men on horseback
who carried each one a cardinal's hat, set on the top of a staff
which was covered with red velvet.'

Before we leave Montaigne let us follow his own experiences as a sightseer. It is encouraging to learn, since we suffer
much from walking in the long galleries and churches, with
their hard marble pavements, that there is some compensation:

'The air is bad for the feet but good for the head. . . . Nothing
is so adverse to my own health as idleness and sloth, and in Rome
I was never without occupation . . . I found it, of all towns in
the world, the one most filled with the corporate idea, in which
difference of nationality counts least; for by its very nature, it is a
patchwork of strangers, each one being as much at home as in his
own country. The authority of its ruler lies over the whole of
Christianity.'

Inside the church of St. Maria sopra Minerva we find
much that is good for the head, if hard on the feet. The effigy
of St. Catherine of Siena under the altar, suitably illuminated, is a beautiful thing. She died, one of the twenty-five
children of a humble Siennese dyer, in her thirty-third year,
after a life of incredible journeyings, fastings, ecstasies,

visions, exhortations and much forceful achievement as a politician. She chided, coerced and encouraged in godly work popes, kings and queens, never for a moment doubting she was the agent of Christ, the Church, and the poor for whom she lived. She died in Rome in 1380, worn out by half-delirious ecstasy, fasting, lack of sleep and intense political excitement. With no education at all, in an age when women had an inferior role, she dominated the moribund Church, revitalised it and re-established it in Rome. It is doubtful whether there is her equal in all history, even considering Joan of Arc, who nobly failed.

On the left of the altar is one of Michelangelo's many unfinished works. This is a statue of Christ carrying the cross. He had accepted the order for it in 1514, but the great neurotic, with illness and nerves, had not begun it in 1518, although the contract stipulated that it should be finished in three years. 'I am dying with shame . . . I have the air of being a thief!' he cried. Thirty years later he was still tormenting himself for not having finished it. He worked on it between 1518 and 1520, and later turned the lifeless failure over to an unskilled pupil, who mutilated it. With his passion for the male nude, again expressed in this *Cristo*, he provoked an outcry, so that a ridiculous bronze kilt was added. A foot also had to be covered with metal to protect it from the wearing kisses of the pious.

Behind the altar are the tombs of two Medici popes, Leo X and Clement VII. It is ironical that the two great Medici, who belonged entirely to the golden era of the Renaissance, should be lying here in the only Gothic church in Rome, and among the least beautiful of all the monuments their age bestowed on Rome. Pope Leo, the son of Lorenzo the Magnificent, became a cardinal at seventeen and pope at thirty-eight. During his rule the Renaissance achieved its greatest glory with Raphael, Michelangelo and Ariosto under his patronage. Strange it is that he did not, like so many other popes, order a memorial by one of the great artists of his age.

Nearby is an outstanding figure in Renaissance letters, the pagan Cardinal Bembo, the friend of Vittoria Colonna, Isabella d'Este and Raphael, for whose tomb in the Pantheon he wrote the epitaph. He was a private secretary to Pope Leo and an historian of Venice.

The left wall presents a laudatory epitaph on Pope Paul IV, a man so hideous to encounter that even the bloody Alva trembled in his presence. The coloured marble effigy conveys something of the nature of this man who persecuted the Jews and made them wear a distinguishing yellow cap. He drew up the papal Bull that created in 1542 the Court of the Holy Inquisition, placing its power in the hands of the Dominicans, and also the Bull against Luther. The cardinal-uncle of the terrible Torquemada, the Spanish Dominican monk who was the Grand Inquisitor of Spain, lies also in this church. The Inquisition racked and burned many times the number of Christians martyred by the Caesars. The epitaph tells us that Paul IV was 'illustrious by his innocence, by his liberality, and by his greatness of soul. He lived eighty-three years, one month, twenty days.' He was in England in 1513–14 as Papal Legate to the Court of Henry VIII.

There is a singular story connected with Paul IV and Queen Elizabeth of England. It is alleged she sent an embassy to him hoping to obtain papal sanction for her succession to the throne, fearful perhaps of Mary Queen of Scots, a Catholic whose cause was championed by France and Spain. Elizabeth's mother, according to Holy Church, had never been Henry VIII's legitimate wife, and therefore Elizabeth was illegitimate, and in 1533 Clement VII had excommunicated her father.[2] In return for the Pope's recognition of her right

[2] The title 'Defender of the Faith' carried by English kings was conferred upon Henry VIII by Pope Leo X for a tract which he wrote against Martin Luther, *Assertio septem sacramentorium contra M. Lutherum.* The Vatican library contains the autographed manuscript sent by Henry to the Pope in 1521, in which the King claims indulgence for any literary shortcomings on the score of his military occupations! M. de Montaigne saw this manuscript with much interest on his visit to Rome in 1581. The Library also possesses seventeen letters written by King Henry to Anne Boleyn while courting her.

to the throne she offered to make an act of obedience. But Paul IV was no diplomat. He returned a blunt refusal, telling Elizabeth she was born out of wedlock and had no right to the crown without consent of the Apostolic See. If the Pope had agreed to Elizabeth's proposal England might have reverted to the Roman Catholic Church, from which her father had divorced it. Elizabeth, after her dangerous and unsuccessful overture, turned to the Protestants for safety and supported the spreading heresy that the Inquisition savagely sought to check. The Italian historian Muratori and others confirm this story. Lingard, the English Roman Catholic historian, denies it.

The other pope buried here is Clement VII, the son of Giulio de' Medici, murdered in the Pazzi conspiracy at Florence. He saw Rome sacked and England break away from the Church. It is said that, together with Leo X, to whom he was an illegitimate cousin, he can be seen in the beautiful fresco by Filippino Lippi that tells the story of St. Thomas Aquinas, the 'angelic doctor'.

Among the artists connected with this church one above all will cause us to pause. In the left transept, under a simple slab depicting a Dominican brother, carved in relief and worn by countless passing feet through the five centuries, lies Fra Angelico, the saint who painted saints, the gentle artist whose life justified the breaking of the rule not to erect monuments to those dying in convents. They placed him here in 1455, and his friend, Pope Nicholas V, who revered him, wrote his epitaph. A lamp now hangs over the memorial of one who was lovely in all his ways.

There is a large convent attached to the church, with historic memories, but, alas, it is used as a Government office. Happily, on the day of my visit an Italian artist from Paris had hired a room in which to give an exhibition of his pictures. He was a shy, gentle young man, and had he been garbed in a monk's habit he might have passed for a reincarnation of Fra Angelico. His work was as tender as his

VILLA MEDICI

PRINCE CHARLES STUART AS A BOY IN ROME

smile. His exhibition enabled me to see the cloister and the great hall of this headquarters of the Dominican Order. In this hall two Conclaves were held at which Eugene IV and Nicholas V were elected popes. But these memories are almost effaced by the fact that it was here that the Holy Inquisition sat and exerted such dread and tyranny over the lives of men. When Paul IV lay dying, the angry mob assailed the prisons of the Castle of St. Angelo, the Corte Savelli and the Tor di Nona. The frightened gaolers released four hundred condemned prisoners. The mob then went to the Ripetta, the prison of the Inquisition, released seventy men who had lain there for years and burned the hated place to the ground. The Convent of Minerva would have met the same fate but for the restraining hand of Marcantonio Colonna, who advised the avengers to bide their time.

In the list of the Inquisition's victims brought to this hall to appear before its fanatical members two names are outstanding, those of Bruno and Galileo. Here on February 8th, 1600, after a protracted trial, the blameless philosopher, Giordano Bruno, was condemned to death. There are few stories sadder than that of this scholar whose thought was four hundred years in advance of his times. He had been a Dominican friar, in the very cloister in which St. Thomas Aquinas had lived. Driven abroad by the hostility of the Church to the advance of learning, he had, in turn, been an honoured teacher in many universities, and had travelled in France and England, where he enjoyed the friendship of Sir Philip Sidney. Invited to Venice by Giovanni Mocenigo, he was foully betrayed by his host and handed over to the Inquisition, which kept him in prison for eight long years of mental torture and questioning, but failed to make him retract his beliefs.

Before the reading of the death sentence he was covered with the Sanbenito, a sleeveless gown for heretics, with red devils over its yellow ground. He stood there amid the throng of monks, priests and soldiers, and when the words condemning him to perish at the stake had been pronounced, Bruno, without emotion, addressed the Inquisition, saying, 'You have more fear in uttering such a sentence than I have in receiving it.' He was then degraded, excommunicated and handed over to the Governor of Rome with the usual recommendation that he be punished *citra sanguinis effusionem*, 'without effusion of blood,' the formula for burning at the stake.

For another eight days he was kept in prison, a man broken in health but steadfast in his witness to Truth, while he was hounded by seven priests of the Company of Mercy, instituted for the purpose of accompanying heretics to the place of execution and of encouraging them to repent. It was also their office to hold up holy images for the victim to kiss until the faggots were lit. The cruellest methods were used to effect an appearance of kissing these, or of repentance. Bruno refused to recant. To prevent him from making a speech his tongue was tied. When they held up a crucifix before him, as the flames mounted, he turned his eyes scornfully away from this travesty of piety.

The burning took place in the year of the Jubilee, and it was just one more spectacle for an enormous crowd of pilgrims. So little notice was taken of the event, a common one, that for years afterwards the Church denied that it had burnt him. His ashes were scattered to the winds. There is a fine statue of Bruno in the Campo di Fiori, now famous as a secondhand market, where the execution took place, as well as that of many other heretics and Jews, victims of the terrible *autos-da-fé*.

II

The next great figure to appear before the Inquisition in the hall of the Convent is Galileo Galilei. He was born at Pisa in 1564, the year in which Michelangelo died. When seventeen, his father, a notable musician, sent him to study at the University there. He soon distinguished himself as a writer, musician and artist, so that his father, wisely deciding that commerce was not a proper calling for his son, allowed him to continue his studies with a view to becoming a doctor.

One day while praying in the cathedral Galileo's attention was drawn to the swinging of a great lamp after a sacristan had lit it. He checked the time of the swing with his own pulse and discovered thereby the principle of the pendulum—isochronism—that made all modern clock-making possible. Yet this was a by-product, for, a medical student, he had sought to time the human pulse and its regularity. From that day physics and not medicine dominated his studies. At twenty-six he was appointed Lecturer in Mathematics at Pisa University at a salary of £13 a year. His shrewd father was appalled. A Professorship of Medicine, for which he had planned his son's education, was worth £100 a year.

By this time Galileo had read the works of Bruno, confounding the Aristotelians and the fixed-earthists. His adoption of the heretical Copernican theory, that the planets were in motion, aroused fierce opposition, and he was driven out of Pisa. He turned to Venice. The independent Venetians had never taken much notice of the fiats of the Church. They invited Galileo to accept a chair at Padua University. Thither he went, and enjoyed enormous success. 'I count myself happy in the search after truth to have so great an ally as yourself. . . . It is really pitiful there are so few who seek truth,' he wrote to Kepler, acknowledging the gift of his new book.

Galileo invented the thermometer, lectured on a new star, and definitely rejected the Ptolemaic system. He also invented the telescope, founded on a Dutch optician's discovery of the lens, and thereby increased by ten times the field of heavenly bodies. His lecture-room was packed. He spoke and wrote clear, fluent Italian. Venice insisted on having a demonstration of the new telescope. He took it there and exhibited his wonder to the Signoria. Old Senators climbed breathlessly up the tower to look at the new world. The State doubled his salary and lengthened the period of his appointment. Galileo made a new telescope, and the Milky Way, instead of being a mysterious fog, was seen to be composed of stars. He also found mountains in the moon. But, wise in so much, he was foolish in one fatal thing. Like Dante, he could not dismiss his love for Florence, ever ferocious and brutal. He was invited by the Grand Duke of Tuscany to return there. In 1610 he left Padua, somewhat ungrateful to Venice, which had supported and honoured him for eighteen years. It was the beginning of all his misfortunes. He should have remembered that Venice was never dominated by Rome. She expelled the powerful Jesuits, she defied the papal interdict, gloriously supported by Paolo Sarpi, the monk-historian, whose writings had so shaken the Papacy that it hired assassins to attempt his life. Knowing all this, Galileo should not have left the safe harbour of Venetia. True, in a weak moment Venice had surrendered Bruno, seventeen years earlier, but it would not bow again to Rome.

The universal Church was in conflict with universal Truth, which seemed to challenge its dogmas. It was resolute in defending itself, and in so doing Bruno and Galileo were crushed in the conflict. Not only the Church and the Aristotelians, but most of the scientists and philosophers bitterly opposed Galileo's attack on the established dogmas of theology and physics. The honour in which excommunicated Venice had held Galileo increased the opposition to his theories. The Church was compelled to prosecute heresy, believing what it did, or go down to defeat. The Jesuits joined forces with the Aristotelians and the travelling jackals. Galileo was a heretic who must be made to recant or be destroyed. He had now found spots on the sun to add to his monstrous mountains on the moon.

At the Tuscan court Galileo was honoured and flattered. Free of the professorial chair, he had more time for study. Above all, he was in his beloved Florence. His two daughters were nearby in a convent. A devout Catholic, he was glad for them to have this retreat. In that age it was the only alternative to marriage.

Galileo had never intended to challenge the Church. He had pointed out that Joshua's miracle could be more easily achieved by stopping the earth's rotation than by stopping the heavens, as in the Ptolemaic system. But his enemies never rested. His heresy at Pisa was recalled. In 1615 Pope Paul V asked him to come to Rome and explain himself. Happily he had a friend in the powerful Cardinal Barberini. The visit was successful. There was a pleasant interview with the Pope, and they parted good friends. Before he left for home a startling development took place. Copernicus's book was banned. Galileo was forbidden to teach the motion of the earth.

In 1621 Paul V died, and two years later his friend Cardinal Maffeo Barberini became Pope Urban VIII. The ban might now be withdrawn. He went to Rome to congratulate his friend, and had a cordial reception. 'We have very lovingly embraced him; nor can we suffer him to return to the country whither your liberality recalls him without an ample provision of Pontifical love,' wrote the Pope to the Grand Duke in Florence.

Galileo returned home and published his epoch-making book, the *Dialogues on the Ptolemaic and Copernican Systems*, passed by the papal censor in a careless moment. A great storm blew up. The book was banned. The old scientist was summoned to Rome. In reply to Galileo's appeal the Pope was obdurate, saying he had previously warned him of his danger. Galileo knew, and his distracted daughters knew, what a trial for heresy meant—torture, if necessary to secure a recantation, and burning at the stake, if obdurate. Seventy years old, ill and forced to travel through a plague area, he arrived exhausted, on February 13th, 1633, and was housed by the Tuscan ambassador in the Villa Medici. He was permitted to take the air of the Pincio in a closed carriage only. He could have been cast into a dungeon, as were many others under examination. Some eight years earlier there had been the trial of Antonio de Dominis, Archbishop of Salpetria, supporter of the Venetians against the Pope, who fled to England and became a Protestant Dean of Windsor. He had foolishly returned to Italy to recant, and had been sentenced to death. He cheated the stake only by dying in the dungeon where he was held during six years of torture and questioning.

Galileo's ordeal dragged on, from February to June. The prosecutors, not content with forging a document to prove that Galileo had persisted in his teachings after solemn admonition in 1616, had also represented to the Pope that he was one of the characters held up to ridicule in the famous *Dialogues*. This may have been the chief or a contributing cause of the withdrawal of the Pope's favour and of his order for the trial to proceed.

On April 12th, 1633, he was removed to the cells of the Holy Office in the convent of St. Maria sopra Minerva and repeatedly examined. When he appeared again on April 20th he was forbidden to say what horrors he had faced. There were five known stages of the ordeal of the rack: the threat of its use in court; the conducting to the door of the torture-chamber and the repetition of the threat; the taking inside and exhibition of the instruments; the stripping and binding on the rack; and finally, if all these had not produced the required confession, there was *territo realis*—the torture itself. Whether he suffered the last degree will never be known, but the hernia from which he afterwards suffered is held proof that he did. His advisers repeatedly urged him to recant, knowing what otherwise would befall. At last he recanted, and those who blame him—a shattered man of seventy, bullied, cross-examined, remanded, brought out of confinement repeatedly, and probably tortured—ask too much of human nature. Old and broken he cried: 'I am in your hands and will say whatever you wish.' He was removed while the document of his perjury was drawn up and twice sworn to.

On June 22nd, 1633, dressed as a penitent in the hideous *Sanbenito*, he was taken again to the Convent of the Minerva to face the cardinals and priests in the court crowded with his exultant enemies. He was sentenced by the Holy Office to abjuration of all false doctrine, imprisonment for life and to recite the seven penitential psalms each week. There were ten cardinals present, of whom three, to their honour, refused their assent to the conviction. Let us set forth the names of these: Cardinals Caspar Borgia, Landivio Zacchia and Francesco Barberini, the Pope's nephew. From the Pope, Urban VIII, Galileo's 'loving friend', came not a word.

Here in this hall Galileo, hideously garbed, on his knees, read aloud, word for word, his recantation, a long, monstrous document:

'. . . I held and believed that the sun is the centre of the universe and is immovable, and that the earth is not the centre and is movable; willing therefore to remove from the minds of Your Eminences, and of every Catholic Christian, this vehement suspicion rightfully entertained towards me, with a sincere heart and unfeigned faith, I abjure, curse, and detest the said errors and heresies, and generally every other error and sect contrary to the Holy Church.'

There is the story that as he rose to his knees he muttered *Eppur si muove* ('and yet it moves!'). It is very unlikely. It would have been fatal for a broken and disgraced man. Nor had they yet finished with him. Unlike Bruno and de Dominis, and hundreds before them, he had escaped the stake, but the strong hand of the Inquisition still gripped him. He was held for some time in a prison in Rome. His recantation was proclaimed in the cathedral of Florence and sent to all the universities to be publicly read. His books were proscribed. The life sentence was commuted by the Pope, and Galileo was confined in the grounds of the Trinitá dei Monti. Later he was removed to Siena and confined in the Archbishop's house. He was never totally liberated or pardoned.

Requests to return to Florence were repeatedly refused. Then, in March, 1638, when completely blind, he was permitted to go to his house there, but was not allowed to go out of the city. His daughter, on her deathbed in a convent near Arcetri, wrote to say she was reciting the penitential psalms for him, thus sparing him the task. He returned home in time to embrace her just before her death.

Strictly confined to his house, he might receive only Catholic visitors, after their approval by the Jesuit controller. Any infraction would have caused him to be sent to a dungeon in Rome. A last request to the Pope, for complete liberty, on April 28th, 1638, was refused, but later he was permitted to live in his villa, Il Gioiello, at Arcetri, some three miles out of Florence. Nearby, in her convent, lived his surviving daughter.

The Holy See could forbid him to teach or publish. It could not stop him thinking or writing. In his enforced seclusion he pursued his studies. He wrote his famous dialogue on the laws of motion. When he became blind he wrote to a friend:

'Henceforth this heaven, this universe, which by wonderful observations I have enlarged an hundred and a thousand times beyond the conception of former ages, is shrunk for me into the narrow space which I, myself, fill in it. So it pleases God; it shall therefore please me also.'

II

Galileo had faithful pupils about him. On a spring day of 1639 an ardent young Englishman of twenty-nine, having received permission, came to the Villa Gioiello at Arcetri to pay homage to the blind old scientist.[3] His name was John Milton. In his father's house at Horton the author of *Comus:*

---

[3] Arceteri is in the zone of Pian dei Giullari. The Villa Gioiello is still there. Nearby is the house to which Savonarola often retreated. Pian dei Giullari (Meadow of the Jesters) takes its name from the fact that the jesters and minstrels at the court of the Medici were trained there and often sent as presents to different European courts.

a Mask had gained some fame. He had also written *L'Allegro* and *Il Penseroso*. He had been studying Italian, which may account for these titles. Then, on the death of his young friend King, he touched the peak of his lyrical genius with *Lycidas*. Its last line is 'Tomorrow to fresh woods, and pastures new.' Milton was beginning to think of foreign travel. His mother had died in 1637, his brother and wife had come to live at Horton with old Mr. Milton, so he felt free to move, in which his father concurred. It was estimated that with a servant one could travel abroad for a year for some £350.

One day handsome young John Milton walked across the daisied meadows to Eton, to consult old Sir Henry Wootton, now Provost of Eton College, formerly an ambassador in Italy. Milton gave him a copy of *Comus: a Mask*. He told John Milton, perhaps aware of his indiscreet temperament in matters of religion, of some advice he had himself received as a young man in Siena from an old Roman courtier who knew the perils. '*Signor Arrigo mio*,' he had said, '*I pensieri stretti ed il viso sciolto*' (thoughts close, countenance open) will go safely all over the world'. In other words, a visitor from a Protestant country to a Catholic country terrorised by the Inquisition should be careful not to talk too much. Milton should watch his dangerous tendency to speak out too freely.

He arrived in Florence from Nice and Genoa in August, 1638, and spent two most agreeable months there. Handsome, learned, well introduced, he was much entertained and made an impression on the local learned societies. He recited some of his Latin verses, and in return had a complimentary ode addressed to him. On this occasion he was not able to visit the famous Galileo. In October he went on to Rome. He found the atmosphere not so sympathetic. It would seem he forgot Wootton's advice, and by his resolute defence of Protestantism gave offence to the English Jesuits and others, who subsequently shunned him. He was present at a sumptuous entertainment at the English College, where he dined with the brother of the gallant Lord Falkland. He pursued his passion for music, and at Cardinal Francesco Barberini's great palace[4] just completed by Bernini, he heard the famous Leonora Baroni sing, and was swept off his feet, apparently as much by the lady herself as by her voice. She was then the rage of Italy, which she toured with her two daughters, and they were reputed between 1637 and 1641 to have the finest voices in the world. Milton wrote three Latin poems in honour of the lady, one entitled 'To Leonora, singing at Rome.' Likening her to a winged angel, he concludes:

> _Quod si cuncta quidem Deus est, per cunctaque fusus,_
> _In te una loquitur, caetera mutus habet._[5]

Young, susceptible to beauty, the poet who even in cold England desired to 'sport with Amaryllis in the shade,' was deeply stirred by the warmth and beauty of the Italian specimens, and although he assures us that in all his tours abroad he lived a pure life, the language of these poems voices a passion desperately restrained. Another lady drew forth an ardent poetic tribute, but Leonora above all appears to have enamoured him. Passionately fond of music, Milton could not have come to Italy at a better time. Opera and oratorio had swept the country. Cardinals kept musicians at their courts. Milton, an organist of some merit, undoubtedly met and heard the famous Frescobaldi, organist-composer and choirmaster at the Lateran. The Barberini nephews, two of them cardinals, and one the Prefect of Rome, used their great

---

[4] Urban VIII built the great palace, and, wishing to found a dynasty, issued a Bull entailing the Barberini name, palace and estates on any living male descendant, legitimate or illegitimate, child of prince or priest. 'He used to complain that he had four relations who were fit for nothing; first Cardinal Francesco, who was a saint and worked no miracles; secondly Cardinal Antonio, who was a monk and had no patience; thirdly Antonio, the younger, who was an orator and did not know how to speak; while the fourth was a general, who did not know how to draw the sword.' Barberinis lived in the palace of that name until they sold it in June, 1949.

[5] 'If however, God is in all things, and through all diffused, in thee alone He speaks; all else he inhabits mute.'

wealth to stage in the immense *salons* of their palaces sumptuous productions. Eventually, with growing ambition, they built a theatre holding three thousand guests and employed Bernini to make the costumes and sets. The master of baroque was also an enthusiast in this era of opera, superbly staged, with enchanted palaces, heroes on the backs of winged dragons, chariots drawn by serpents, with horses, camels and even elephants paraded across the stage. Bernini not only built a theatre but painted and carved the scenery, wrote the plays, composed the music and acted and sang the principal parts himself. Leonora Baroni had to enthrall her audience off the stage. The convention would not allow women to act and sing. The female parts were played by handsome boys, often with the purpose of finishing their musical education. They looked the parts extremely well, and a century later delighted Goethe, who saw Tuscan lads play *Armida and Chloe*. The Romans were critical but paternal, and administered the rod to ambitious musicians. It was therefore an honour to win their approval.

All this must have astonished and delighted Milton. He was present at a performance of *Chi soffre speri*, written, to music by Mazzocchi and Marazzoli, by Monsignore Rospigliosi, later Pope Clement IX. Milton heard in this Barberini production *recitativo secco*, dialogue half-sung, half-spoken, an innovation. The opera was given 'with true Roman magnificence,' says Milton. He was introduced to Cardinal Barberini by the Vatican librarian, an old Oxford friend and, alas, an abjurer of Protestantism. Much flattered, he wrote: 'The Cardinal himself stood at the door to receive me, sought me out in the great crowd and pressed me to enter with every mark of honour.'

Milton bought a considerable amount of music in Italy, and had it shipped from Venice when he reached there later. After two months in Rome he journeyed to Naples in November, 1638, where he met the septuagenarian Count Manso,

Tasso's biographer and friend, who acted as cicerone, but was scared by being seen with Milton. The Inquisition was active, and in apologising to his young guest he suggested he should be more tactful in his remarks about religion.

The news from England became perturbing, and Milton felt it would be 'dishonourable to be enjoying myself at my ease in a foreign land, while my countrymen were striking a blow for freedom.' So he cancelled a projected tour of Sicily and Greece and started homewards, but leisurely. He stayed in Rome throughout January and February, 1639, and was again warmly welcomed in Florence, where he lingered through March and April. He attended three meetings of the Academies, but the great event of this second visit was his meeting with Galileo at Arcetri. He sought and received permission to talk with the blind savant, old and frail, but still mentally alert. What a moment in history that was![6] All unknown that his name and fame would be recorded in verse by one of the greatest of poets, and destined, like him, to blindness, Galileo thus linked his own immortality with that of his young English visitor. And Milton, alert to the greatness of his host, sitting in the villa and observing the savant's instruments, gained an indelible impression, to be used in later years in *Paradise Lost:*

> As when by night the glass
> Of Galileo, less assured, observes
> Imagined lands and regions in the moon.

Moreover, Milton had stayed at that convent at Vallombrosa where the young Galileo and his schoolfellows

---

[6] This meeting greatly affected Milton's thought and writings. He alludes to the event in his *Aeropagitica*—'Italy . . . there it was I found and visited the famous Galileo grown old, a prisoner to the Inquisition, for thinking in Astronomy otherwise than the Franciscan and Dominican licensers thought.' Galileo is the only contemporary mentioned in *Paradise Lost*.

This visit aroused his curiosity, as in IV. 592. Milton, like Europe, was not sure whether to support the Ptolemaic or Copernican theory, but leaned to the latter; the Archangel will not decide—VIII. 122. Satan (Ignorance) is made definitely Ptolemaic, (astronomy is geocentric and astrological, IX. 103) as are the Inquisition and others, III. 478.

> lay entranced
> Thick as autumnal leaves that strow the brooks
> In Vallombrosa, where the Etrurian shades
> High over-arch'd embower;

The pattern of Fate is here finely drawn. As with his host, Milton would inherit the reward of fame and the infliction of blindness. Here on the hilltop he bids farewell to Galileo, whose life has less than three more years to run, to take his own stormy part in a riven England. He was to witness how Truth, despite interdicts and Inquisitions, marches triumphantly on. In that same year of the death in Italy of Galileo, who gave us the laws of motion, there was born in England Newton, who gave us the laws of gravitation. The forerunner lies honoured in Santa Croce, the Westminster Abbey of Italy; his successor lies in Westminster Abbey, the Santa Croce of England.

VIII

THE PRINCE, THE LADY, THE POET

I

'I WANT to go to the Via Vittorio,' I said one morning to my companion, who had the merit of being a tireless walker.

'How odd! That's exactly where I want to go,' she exclaimed. 'What takes you there?'

'Bonnie Prince Charlie.'

'What has he to do with the Via Vittoria?'

'And what have you?' I queried, avoiding any explanation, which would have been difficult and long.

'I want to get a ticket for Rubinstein's recital in the Academy of St. Cecilia there,' she replied.

We set off, descending by the steps of the Trinità dei Monti. The morning was perfect. We lingered on the steps awhile to listen to a small boy with the head of a Murillo cherub playing the accordion. All over the tourist tracks in Rome, up on the Pincio, along the leafy parade before the Villa Medici, down the steps to the Piazza di Spagna, by the Forum and the Colosseum, by any café with chairs set in the sun or, at other times, in the shade, these nimble-fingered boys, large accordions slung round their slender necks, fill the air with strains of Verdi, Puccini, Mascagni, Léhar, Strauss and, yes, Gershwin, whose *Rhapsody in Blue* one hears floating through the rose and violet of a Roman sundown, or in the freshness of morning.

These boys have an inexhaustible repertoire. Where do

they learn to play? Their instruments are usually hired by the hour. They are always attended by a bedraggled little girl who approaches with a collecting-tin. Poverty marks them for its own.

No, he had never had a lesson, he told us. He did not know just how many pieces he could play—but he could go on all day. The little girl was not his sister. He had seven brothers and four sisters. He lived in Trastevere. While we elicited this information his fine fingers never ceased to run over the ivory keys, or his bright eyes and teeth to flash. Snatches of *Butterfly*, *Rigoletto*, *O Sole Mio*, *Way Down Upon the Swannee River*—this at the sight of two American ladies mounting the steps—a fox-trot, then *Celeste Aïda* came forth in a stream. We put some money in the collecting-tin and passed on down the steps to the blazing flowerstalls under the windows of Keats's lodgings, now a memorial museum.

'I always utter a prayer for dear M'sieur Gueffier,' I said, as we came to the end of the steps and launched ourselves into the Piazza.

'M'sieur who?' demanded my companion.

'Gueffier. All we know of him is that he had the beautiful idea of completing a French donation. A French king gave the church at the top, and Gueffier had the idea in 1721 of building these steps. He got a man of genius, Alessandro Specchi, to design them, and built them up through what had formerly been a hillside garden, part of the place where Lucullus used to give his famous banquets. And, unlike the Popes, he refrained from placing a plaque anywhere to boast about his gift and immortalise himself.'

'But who was M'sieur Gueffier?' persisted my friend, as I held her back from a suicidal step into the maelstrom of traffic that whirled before us.

'When Innocent XIII was Pope,' I answered, 'he was secretary to the French Embassy. He unwittingly provided all the artists' models of Rome with sunny shelves on which to display themselves. Look at this,' I added, pointing to a marble plinth, on which were carved the lilies of the Bourbons and the eagle of Napoleon. 'A little French history on a scene to which they contributed. Incidentally, M'sieur Gueffier provided a magnificent approach to the Villa Medici, the French Academy of Art in Rome. Lord Dufferin, once our Ambassador in Rome, on being moved to Paris told Rennell Rodd that his idea of an ideal life was to be, from twenty to twenty-five a reigning beauty, from twenty-five to thirty a successful French General, from thirty-five to fifty a wealthy English nobleman, and the rest of life a Roman cardinal. As he could not be the last, he would like to have remained the next best thing, an Ambassador in Rome. Well, since all of these are quite out of the question for me, I've my own idea. I would probably trade the Ambassadorship for a French studentship and the Prix de Rome. To be young, rewarded, to live for one's art, in that most beautiful villa—and surely to be in love, like Raphael with some little Italian madonna who comes to pose, is my idea of felicity, and it was Henry James's!'

My companion laughed. 'You should be very content with what you are. You wander round the world with a fountainpen and get paid for expressing yourself. That's my idea of felicity.'

Descending the steps of the Trinità dei Monti I always have in mind Charles Dickens's description of the models he saw there for hire.

'The first time I went up there I could not conceive why the faces seemed so familiar to me; why they appeared to have beset me for years, in every possible variety of action and costume; and how it came to pass that they started up before me, in Rome, in broad day, like so many saddled and bridled nightmares. I soon found that we had made acquaintance, and improved it, for several years on the walls of various Exhibition Galleries. There is one old gentleman with long white hair and an immense beard who, to my knowledge, has gone half through the catalogues of the Royal Academy. This is the veritable patriarchal model. . . .

There is another man in a blue cloak who always pretends to be asleep in the sun and who, I need not say, is always very wide awake, and very attentive to the disposition of his legs. This is the *dolce far niente* model. There is another man in a brown cloak, who leans against a wall, with his arms folded in his mantle, and looks out of the corners of his eyes, which are just visible beneath his broad slouched hat. This is the assassin model. . . . As to Domestic Happiness and Holy Families, they should come very cheap, for there are heaps of them all up the steps, and the cream of the thing is, that they are all the falsest vagabonds in the world, especially made up for the purpose, and having no counterparts in Rome or in any other part of the habitable globe.'

There are no artists' models now, only cameras clicking in the hands of the tourists, with Keats's deathplace on one side, a favourite English tea-room on the other, the flower-stalls between, the steps behind, and in the middle of the square the fountain in the form of a stone boat. It is the work of the great Bernini's father. Opposite is the Spanish Embassy to the Vatican, which gives its name to the Piazza.

'We shall come back later and call there,' I remarked, indicating the Embassy. 'Alfieri once lived at the top of the steps and triumphed at the bottom.'

'How? Why don't you satisfy my curiosity, instead of arousing it?' complained my friend.

'The art of story-telling is the art of suspense,' I replied, teasingly. 'It will all be made clear in the Via Vittoria, I think.'

As we waited for the traffic I reflected how often in Rome any halting spot crowds one with memories and reflections. The city is a palimpsest. Centuries of man's activities overscore each other. On this blithe morning the music of the accordion-player filled the air, the flowers were ablaze on the stalls. At this very moment I had in my pocket a letter from a young friend at Eton who wanted to know what I was doing in Rome. Well, just now I was calling up the ghost of one of his ancestors, Mr. W. C. Cartwright of Aynho, a Northamptonshire squire who lived much in Rome and became the close friend of Robert Browning and Frederic Leighton. One day, in 1850, Mr. Cartwright was walking across this piazza with John Gibson, the sculptor, who worked in Canova's old studio. Gibson stopped him and told him how one morning, on a balcony opposite, he had seen Lord Byron, who had lodgings at No. 66, across from Keats's house. A Roman bank had the address of their famous client entered upon its books, but in those days of expansive elegance one did not have to call at a bank to find who had arrived in Rome. The wide end of this piazza was filled with the private coaches, piled up with travelling utensils, bedding, furniture and the personal servants of the owners. By these the watchman could always tell one what notability had arrived from across the Alps. To-day, in the same piazza, Americans call at the American Express Agency to find who has crossed the Atlantic.[1]

The piazza was for a long time the heart of the tourist traffic, especially of the English tourists, always in the majority throughout the nineteenth century. Winter in Rome was the mode. It has never been improved upon, whether the competition comes from the sporting snows of Switzerland or the dazzling azure seas of the Bahamas—at least it must seem so to those with a mind to nourish as well as a body to exercise. Dickens has reported from the piazza. Now let Thackeray speak. He was here in the full flood of fashion and made a record, with an ironic note:

'Every winter there is a gay and pleasant English colony in Rome, of course more or less remarkable for rank, fashion and agreeability, with every varying year. Thrown together every day, and night after night: flocking to the same picture galleries, statue galleries, Pincian drives and church functions, the English colonists at Rome perforce become intimate, in many cases

[1] 'Rome is full of English. We could furnish exceedingly respectable Houses of Lords and Commons. There are at present twice as many coroneted carriages in the Piazza di Spagna as in St. James's parish.' (Macaulay, in a letter to Lord Lansdowne, 1838.)

friendly . . . on Wednesday there will be music and vespers in the Sistine Chapel; on Thursday the Pope will bless the animals—sheep, horses and what not; and flocks of English accordingly rush to witness the benediction of droves of donkeys. In a word the ancient city of the Caesars, the august fanes of the Popes, with their splendour and ceremony, are all mapped out and arranged for English diversion.'

Byron was in Rome from May 5th to 21st, 1817. He was then planning the Fourth Canto of *Childe Harold*, and sat for his bust by Thorwaldsen, the Danish sculptor then living in Rome, and the great Canova's contemporary. He lived for twenty years in the Via Sistina, above the Spanish Steps, a street in which at various times Chateaubriand, Stendhal, Piranesi, Zuccari, Gogol and D'Annunzio have lived.

Hans Andersen met Thorwaldsen in Rome for the first time, though often when a poor boy in Copenhagen he had seen the sculptor. Years later Thorwaldsen, exchanging reminiscences, told Andersen of his experience with Byron.

'In Rome when I was about to make Byron's statue, he placed himself just opposite to me and began immediately to assume another countenance to what was customary to me. "Will you not sit still?—and you must not make these faces," I said. "It is my expression," replied Byron. "Indeed," said I, and I then made him as I wished, and everybody said when it was finished that I had hit the likeness. When Byron, however, saw it, he said, "It does not resemble me at all. I look much more unhappy." He was above all things so desirous of looking extremely unhappy,' said Thorwaldsen with a comic expression.

From Rome Byron sent to his publisher the third act of *Manfred* and *The Lament of Tasso* inspired by the scene of Tasso's death, for which he demanded six hundred guineas.

The water of the fountain shaped like a boat, whose cool sound is grateful to the ears as one crosses the Piazza di Spagna, comes from an ancient source. Twenty centuries ago Marcus Agrippa sent his engineers to look for water for the baths he was building near the Pantheon. On a farm eight miles out of the city they came upon a country girl who showed them a spring. *Aqua Virgo* they thereupon named the water, which they conducted under the site of the Villa Medici to the foot of the Trinità dei Monti steps, where it serves the fountain. It is still carried by conduits along the Via dei Condotti, the Street of the Conduits, until it emerges again in the cascading Fountain of Trevi. In Agrippa's day it crossed the Via Flaminia, now the Corso, in an aqueduct over the Arch of Claudius, to the Baths of Agrippa. The aqueducts that supply the many fountains of Rome are among the most striking features of the approach to the city from the surrounding country. They also form one of the chief witnesses to the Roman genius for building. Being the first people to devise the arch, they could build their great aqueducts crossing many miles of the landscape. These carried the water of the springs from long distances, distributing it to reservoirs from which the various parts of the city were supplied. The water was seldom pressure-fed, but ran in open channels, the Romans not having the means of making iron pipes, or lead ones, both metals strong enough to withstand great pressure, and too costly, heavy and scarce for long distances. The open conduits entailed extremely skilful surveying to preserve the gradient of descent and to bring the water from the hills and across the plains to the reservoirs. Over-rapid descent had to be avoided, so that the line of the aqueduct was sometimes lengthened, much as a railway line is lengthened. Tunnels had to be cut and high arches built over valleys, to keep the gradient moderate. The water-channel itself was lined with *opus signinum*, which was easily fractured. This involved constant inspection and repair, for frost, earthquake, bombardment, as well as wear and tear, could create leaks. Thus it was that medieval Rome, unlike the city of the Caesars, which had a supply of some 1,200,000 cubic metres a day, ample for its great baths, fountains and domes-

tic supply, suffered much from barbarian invasions, resulting
in the destruction of the aqueducts. Rome, deprived of its
water, was then compelled to resort to the polluted River
Tiber.

II

In a lull of the traffic we crossed the piazza. At its narrow
end rises a cipollino column, surmounted by a statue of the
Virgin. In 1854 Pius IX declared the dogma of the Immaculate
Conception to be a canonical doctrine of the Church.[2]

The column pays honour to the dogma; it also marks a forgotten phase of the State's conception of punishment for
transgressors. This column was dragged to its base and raised
on its pedestal by hundreds of wretched galley-slaves who,
as late as 1854, were farmed out in their striped brown uni-
forms to contractors, who naturally underfed and overworked
their victims. By this compulsory labour the Government
carried out many of its grandiose building projects. The
Forum itself and the vast ruins of the Baths of Caracalla were
excavated by this prison labour. 'Never was such a wretched,
decrepit, broken-down set of labourers seen gathered together,' wrote W. W. Story, author of *Roba di Roma*, a witness of the scene. 'Falstaff's ragged regiment was a powerful
and mighty body compared with them. They bore the same
relation to our able-bodied workmen that the ruins in which
they excavated bear to a thoroughly constructed house. They
were ruins themselves, working among ruins.'

Entering the Via Condotti I took my friend for morning
coffee into the Café Greco. I like to sit here a while and con-
jure up ghosts of the past, for this was the gathering place of
famous visitors to Rome. Here came, to gossip and be seen,

[2] 'It is the Feast of the Immaculate Conception of the Virgin Mary; a day
held in prodigious honour by the Franciscans, who first, I believe, introduced
this absurd notion, which even within the Catholic Church the Dominicans have
always combated, and which the Council of Trent, if I remember Fra Paolo
right, refused to pronounce orthodox' (Macaulay, Rome, 8th December, 1838).

Goethe, Liszt, in his Abbé's black soutane, Thorwaldsen, Wagner, Alfieri, Rossini and old Goldoni from his lodging down at the other end of the street, overlooking the little square now named after him. Gold-topped canes, snuff, manuscripts, tricorne hats and black brocade—they all come back with the aroma of ground coffee that still pervades the little place.

In the late afternoon the long Via dei Condotti, with its exclusive shops, is in a purple shadow. Looking along it, one sees the sunlit flight of the steps, crowned by the golden church of the Trinità dei Monti, with its twin towers, and the tall obelisk on the platform before it. It is a setting so dramatic, so rich in the subtle hues of amber stone rising from shadow below into the sunlit gold and blue above, that in order not to miss this divine hour of falling light I often timed my return to coincide with the waning afternoon.

One might write a volume on the obelisks of Rome. Their history makes the ancient city in which they stand a *parvenu*. The oldest, in the Piazza di San Giovanni, dates back to 1449 B.C. The one by the Trinità church marks the place from which an unforgettable panorama of the Eternal City is seen. This exile from the banks of the Nile, which may have witnessed the labours of Joseph's countrymen, stood in the *spina* of a circus, amid the roar of the populace and the crash of colliding chariots. To-day it throws a slender shadow where old men and women, nursemaids and their charges, sit in the afteroon sun of a winter's day warming themselves on a ledge below the balustrade of the church. It is immense and unforgettable when seen down the Via Sistina, a black silhouette against the violet and emerald sunset.

A turning out of the Via dei Condotti takes us into a side street, the Bocca di Leone, along which we go until we reach the corner of the Via Vittorio, our goal. Here again one is delayed by a throng of memories. It was on this very corner that the Comparini house once stood. Here lived Pompilia,

with her foster parents, whose tragic story is immortalised
in Browning's *The Ring and the Book.*[3]

A little distance away, across the Corso, is the church of
St. Lorenzo in Lucina, in which she was married. The thir-
teenth-century stone lion devouring a man, symbol of the
Church's severity towards the heretic, is still in the church
portico, as when Pompilia saw it and wondered about it.
With its companion lion it has been there for some seven
hundred years, worn smooth by the patting of children's
hands.

I am just seventeen years and five months old,
And if I lived one day more, three full weeks.
'Tis writ so in the church's register. . . . This S. Lorenzo seems
My own particular place I always say.
I used to wonder when I stood scarce high
As the bed here, what the marble lion meant,
Eating the figure of a prostrate man.

When she and her parents were murdered, their bodies
were exposed in this church. Here she was buried.

It was quite by accident that Robert Browning and his
wife took a place, for the winter of 1853, at 43 Via Bocca di
Leone. Their lodgings were undoubtedly passed by Pompilia
on her visits to the church. Here on the first floor of the palace
standing on a corner, the Brownings entertained. The poet
was exploring the city, unwittingly gathering impressions
he would call upon when he began to write the saga of that
tremendous drama which he had found 'one memorable day
in January, 1862' at a Florentine bookstall, in 'the square
old yellow book,' containing the record of the murder of

---

[3] It is singular that the two great English poets, Shelley and Browning, based
their finest achievements, the drama of *The Cenci* and *The Ring and the Book*,
on the manuscripts of two famous Roman trials for murder. *The Ring and the
Book* was almost not written, for Browning offered the manuscript book he had
picked up on a stall in Florence to his friend, Mr. Cartwright of Aynho. The
symbol of the ring he took from one purchased at Castellani's, the famous
jeweller's near the Fountain of Trevi, which his wife had worn, and which after
her death he carried on his watch chain.

Pompilia, his girl-wife, and her parents, Pietro and Violente Comparini, by Count Franceschini, in January, 1698.

The Brownings were invited everywhere. Thackeray was in Rome with his two daughters. The novelist and poet saw much of each other; they may have gone together to one of those benedictions of droves of donkeys that Thackeray made fun of. They made excursions to the Campagna, usually with the famous Fanny Kemble, who filled most people with awe, but not the Brownings' infant son, Pen. 'I am afraid of nossing,' he asserted. The poet was inspired by the deserted expanse of the Campagna, traversed by the Appian Way. He wrote the superb *Love Among the Ruins* and *Two in the Campagna*.

> The champaign with its endless fleece
>   Of feathery grasses everywhere.
> Silence and passion, joy and peace,
>   An everlasting wash of air—
> Rome's ghost since her decease.

Those parties on the Campagna included young Frederic Leighton, the artist, an Adonis of twenty-two. He was a frequenter of the *salon* of Mrs. Sartoris, the ex-actress sister of Fanny Kemble, who entertained lavishly. There Leighton met Thackeray's daughters and the Brownings. Leighton had arrived in Rome in 1852, and lived there for three years. It was from his studio there that the young artist conquered England. One day he carried off Browning to look at a canvas, seventeen and a half feet in length, on which he was painting his first picture, a historical piece, 'Cimabue's Madonna being carried in triumph through the streets to the Chapel of Santa Maria Novella.' It was the era when every picture must tell a story. It was hung in the Royal Academy Exhibition in 1855, and made a sensation.

One morning the astonished painter received a letter from the President of the Royal Academy informing him that Queen Victoria had bought the picture for six hundred guineas. His Roman colleagues gave him a festive dinner, and the kindhearted Leighton immediately bought the pictures of three of his friends to help them. His life from that hour was an unbroken success story. He was elected President of the Royal Academy at forty-eight, and proved to be the most popular president in all its history. Handsome, eloquent, kind and of perfect courtesy, his works, mostly in the classical genre, were acclaimed as masterpieces. To-day we know they are second-rate, a series of moulded figures in classical draperies, devoid of cohesion and movement, with dead faces and eyes that look nowhere, stuck on to historical backgrounds, the whole in flaming colours. But when he died, lamented, renowned, and was buried in St. Paul's among the great, the architect-pasteboard school was still in favour and no one foresaw it would become ludicrous with Alma Tadema's marble mosaics of Roman languors.

Browning's greatest friend in Italy was probably W. W. Story. As a young American of varied gifts he had arrived in Rome with a commission to make a statue of his father, Judge Story. He fell in love with Italy, and most of his life was spent there. He was a well-known figure in Rome, where he had a studio, and became famous, his sculpture apart, as the author of *Roba di Roma*, a goldmine of folklore. He is best represented in England by his statue of George Peabody, the American philanthropist, at the Royal Exchange, London. When the Brownings first went to Rome in 1853 it was Story who found them their lodgings in the Bocca di Leone. On the death of Elizabeth Barrett Browning the Storys were the first to go to Florence to be with the bereaved poet. They were destined to be close friends to the end of Browning's life. They spent a last holiday together at Asolo, and as Browning left for Venice he held Story's hand, saying, 'We have been friends for forty years.' A few days later he was dead.

In Rome the Storys and the Brownings were inseparable, as also at Siena and Bagni di Lucca, where they spent holidays together. The Storys had an apartment in the Palazzo Barberini in Rome. There was a children's party given there one Christmas day that must have been gratefully recalled by the fortunate young guests, for Hans Andersen, then being greatly fêted in Rome, read to them his fairy-tale, *The Ugly Duckling*. Browning followed with *The Pied Piper*, and Story, playing on a flute, led the delighted children round the great *salon*.

Hans Andersen was a frequent visitor to the Storys at the Palazzo Barberini, that vast edifice built out of stone taken from the Colosseum. He was a lovely character, to whom children from all over the world sent their old tin soldiers and broken toys. Young Edith Story was a great favourite with him. This same child had another devoted attendant in Thackeray, who, when she was sick, wrote for her and read to her *The Rose and the Ring*. The first edition of this book carried a drawing of an obsequious flunkey presenting a little rose and a little ring on a salver, with an inscription of the author's 'most respectful compliments to Miss Edith Story.' The Browning–Story friendship was continued into the second generation. When Browning's son died at Asolo in 1902, Edith Story was with him. Henry James wrote a two-volume life, *William Wetmore Story*, of his New England compatriot. He failed as biographer, since James kept breaking in, but always delightfully and rewardingly.

At last we arrived at the doorway of the Academy of St. Cecilia in the Via Vittorio.

'Here's where I get my ticket for Rubinstein's concert,' said my companion.

I followed her in, and something I wished to find was there.

'Excuse me a moment,' I said, and rushed out into the street.

I examined the windows. They had heavy iron grilles,

probably seventeenth-century work. I went inside and re-joined my wondering friend.

Having purchased tickets, she asked if she might view the concert-hall. It was a large, pleasant room with Venetian glass chandeliers, an organ and a Royal box. It would have been as fitting for a recital by Baldassare Galuppi as for one by Artur Rubinstein. We passed a cloister on our way to the hall.

'This is it, without any doubt!' I exclaimed excitedly.

My patient companion looked at me with amusement.

'Will you tell me just what is what? You have been holding something back all the morning. What is it all about?' she asked.

'That is a long story,' I said.

III

It begins one morning in the summer of 1715 in Soho Square, London. In a house in that square lived ex-Governor Gabriel Roberts, Member of Parliament for Marlborough, and a retired Governor of the East India Company, whereby he had made a fortune in India. He had for a neighbour in that fashionable square Sir John Newton, who had a pretty granddaughter of sixteen, his ward, Anne Coke. She was an heiress, and came of a remarkable line. Her ancestor was none other than the famous lawyer, Sir Edward Coke, who, in turn, was Recorder of Norwich and London, Solicitor-General to Queen Elizabeth, Speaker of the House of Commons, Attorney-General and, later, Lord Chief Justice in the reign of James I. As Attorney-General he conducted the prosecutions of Essex, Raleigh and Southampton, and was notorious in these proceedings for his bluntness of speech, his choleric temper and, later, for his habit of browbeating the prisoners brought before him. Not only was he the greatest lawyer produced by his country, but he was incorruptible, fearless and ready to defy the King, if justice so dictated.

Rather than compromise his reputation, he opposed King James and his fellow-Justices, and was dismissed from office. He lived to be a parliamentary leader in the stormy days of Charles I, and before dying, at eighty-three, framed the famous Petition of Right that led to the Civil War. He married into the great Paston family. His passion having been the acquisition of land, he left his son a man of vast wealth.

Thus it was that Thomas Coke, his great-great-great-grandson, enjoyed a fortune with which he built the palace of Holkham and filled it with treasures. At the age of fifteen, having inherited the Holkham estate, he was sent by his grandfather on the Grand Tour. He set forth to complete his education at Turin and elsewhere with an entourage consisting of a chaplain, a Gentleman of the Horse, a steward, a valet, numerous grooms, a coach-and-six and attendant carriages. It was a semi-regal progress in which he was joined by the young Earl of Burlington, builder later of Burlington House for his Italian treasures. Coke was abroad six years, made an extensive tour of six countries and became famous throughout Italy as the Cavaliero Coke. He was avid of learning, highly intelligent, discerning in taste and a shrewd buyer of *objets d'art*. Thus it was that in 1718 he brought back to Holkham priceless treasures in the form of pictures, sculptures, books and manuscripts. The works of Raphael, Titian, Caracci, Veronese, Domenichino and Holbein decorated the great *salons* of Holkham.

Coke shared the renown of being the greatest patron of art and the greatest cock-fighter of the age. At twenty-one he married eighteen-year-old Lady Margaret Tufton, a beauty and an heiress. He was raised to the peerage as Baron Lovel of Minster Lovel, and later as Earl of Leicester. But Fate mocked him. His only son and heir was a gambler, a debauchee and a drunkard. They married him to Lady Mary, youngest daughter of the Duke of Argyll. Edward, Lord Coke, as he was styled, left her on even her wedding day to

join his roystering friends. At thirty-four he was dead. His
father, the Earl of Leicester, was killed in a duel, his great
house unfinished, his title without an heir. Lady Leicester
completed her husband's work at Holkham and sat alone,
imperious and austere, conscious of her position, a woman
of great wealth. There was bitterness in her heart when she
contemplated that Anne Coke's grandson would inherit all
this vain splendour.

When Philip Roberts, son of Governor Roberts, saw Anne
Coke tripping down the steps of Sir John Newton's house one
summer's day in 1715, he fell in love at sight. He was young,
extremely handsome, and soon to be commissioned as a
Major in the 2nd Troop of the Horse Guards. He was the eld-
est son and heir. Within six months he had married Anne
Coke, young, pretty and a considerable heiress in her own
right. They had six sons and one daughter. The eldest, Wen-
man Roberts, assumed his mother's surname. His son, Thomas
Coke, was destined to fame as the Great Commoner, later
Earl of Leicester of a new creation. The time came when,
like his great-uncle, young Tommy Coke was sent on the
Grand Tour. Reynolds had painted him when a child as
'Young Hannibal,' but he grew into no autocrat. 'Now remember, Tom, as long as you live, never trust a Tory,' said
his grandfather, Philip Roberts. 'I never have, and by God,
I never will!' declared Coke in his old age. When the youth
left Eton, and his father contemplated sending him to Oxford, a letter arrived from Lady Leicester:

'Sir,
   'I understand you have left Eton and probably intend to go
to one of those Schools of Vice, the Universities. If however you
choose to travel, I will give you £500 per annum.'

It was not wise to ignore the autocrat of Holkham. He
chose to travel, but first he went to visit this relation of whose
wealth and estates he was the ultimate heir. The dutiful visit
was made, and after this grim ordeal Thomas Coke set off on

his tour. He followed, in a less lavish style, the trail of his great-uncle, the Earl of Leicester, first studying at the University of Turin. Extremely handsome, tall, with an attractive personality, the heir to a huge estate, the seventeen-year-old youth excited attention wherever he went. They dubbed him *Le bel Anglais*. He was warmly welcomed at the Turin court of the King of Sardinia, and there met the King's daughter, the Princess of Savoy. When a Court ball was given prior to her departure to marry the Count d'Artois, young Coke had the honour of leading the Princess out. He found favor in the young lady's eyes, for later he formed one of her escort to Cambrai. Beautiful young princesses seemed to gravitate towards the handsome English youth, for soon there was news of his journeying south in the company of the Princess Louise of Stolberg.

This episode in the life of young Coke has exasperating gaps, but there is sufficient material with which to fill in the outline. It was a story that set tongues wagging in Rome and soon assumed disturbing proportions.

The Princess Louise Maximilienne Caroline Emmanuele Stolberg was the daughter of the late Prince Gustavus Adolphus of Stolberg-Gedern, and through her parents she was related to the princely houses of Europe. By virtue of the fact that she was the granddaughter of Lady Charlotte Bruce, she could claim to have Scottish royal blood in her veins.

In Rome the Young Pretender, Bonnie Prince Charlie, now self-styled King of England, had looked around for a bride with the purpose of producing an heir to the coveted English throne. He was no longer bonnie, nor a figure of romance, as in the stirring days of the rising of '45. He was now fifty-two years of age, portly, testy, embittered with his fortune, and as his dignified brother Henry, Cardinal Duke of York, lamented in a confidential letter, sadly given to 'the nasty bottle, that goes on but too much, and certainly must at last kill him.' The fear was fulfilled, but before that time there were to be many stormy years in the great gloomy Palazzo Muti in Rome that housed the exiled Court.

The Vatican had lost all faith in the restoration of the Stuarts. They pensioned them and housed them, but whereas the Pope, who had recognised the father as James III of Great Britain, and had given him a Papal Guard assigned to his palace, His Holiness denied this recognition to his son Charles Stuart, anxious not to offend the reigning Hanoverian House. The young Pretender, deeply humiliated, in no way abating his claim to be the rightful King of England, had to be content with styling himself the Count of Albany. After the collapse at Culloden of the Stuart cause, with its terrible penalties visited upon his loyal supporters, Charles had returned to France. He was well received at the French Court, but nursed in his heart the bitterest resentment at what he considered to be French treachery in the matter of failing to fulfil promises of support. He was joined by Prince Henry, who had waited in vain during those stirring days to cross the Channel and help his brother.[4] The Young Pretender was then living in a house at Clichy assigned to him by King Louis. Henry lived nearby. One evening Charles, invited to dine by Henry, arrived, but found no host there, despite a table all set in readiness. Henry, disgusted with martial adventures, and more and more inclined to the Church, had slipped away to Rome, where, at the early age of twenty-two, he received in the Sistine Chapel the red hat of a cardinal, while the artillery of the Castle of St. Angelo thundered in his honour.

Charles could forgive neither his brother nor his father in Rome, who had supported this 'betrayal' of the Stuart cause. For eighteen years the two brothers, who throughout boyhood and youth had been on the most affectionate terms with

---

[4] He was an indifferent soldier. Aged twenty, he was nominal Commander of the Forces at Boulogne and Dunkirk. He kept a Council of War waiting while he attended Mass, which provoked the taunt from the Duke of Richelieu—'You may perhaps gain the Kingdom of Heaven by your prayers but never the Kingdom of Great Britain.'

each other, had no communication. But with the death of James III, the rise to power and affluence of his brother Henry, who showed great zeal in promoting his cause in papal circles, together with a gracious invitation from the Pope, who continued the pension paid to his father, Charles considered the time had come when he should set forth for Rome.

The meeting between the two brothers was cordial. The Cardinal drove out to meet him at an inn some miles beyond the Porta del Popolo. Eighteen years had not greatly changed the Cardinal Duke of York, except that the flowing robes, the jewelled cross and the stately bearing emphasized a Prince of the Church as well as of the Blood. Charles was scarcely recognisable by his brother. He moved slowly on swollen legs, breathless, portly, middle-aged, haggard in expression. Could this be the dashing young Prince whose exploits had thrilled the world? They dined together, and in the gathering dusk drove into Rome. It was past midnight when they reached the Stuart palace, but at the Porta del Popolo, which through the centuries had witnessed many of the pageants of arrival and departure, and all along the Corso, the people waited to see the returned 'King.' The household of His Majesty, as it regarded him, flocked to kiss his hand. But this return had no triumphant ring for the bloated man who entered the palace from which he had last emerged, nineteen years earlier. He was then a confident, handsome young prince setting forth to win a kingdom. He now nursed in his mind the bitter facts just imparted by his brother. All efforts had failed to induce the Pope to give him the royal status of his father. He was to be received cordially everywhere, but without any recognition of his royal claims. He had to content himself as the self-styled Count of Albany.

Stuart obstinacy revealed itself in the ensuing years. Neither of the brothers wearied in their battle for recognition. The Cardinal, a gracious, devout man, generous with the considerable wealth that came to him as a prince of the

Church—he had an income of £40,000 a year—sought nothing for himself, but never ceased to press upon the Pope his brother's claim. It was all in vain.

Meanwhile the necessity of preserving the Stuart line, Henry being withdrawn into the Church, began to obsess the Count of Albany. He had a child—a girl, illegitimate—by the mistress he had repudiated. She and her child were pensioned by the kindly Cardinal. Negotiations were begun, and, after many delays, successfully concluded, for the hand of the Princess Louise of Stolberg. The French Court assisted, not reluctant to annoy the Hanoverian King of England. The bride was a vivacious girl of nineteen, more French than German in appearance, with a turned-up nose, a dazzling white complexion and dark blue eyes. 'She was enough to turn all heads,' said a diarist at the German Court. Such was the young woman, chosen unseen, by whom Charles Stuart hoped to perpetuate, legitimately, his line.[5]

The first marriage ceremony, by proxy, took place under the auspices of the French Court in Paris on March 28th, 1772. Another ceremony was to be held at Macerata, near Ancona, to which Charles would proceed. There in the family palace of Cardinal Marefoschi the marriage would be consummated. Charles had not thought it necessary to inform his brother of all these preliminaries, and it was by a special courier that the Cardinal learned of Charles's departure for the ceremony at Macerata.

The destined bride started her journey south. In a manner of which the details are lost she encountered the handsome English youth, Thomas Coke, *le bel Anglais*, and for two weeks their cavalcades moved downwards through Italy together. Owing to the fact that Louise was a protégée of the Empress Maria Theresa, and her consent had not been asked, and would not have been given, since Austria opposed the

[5] Her mother, 'old Princess Stolberg,' was daughter of Prince de Horne, by Lady Charlotte Bruce, daughter of the Earl of Ailesbury. Her elder daughter was Louise; the younger married, in 1771, Charles, son of the third Duke of Berwick, who was grandson of the Old Pretender's natural brother.

Stuart ambitions, the journey, as the marriage by proxy in Paris, was made in some secrecy.

Given a vivacious lovely princess of nineteen, a handsome, bright youth of almost eighteen, both of them with the attributes of family and wealth, travelling through the enchantment of an Italian spring, it is not a wild surmise that there were moments touched with the ecstasy of young love. The pretty bride, a victim of political ambition and family pride, could have had no illusions about the husband awaiting her. He was Royal, of an exiled house that had not surrendered its hopes of gaining the throne of a great kingdom, but he was a man of fifty-two, infirm in his legs, degraded, choleric in temper, an habitual drunkard sunk in resentment against the treatment of the English, French and papal Courts. Whatever awaited the Princess, it was the death of romance, and if now, in youth and springtime, she succumbed to the attraction of her handsome young cavalier, can one wonder?

The wedding took place at Macerata at midday on Good Friday, April 17th, 1772, in the private chapel of the Cardinal's palace, to which she had been conducted by Charles Stuart, who had journeyed to Loretto to meet her. The wedding was witnessed by a large number of the Italian nobility and a few of the British who could not resist the spectacle, despite the severe ban on all contacts with the Stuarts. It was treason even to be received in their palace in Rome.

The wedding party remained at the Palazzo Marefoschi for two days, where a great reception was held for guests and visitors. Charles and his bride held a kind of court. Then on Easter Sunday, April 19th, they started for Rome with their entourage.

The bridegroom abated no jot of his claims, papal displeasure notwithstanding. He signed the marriage register as Charles III, and made his wife inscribe herself as Queen. Immediately on arrival in Rome, Charles added offence to indiscretion by sending a message to the Pope's Secretary of State announcing the arrival of 'Their Majesties the King and

Queen of Great Britain, France and Ireland.' The rebuff was forceful and immediate. The answer came back that no such person could possibly be in Rome.[6]

The movements of the Stuarts in these days were not devoid of a sense of pageantry and tradition. The splendid Cardinal Duke of York, urbane, handsome and widely beloved for his qualities of gentleness and generosity, moved regally through the papal Court, ever alert to further his brother's interest, though never successful in his chief aim of having the same rank as a monarch accorded to his brother as to their royal father, who had been received always as James III. In all his acts, however annoyed or shamed by his contemptible brother, he contributed the reverence of *majestie* to the head of the House of Stuart. Thus it was that, swallowing his resentment at being kept ignorant of the marriage, he behaved punctiliously when the approach of the royal cortège to Rome was announced. He sent the Marchese Angeletti, his chamberlain, in his coach and six, to intercept the royal pair at the Ponte Molle, the ancient Pons Milvius, which crosses the Tiber a mile and a half northward from the Porta del Popolo, where in 63 b.c. Cicero captured the emissaries of the Catiline Conspiracy, where the Emperor Maxentius was thrown into the river during battle with Constantine, and where Henry VII forced his way towards Rome with his barons and bishops in May, 1312. The old bridge had seen many glittering cavalcades. It now witnessed four couriers riding in advance, dressed in scarlet liveries, and the postilions and equipages of their Majesties, of the Cardinal Duke, of the Cardinal Marefoschi, of the Neapolitian Ambassador and of Mr. Thomas Coke. The procession went onwards with royal pomp. A great crowd cheered them at the Porta del

---

[6] 'His insisting on her assuming the title of Queen, contrary to her own and his brother, the Cardinal Duke of York's, earnest entreaties, was a cruel circumstance on her, as it condemned her to live in solitude with him, who was drunk half the day and mad the other; for as the Pope would not acknowledge him or her for King or Queen, the Roman nobility, sufficiently proud, would not pay her the honours he required, and consequently could not visit her' (Horace Walpole, *Journal*, April 4, 1772).

Popolo and all the way down the Corso to the Stuart palace in the Piazza dei Santi Apostoli.

The next day the Cardinal Duke drove in from his palace at Frascati, with two running footmen before his coach. He was charmed by the pretty young bride, and all his anger vanished in the freshness of her presence. The sad old palace where he had grown up from a boy, which had seen the tragedy of his father, an exile whose hopes and intrigues had been all in vain, took on a new life. The Cardinal brought his wedding gifts, a gold box encrusted with diamonds, a beautiful court dress with fine lace and jewels, for the bride; and since he was never neglectful of his brother's needs, a useful banker's order for ten thousand *livres* for Charles. He stayed for dinner, which was splendidly set, with the nobility of Rome around the great table. He found the young Queen intelligent as well as vivacious. He departed thinking an era of happiness had dawned for his brother.

A few days later he gave a banquet in honour of the bridal pair at his fortress-palace at Frascati. All Rome was delighted with the young bride, who, since she might not be called Queen of England, according to the ruling of the Pope, they dubbed 'Queen of the Apostles,' from the situation of the Stuart palace.

Through all these days of high entertainment young Thomas Coke, accompanied by another youth encountered at Turin, Thomas Kerrick, went everywhere. Often he was in the presence of the Pretender's wife, and the alert Romans soon began to notice the pleasure the young couple found in each other. They were both too striking and notable not to be observed wherever they went. High-spirited, the Pretender's wife became reckless concerning the whispering that began to run around the *salons* of Rome. There was a great fancy-dress ball at which all Rome was present. Young Coke appeared dressed as a Cavalier and danced frequently with Louise. They held the floor with their youthful beauty.

We can surmise to-day what the English lad looked like on

that far-off night in 1773, for Louise commanded from Batoni, the fashionable portrait-artist of the day, a life-sized portrait, which she gave to young Coke. Tall, superbly built, the artist caught the Cavalier in a graceful pose. With a high brow, fair hair, and eyes revealing fire and intelligence, he stands dressed in a pearl-grey satin vest and breeches, plumed hat in hand, an ermine-tipped, rose-coloured cloak over one shoulder, against a classical background of columns, and a dog at his feet. One detail gave the scandalmongers all and more than they required. The infatuated young lady made a fatal slip in a direction she gave to the artist. In the background of the portrait Batoni had placed the sculptured figure of the reclining, love-lorn Ariadne, a reproduction of the famous antique in the Vatican, representing her in her agitated sleep after the desertion of Theseus. It is the same statue that we see in Velasquez's sketch of the garden of the Villa Medici. It was no secret that the Princess Louise of Stolberg had often remarked on the singular resemblance between her own face and that of Ariadne's. It was all too obvious what the distressed Ariadne behind the gallant young Cavalier implied. Her lover was soon leaving Rome, and she had her despair thus symbolized. The gossip even got as far as England. Horace Walpole commented on the singular fact that Mr. Coke had returned with a painting in which the Pretender's Queen had let him have her portrait. 'I hear that the young Mr. Coke has returned from abroad in love with the Pretender's Queen,' he wrote in 1774.

It was indeed time for Mr. Coke to leave Rome. Perhaps someone gave him the hint, perhaps he needed no hint. He announced his departure for Naples. Louise never saw him again. Forty years later Coke's eldest daughter met the Queen, now known as the Countess of Albany, in Florence, where she was living. She talked eagerly and with some emotion of the handsome young Mr. Coke, now the Earl of Leicester, still vivid in her mind after all the intervening years.

Before Coke left Rome he was received, with his friend Kerrick, in audience by the Pope, Clement XIV. In a letter home young Kerrick gives a vivid account of their experience. The Pope was an old man, the son of an apothecary, and it was said he had been elected, after a Conclave lasting three months and three days, as a compromise between the fierce ambitions of the cardinals because he was nobody's friend, was infirm and easily controlled. They made a mistake regarding the last characteristic. When the cardinals complained of his secrecy he replied, 'I sleep sound when my secret is my own.' When the Vatican cook begged to be continued in service to the new Pope, Clement said dryly, 'You shall not lose your appointment, but I will not lose my health to keep your hand in.' He was the last pope to take part in the 'Cavalcata,' the procession from the Vatican to the Lateran, riding upon a white palfry that was covered with a gold-embroidered saddle-cloth of crimson velvet, the horse led by a member of the Colonna family. A strong personality, upright and autocratic, he aroused tremendous enmity by his fearless suppression of the Society of Jesus in 1769. It was believed this act sealed his doom. Though in robust health in April, 1774, he fell suddenly ill in a manner that pointed to subtle poison, and upon his death a few months later none doubted but that the Jesuits had encompassed his end. The fear of poisoning had long caused him to allow only an old Brother, whom he had known when he was a poor man and lived in a convent, to dress his meat. Such was the Pope who gave an audience to the two English youths. Kerrick wrote:

'Ye Pope seems to be an exceedingly good sort of man and particularly civil to ye English; he asked us if we had got good lodgings, and hoped we should meet with no affronts in his territories; if we should, he begged we should immediately make our complaint to him and added, by way of compliment, I suppose, that he does not expect we shall have much occasion for his assistance, as the English are no geese and can usually speak for themselves.'

The young Englishmen were in Rome when the sad news

came of the death of Pope Clement on September 22nd, 1774, and Kerrick sent the news home.

'You know, I suppose, by ye papers that we have lost poor Clement XIV, I say "we" for I believe ye English are ye people the most sorry for his death. I believe I told you in a former letter how much attention and civility he showed to all ye people of our country, and indeed it was so much at times as to make our own subjects grumble. One of ye last actions of his reign was ye making an Englishman master of his Galleys, a place which I am told will bring him in near two thousand a year: it is ye nephew of an English picture merchant he had a great regard for. Nobody seems to doubt but he was poisoned and it is certain he himself had for many months suspected it would be attempted.

'He looked into everything himself, grew very active, and was one of ye most hearty greybearded old men I ever saw. He used to go every evening to a house he was very fond of and I used to see him frequently in ye Summer walking home again as briskly as a much younger man, before his coach, his guard following him on horseback, his Gentlemen attending with their hats off, etc; for he was very exact in keeping to ye dignity of his character when he appeared in publick. In his living he was frugal, ordered his dinner every day at about ½ a crown, which he said he knew would buy as much as he could eat, and he did not like to see more on ye table . . . ye whole bulk of his fortune goes to ye Public, without having reserved even enough to raise him a monument.

'We have had a good deal of ceremony at his funeral, but not all that is usual, for his body putrified almost immediately and they could not keep it long enough . . . I am afraid you will be tired of this letter, which I perceive I have filled with histories of Clement ye 14th; but he talked familiarly with us, laid his hands upon our heads and blessed us, and in some way he is my Pope, and I can't help being sorry for him and full of the story of his death.'

This was the Pope upon whose election the Count of Albany's hopes of recognition as a sovereign were placed, but despite the pleading of the Cardinal Duke of York, the old man was adamant. He refused to treat the Count as a titular king. This pious Pope of humble origin cared little for the pretensions of royalty. It was he who had instructed his Secretary of State to rebuff the Count for the grandiloquent announcement of the arrival in Rome of 'the King and Queen of England.' He refused to recognise the Countess of Albany as a queen. But the arrogance of the Count in no way changed the affection in which Clement XIV held his brother, the Cardinal Duke, who enjoyed his intimate friendship and made frequent visits to Castle Gandolfo during the mortal illness of the Pope.

Mr. Coke departed from the scene.[7] The Countess of Albany, or the Queen-Consort, as the Jacobite circle regarded her, was disconcerted to find that she was to be suddenly removed by her elderly and drunken husband from the gaieties and colourful life of Rome. Enraged by the fact that Clement XIV ignored his peremptory demand for a special box for himself and his Queen on the occasion of the ceremony of the opening of the Porta Santa in the coming Jubilee Year of 1775, the Count of Albany declared, in high passion, that he would move his household from Rome to Florence. He departed, greatly to the relief of His Holiness and of his sorely tried brother, but he continued to draw the papal pension. The blow fell not on the Pope, or Rome, but on the hapless Louise, whose life with her violent husband became a nightmare.

The Count and Countess of Albany, with a train of courtiers and servants, arrived in Florence in the summer of 1774. For the first three years they hired an apartment, and then

---

[7] Lord Coke's widow, Lady Mary, claimed to have married the Duke of York, George III's brother, and when he died at Monaco in 1767 she went abroad, much chagrined by the lack of an acknowledgment of her marriage. Horace Walpole dedicated the second edition of his *Castle of Otranto* to her, and seeing her at Amiens 'was much refreshed by the sight of her, in pea-green and silver.' She was a great beauty, and nicknamed 'Queen Mary.' She was at Florence in 1774 when Coke arrived there on his way home. 'He is a very pretty man and a good deal more fashioned than his sister, Lady Hunloke; as he is to have a very great estate, I am glad he is so worthy of it,' she wrote.

purchased the Palazzo Guadagni.[8] In Florence there were bitter disappointments also. The Count had a reception from the ruling Grand Duke of Tuscany even more chilly than that from the Pope. The neglect of the papal and Florentine Courts, the non-arrival of an heir, rendered the Count daily more morose and brutal. He resorted to 'the nasty bottle,' behaved like a buffoon in public and a tyrant at home. Madly jealous, and demanding, he made a slave of his wife. He stormed at her and would not permit the unhappy young woman to be for a moment out of his sight. 'Drunk half the day and mad the other half,' reported the British Minister at the Tuscan Court. The girl-wife, lonely, a prey to melancholy, terrified by her husband's insane jealousy and brutality, began to lose all the sparkle and sweetness of a fine nature. Her home was a prison, her elderly keeper a besotted tyrant.

It was at this stage in her miserable condition that a ray of light in the form of the dashing young Count Alfieri illumined her gloom. The Prince of Italian Tragedy, the famous poet, handsome and uninhibited, became a frequent visitor to the receptions at the Palazzo Guadagni in the autumn of 1779. Thirty years of age, tall, applauded by all Italy, well-born and highly gifted, he affected a scorn of Society while never ceasing to attract its attention, in which, by some forty years, he anticipated the rôle of Lord Byron. Vittorio Alfieri, born in the city of Asti in 1749, had something in common with the effervescent wine that takes its name from his birthplace. He might well have been nicknamed *Asti Spumante*. His father had died while he was scarcely a year old, and he had one sister, Giulia. He was sent while young to a small academy at Turin, where the Court pages of the Royal House were also lodged. But he learned little, and the future author of the classics of the Tuscan tongue was almost ignorant of pure Italian, since he spoke the Piedmontese dialect.

[8] This beautiful palace, the work of Il Cronaco, (1454–1508), with its elegant courtyard and beautiful staircase, stands on a corner of the Piazza San Spirito. It is now used as a public library. It is regrettable that there is nothing to record that for ten years it was the home of the Young Pretender and his Court.

In 1765 his uncle and guardian, the Viceroy of Sardinia, died, and owing to the singular law of Piedmont that minors ceased to be *status pupillaris* at the age of fourteen, he was absolute master of a considerable income from his patrimony and also from his uncle's estate. The sanest youth in such circumstances might have wrecked himself. Alfieri did not lose his head. He began to travel, and in 1767 was in Paris, the city of his dreams. The dream was speedily shattered. Presented at the French Court, he felt a great dislike for the disreputable Louis XV, and hurried on to England. He was nineteen, handsome, enthusiastic. 'Quite as much as Paris had disgusted me did England and especially London please me at first sight,' he recorded. Balls, supper-parties and fashionable routs filled his days and nights, but after three months of these, satiated, he formed an eccentric resolution. He bought a coach and acted as coachman to a young friend, the nephew of the Spanish Ambassador at the Court of St. James's. He competed with the cockney Jehus, the lackeys and the periwigged coachmen waiting outside houses whose stairs he could have ascended as an honoured guest. Then, tiring of this prank, he went to Holland, and so home. It was not long before the restless young man set off again. Austria, Germany—'I took myself out of that huge barrack called Prussia, abhorring it sufficiently'—Denmark, Sweden, Finland and Russia were visited in swift succession. The last country filled him with hatred.

'No sooner had I set foot in that Asiatic encampment of booths drawn up in line, than, remembering Rome, Genoa, Venice, and Florence, I burst out laughing. . . . So much did I dislike everything there excepting beards and horses) that, during six weeks' sojourn among those barbarians disguised as Europeans, I made acquaintance with nobody.'

At the age of twenty-two this undisciplined but observant youth was in London again. Already a libertine, equipped with Italian fervour and allure, he was soon involved in a love affair with a young married woman of fashion whom he frequently met at the house of Prince Masserano, the Spanish Ambassador. His passion requited, he began to make clandestine calls in the absence from London of the lady's husband. When she was taken by him into the country, Alfieri followed. The husband, Viscount Ligonier,[9] an officer in a Guards Regiment, was often called to town, which provided Alfieri with the opportunity of visiting his mistress. One night he arrived with a dislocated shoulder, having put his horse at a fence on the estate. On his return home a doctor was called in to set it. Despite this he returned the next evening, and stayed some time, unaware that his visit had been observed. Early the next morning he returned to London and, the shoulder being inflamed, the doctor ordered him to stay in bed. Two evenings later, eager for the sight of his mistress, he occupied a seat in the box of Prince Masserano at the opera. While apparently listening to the music, his eyes were on a box opposite when he heard his name called. He rose, and found at the door of the box the husband of his mistress. He was requested to go outside, where he was challenged. They proceeded at once from the Opera House in the Haymarket to a corner of the Green Park, and there, in the dusk of a summer's evening, fought a fierce duel. The challenger was a skilled swordsman, Alfieri was a tyro. 'In the act of drawing our swords he noticed that I had my left arm in a sling, and was generous enough to ask if that would prevent me from fighting. I thanked him but answered that I hoped not, and forthwith attacked him.' A few minutes later Alfieri was wounded above the wrist, whereupon the wronged husband deemed honour satisfied, sheathed his sword and walked away. Ten minutes later, his arm bound up with a handkerchief by the help of his teeth, and his left arm still in a sling,

[9] He was the nephew of Field-Marshal Lord Ligonier, who, by the appointment of his secretary, Richard Cox, as banker of the 1st Regiment of Foot Guards, in 1758 founded Cox's Bank, known throughout the British Army. The original charter granted to Cox as banker to the Regiment is at Lloyd's Bank (Cox's Branch), Pall Mall, London.

Alfieri returned to the box at the opera and took his seat, explaining to his host that he had remembered an appointment.

The injured husband instituted divorce proceedings, citing the Count. In court the guilty wife, whom Alfieri was willing to marry, proved to be so depraved a creature that she actually had had a liaison with one of Viscount Ligonier's grooms. Thirteen years later she married a trooper in the Blues.

The husband seemed to have behaved with singular forbearance towards the wild young Italian, just twenty-two years of age. He refused to ruin the youth with heavy damages, just as he had refused to run his adversary through with his rapier. A wiser but scarcely chastened young man left London. In the next six years Alfieri began the career that was to establish him as one of the great poets of his age. Discovering that a preposterous law in Piedmont prohibited the publication of a book without approval of the Censor, and that no person could leave the State without permission, Alfieri boldly decided to surrender all his estates in Piedmont, sacrificing a large income thereby to his only sister, the Countess of Camiana, and her children after her.[10] At this time in Alfieri's life he had two passions, his horses and his writing. There was soon added to these a third, his love of the Countess of Albany.

IV

A contemporary memoir describes the Countess and her husband as they appeared at the time of their arrival in Florence in 1774.

[10] The day after I wrote this passage on Alfieri I found myself having tea at a palazzo situated in the pleasant Mediterranean resort of Alassio, Italy. My hostess was Donna Anna Ferrero-Ventimiglia. It transpired in conversation that her great-grandfather was the grandson of Alfieri's sister, and she was the poet's nearest descendant. In the library I was shown the poet's manuscripts, a miniature of him, with a lock of his reddish hair, and the sword with which he had fought the duel in London in 1771.

General Napoleon Bonaparte slept in this palazzo in 1796 during his march into Italy, and with him went Alfieri's young nephew, who lost his leg in Prussia. His wooden leg is in the palazzo—'All that was left to him of the glory,' observed my hostess.

'The Queen of hearts is of middle height, with dark eyes, soft blonde hair and a dazzling complexion. To this add the reddest of lips, and the most delicate of forms, constituting together beauty enough to turn all heads. The Pretender, her husband, is tall and lean, as becoming his Scottish parentage, red-faced, good-natured and talkative when sober; likes speaking English, and is given to relating his own adventures. After every sentence he would ask *"Capisce?"*—Do you understand? But this once well-beloved Prince Charlie became in time disgusting to the refined little Princess, his wife. He was not a merry drunkard but had *le vin triste*, and in his mad fits of intoxication beat her and occasionally tried to choke her.'

Alfieri first saw the Countess of Albany at the theatre in Florence, where, appearing with her husband, who took 'the nasty bottle' with him into their box, they naturally were observed of all. Alfieri was immediately captivated by her fresh beauty. Later, riding in the Cascine Gardens, he was presented to the royal pair and invited to call at the Palazzo Guadagni. But he did not accept the invitation at first, and retreated to Siena, hoping to cool his passion. Returning, he ventured to call, only to discover that absence had not changed him in any degree. In the autumn of 1779 he became a frequent visitor to the evening receptions at the palace. His handsome appearance, his vitality, his growing renown and the deliberate eccentricities that made him the talk of the city, awakened in her a glowing passion, encouraged by the contrast with her elderly husband's personality and the ceaseless humiliations and cruelties to which she was subjected by him. In his memoirs Alfieri set down her effect upon him, who, contrary to everybody's expectations, offered her a love lasting through the rest of his life.

'I perceived that I had at last met with the woman I had been seeking, one who (unlike all the others I had known) instead of being a hindrance to literary glory, a stumbling block to useful work, and a deterrent to all high thinking, was an incentive and a noble addition to every great idea, so that I, noting and valuing so choice a treasure, surrendered myself completely to her.'

At first neither of the lovers betrayed to each other the feelings inspired by their contact, but in time a great tensity developed. It was singular that Charles, acutely jealous and suspiciously watchful of all his wife's movements—he would not permit her to sit apart in another room—did not for a long time suspect the attachment so carefully masked by the lovers. But a moment came when concealment was no longer possible, and all the restraints Louise had imposed upon herself, a sense of duty fighting the passion of her heart, proved vain. There were terrible scenes with her drink-maddened husband, whose violence filled her with fear.

On St. Andrew's Day, 1780, when heavy celebration of the national Scottish fête had made the Pretender half insane, he burst into her bedroom, accusing her of infidelity, and attempted to strangle her. Her ladies came to her rescue. Terrified, afraid of a second attack, she turned to Alfieri, beseeching his help to escape from the tyranny of her husband. In concert with two members of the Pretender's suite, whose sympathies were with her, they devised a plan.

It was almost impossible for the Countess to be out of the sight of her husband. He made her accompany him on all his excursions, and would never allow her to go out or to receive alone. One day at dinner Madame Orlandini, her lady-in-waiting, who had obtained the consent of the Grand Duchess of Tuscany to the plan of escape, readily given, since the Court at the Pitti Palace held the Count in contempt, suggested they should visit a local convent renowned for its embroidery work. The suggestion aroused no suspicion on the part of the Count, and after dinner the royal party, consisting of Charles, Louise, Mr. Gehegan, his gentleman-in-waiting, and Madame Orlandini, drove to the convent of the White Nuns, situated in the Via del Mandorlo (Via Giuseppe Giusti). The two ladies went up the steps to the convent door, where they were admitted as prearranged, while the Count and Gehegan waited in the coach. After a time the Count became impatient, and sent Gehegan to summon the ladies. He returned with the strange story that the nuns refused to open the door. The angry husband got out of the coach, climbed painfully up the stairs and hammered loudly on the convent door, demanding admittance. From behind a sliding panel the Superior firmly and curtly informed him that the Countess would not return, that she had entered the convent with the approval and under the protection of the Grand Duchess. The panel slid back again in the face of the astonished Count, who could only retreat, cursing loudly.

The news spread over Italy, Alfieri's part in the conspiracy adding spice to the wife's defiance. The Count of Albany wrote to the Pope and the Grand Duke, demanding the restoration of his wife. The Pope refused to make any order, and enraged the Count by bidding him to deliver his wife's linen and personal effects to the Papal Agent in Florence, for the Countess's use. The Grand Duke declined to interfere in a purely domestic matter.

The Count was defeated. Neither his threats to attack the convent and take off his wife by force, nor to have Alfieri assassinated by hired bravos, had any effect. For although he offered a reward of a thousand sequins to anyone who would kill the poet, the young man lived to write twenty-two tragedies. The Pretender never again saw the Princess he had so brutally treated. In far-away England the news delighted the Hanoverian Court and quenched the last hopes of the vanishing Jacobites. There was now little possibility of the breeding of new Pretenders. With Charles deserted, and Henry a Cardinal, the House of Stuart could cause no more apprehension.

The Countess at once informed her brother-in-law, the Cardinal Duke of York, of what had happened, proof that she had no fears regarding the innocence of her behaviour, despite the gossip connecting her name with Alfieri's, as once it had connected it with Thomas Coke's. She turned to the Cardinal because through all the past eight years she had experienced his affection, and regarded him as her true protector. The Cardinal Duke received the news in his bishop's palace at Frascati with dismay, foreseeing the difficulty of his position. He was a man of piety, integrity and, when called for, inflexible courage. He at once wrote to the Countess, after consulting the Pope. He could, with perfect truth, unburden himself of his opinion on the matter.

'My Very Dear Sister,
    'I cannot express to you the sorrow that I have felt on reading your letter of the 9th of this month. Long ago I foresaw what has now happened, and your escape being made with the approval of the Florentine Court has fully justified your conduct. You may rely, my very dear Sister, on my kindly feelings towards you, for up till now I have always sympathised with your position; on the other hand, I beg you to recall that I had no share whatever in bringing about your indissoluble union with my brother beyond giving my formal consent to the marriage, of which I had received no previous notice. . . .'

Thus gracefully the Cardinal relieved her, and himself, of all blame. A great prince of the Church, he had still his shadowy Royal House to serve, and his solution was neat and proper. He had driven at once into Rome from his See of Frascati. Sixty horses were kept in his stables to maintain a coach service between Frascati and Rome. He covered the intervening miles at top speed in a magnificent coach with six horses, postilion outriders, and two running footmen, chosen, like all his lackeys, grooms and valets, for their commanding stature and pleasing appearance. His adoring flock at Frascati, the villages en route, the crowds in Rome, and the beggars around his magnificent palace, the Cancelleria, were all familiar with the splendour and speed of the Cardinal Duke's equipage as he flashed by on his way. But never was the going so speedy, the mission so pressing, as upon that day of Decem-

ber, 1780, when he drove to an audience with the Pope
Louise's dramatic appeal in his pocket.

The situation was skilfully and smoothly dealt with, following that audience. Fifty-three years ago his mother, Princess Clementina Sobieski, granddaughter of King John III
of Poland, in a period of great tension with her husband, the
Old Pretender, had withdrawn from the grim palace in the
Piazza dei Santi Apostoli, where he, Henry, had been born, to
a safe retreat in a neighbouring Ursuline convent, where she
stayed until she had gained her point. When she died in
1735, in his tenth year, he witnessed how his father converted
the wife he had found irksome into a saint, so that much of
James Stuart's last years had been spent on his knees before
her monument in the church across the piazza, which had
temporarily held the remains of Michelangelo, before their
transference to Florence.

It seemed to the Cardinal Duke that the pattern of retreat
to this convent was a good one for all abused wives. 'You will
reside in the convent where the Queen, my mother, remained
for some time,' wrote the Cardinal to Louise. 'The King, my
father, had a special regard for it. It is the least restricted convent in Rome.'

It is possible that this saintly and simple man, utterly
ignorant of the ways of women, thought that that was the end
of the matter. There she would piously remain until released
by her husband's death, or until the quarrel had been patched
up. The needs of her youth or the possibility of some other
man evoking her love never occurred to him. What did she
think of this solution? Was convent life possible for a beautiful, vivacious woman still avid for the world that offered her
homage, and above all for one in whom an ardent young poet
had stirred a passion more fierce than that evoked by the
handsome English lad who had escorted her to Macerata
eight years ago? She may have lingered, excusably, over one
sentence in the Cardinal's letter. 'It is the least restricted convent in Rome.'

Whatever her thoughts, she agreed to the proposal without demur. On December 30th, 1780, she secretly left Florence in a coach. As far as the Tuscan frontier Gehegan mounted guard, with loaded pistols. One other kept him company—Vittorio, Count Alfieri.

The convent in the Via Vittoria seemed destined to shelter royal ladies troubled either by husbands or revolutionaries. Queen Clementina was followed by Queen Louise, as her husband insisted she was, and she, a few years later, was followed by two distressed royal ladies, Madame Victoire and Madame Adelaide, aunts of Louis XVI, fleeing from the Revolution. It was by virtue of Madame Victoire's retreat there that the street in which the convent was situated subsequently changed its name to that of the Via Vittoria.

The Muse of History, who often writes her chronicles with an ironic note, ordained that this convent of refuge should be founded by Camillo Borghese (Pope Paul V), who also founded the enormous wealth of the family, and built the vast Palazzo Borghese, not a mile from the convent, in which Pauline Bonaparte, married to Prince Camillo Borghese, reigned in great splendour only twelve years after the flight of the *'tantes du Roi'* to Rome.

The arrival of the Countess of Albany at the convent was the talk of Europe. She was given comfortable quarters. The nuns spoke French, and were of distinguished birth. There was a pretty garden in the cloister behind. On the south side, on the ground floor overlooking the narrow street, were windows with iron grilles that on either side of the entrance looked into the narrow Via Vittoria, just a short distance from the busy thoroughfare of the Corso. The street has changed little in apperance, and is the haunt of cabinet-makers.

Special favour was shown to the Countess by His Holiness, perhaps as an inducement to enter convent life. She was allowed the use of a carriage, which at once gave a meaning to the definition 'least restricted,' and the Papal Treasury took from its pension to Charles Stuart one half of the yearly sum of 12,000 crowns and gave it to his wife. Clearly neither imprisonment nor privation was intended.

It was not long before the vivacious young lady, whose spell upon the Cardinal Duke had been increased rather than diminished by recent events, had persuaded the unsuspecting old gentleman that she would be happier, and equally protected, by residing in his Roman palace. To this suggestion he assented, persuading the Pope to acquiesce. In the Palazzo della Cancelleria he would be able to enjoy the feminine graces and cheer she brought to that vast palace, for his affection was very genuine towards the ill-used young wife of his brother. Something of a saint's piety, as well as the hereditary narrow-mindedness that kept him untainted by the world, prevented him from knowing what was happening under his ducal nose. Alfieri had moved from Florence to Rome, and while the Countess was living in the convent he rode up on his horse and talked to the immured lady through the grille. Years later he wrote in his *Memoirs:* 'O God, my heart seems to break at the recollection—a prisoner behind a grating! We were separated, and who could tell how long it might last?'

The Cardinal Duke knew, of course, that the famous poet was in Rome, but he was oblivious of the true state of affairs. The furious husband in Florence learned that Alfieri, in his youth guilty of outrageous diatribes against the Papacy and priests, had been received in special audience by Pius VI. This seemed a deliberate insult to the Count of Albany, who made the strongest protest, only to be told that Rome was honoured by the presence of the poet. Moreover, before Alfieri proceeded on his way to Naples he was accorded a special interview with the Countess.

It cannot have occurred to the unsuspecting Cardinal Duke that his sister-in-law would take advantage of his innocence and kindness, and while under his roof carry on an intrigue with Alfieri, who soon returned from Naples. The poet found her splendidly established in the great Palazzo della Cancelleria, one of the finest buildings in what is now the Corso Vittorio Emanuele leading across the Tiber, to St. Peter's.

A cardinal at twenty-two, Bishop of Frascati at thirty-six, Henry, Cardinal Duke of York, at the age of forty-two was appointed to the Vice-Chancellorship of the Holy See, in compensation, it was thought, for the Pope's refusal to recognise the royal title of his brother, Charles Stuart. With this highly coveted post went the magnificent Palazzo della Cancelleria. It was considered the most beautiful example of Italian Renaissance architecture in Rome. Antonio de Montecavallo designed it in 1494, and the great Bramante is believed to have built the splendid courtyard. It is an example, however, of the plundering of ancient Rome under Sixtus IV, by whose nephew, the gay young Cardinal Riario, it was built with sixty thousand *scudi* won in one night's gambling from the nephew of Innocent VIII. It was largely constructed of material taken from the Colosseum, and enriched with marbles from the Arch of Gordianus. The plunderings of an earlier pope are visible in the forty-four granite pillars of the colonnade, brought from the Library of San Lorenzo, built by Damascus, A.D. 366–384, who took them originally from the Theatre of Pompey, in the vicinity. The interior is worthy of the exterior. The frescoes of the great *salon* have scenes from the life of Paul III.

Such was the Cardinal Duke's Roman residence for more than forty years, although he preferred to spend his time at his beloved Frascati, in his episcopal fortress-palace[11] of La Rocca with its magnificent view over the Campagna to Rome, or, in the hottest months, in the nearby palatial Villa Muti.

Louise on her removal from the convent was assigned her own magnificent suite. She had servants and carriages at her command. She became again a figure in Rome, no longer restrained in her society life by the husband now absent in

[11] Two bombs destroyed the courtyard in the heavy bombing of Frascati in 1944. The old palace has been restored. A street at the side is called Via Duca di York.

Florence. In May, 1781, Count Alfieri was back in Rome. At first he hesitated to call upon his 'Donna Amata,' or 'Psipsia,' as he called her in the high-flown affectation of the age. He was a little fearful of the reaction to his return, but, to his surprise, no objections were raised. He took up residence at first in a house above the Piazza di Spagna, and could be seen in the early morning sitting by the cascading waters of the Fountain of Trevi in deep meditation, or riding across the Campagna on one of his splendid horses, for he anticipated all the Byronic poses except that, in place of a studied moroseness, he displayed a dashing gaiety. Later he moved with his books and horses to the Villa Strozzi, charmingly situated amid the vineyards and gardens on the Esquiline, later swept away for the great railway station and the new streets of frightful stucco houses. The building mania had not then struck Rome, and its princes had not begun to sacrifice their beautiful villas and gardens in the wild estate gamble that ruined many of them. In the time of Pope Pius VI the Villa Strozzi was secluded, a country place although within the Aurelian Wall containing the city, and only a mile from the Palazzo della Cancelleria.

'During these two years in Rome,' he wrote, 'I led a truly happy life. The Villa Strozzi, near the Baths of Diocletian, afforded me a delightful retreat. The whole long mornings I passed in study, never moving from the house, except for an hour or two spent in riding over those immense solitudes of the uninhabited neighbourhood of Rome that invited me to reflect, to mourn and to compose verses. In the evening I descended into the city, and restored from my fatigues of study by the lovely sight of Her for whom alone I existed and laboured, I returned from it more contented to my hermitage, whither I retired never later than eleven at night. An existence more gay, more free, more rural in the confines of a great city one could never find, nor one more agreeable to my nature, character and occupations.'

Thus, once more seeing his Donna Amata, in love, in the

springtime of life, famous, handsome and fulfilling his three passions, for books, horses and his donna, he found Rome as near a paradise as ever he was to attain.

The Countess, alas, free from restraint, grew daily more reckless. By this time all Rome was aware of the love affair carried on under the nose of the unsuspecting Cardinal. Alfieri himself had called on him, in a manner artfully devised by the Countess. The Cardinal had a passion for books. Having procured a fine edition of Virgil, she sent it to him via the Count, who found himself most cordially received at Frascati. Young, well-born, brilliant in conversation, it is not surprising that the Cardinal Duke found him an interesting addition to his much-frequented table. A little later, through the Cardinal's good offices, the Count was granted a special audience by the Pope, who expressed interest in the writings of a Republican poet, now converted he hoped, and, after playfully patting the young man's cheeks, dismissed him with a papal blessing.

All these assurances and favours made the two lovers increasingly indiscreet. The Countess visited the Villa Strozzi, and during the absence of the Cardinal at Frascati Alfieri was constantly at the Palazzo della Cancelleria. They drove out together in her carriage along the streets of Rome, they rode gaily over the Campagna. He seemed to have an ample fortune these days, with a stud of superb horses brought over from England, and grooms in attendance. He knew the art of publicity and gained great popularity by the possession of fine horses run in the public races.

Every year there was the Carnival, with its great race down the Corso, from the Piazza del Popolo as far as the Palazzo Venezia, where, before the clearance made for the colossus of glaring marble erected to the glory of Victor Emanuel, a wing of the Palazzo Venezia narrowed the Corso. Here a large cloth was hung across the street to stop the riderless Barbary horses dashing themselves to pieces against the Palazzo. The Carnival went back to medieval times, and

after Paul II had instituted the races along a thousand yards
of what was then the Via Flaminia, it took the name of the
Corso. The foot races, in which naked old men and Jews were
compelled to run, to the jeering of the crowd—a spectacle
that disgusted Montaigne—had changed into those for horses
only. Alfieri's Barbary horses were entered in these Carnival
races, and the flamboyant poet was cheered by the excited
populace. His renown as a horseman was widespread.

For two years Alfieri and the Countess were seen everywhere together in Rome. Society, so far from being scandal-
ised, was amused. In the world of fashion the Countess of
Albany had never been more popular. She was under the protection of the Cardinal Duke of York, Count Alfieri had been
received in audience by the Pope. Why should anyone interfere with such a charming romance, played out before
their eyes by a famous poet and a pretty, ill-used woman
denied her royal status? Her great receptions in the Cardinal's magnificent palace were thronged by the rank and fashion. Carnivals, balls, concerts and private theatricals filled
the days and nights of a gay century sweeping onwards to the
mutterings of the Bastille, the blood-frenzy of the Revolution,
and the rise of the young Corsican who was to strip Italy of
her freedom, her wealth and her treasures of Art. The festivities grew apace, and seemed to find their apex at the close
of 1782, when Alfieri's new play was presented before an audience packed with the fashion of Rome. Alfieri produced and
acted in his own play. It was a tragedy called *Antigone*. The
beautiful Duchess Zaragola, sister of Prince Rospigliosi,
played the title-rôle. The author played Creon, the Princess
Giustiniani was Argia, the Duke of Ceri, Emone. The chosen
theatre was in the palace of the Spanish Ambassador to the
Papal Court, himself an enthusiastic amateur actor.

For many weeks the forthcoming production was the talk
of the city. Alfieri had read parts of the play in the Roman
palaces. There was a scramble for seats in the restricted
theatre in the Spanish Embassy in the Piazza di Spagna. The

great evening arrived. Flambeaux burned in the sconces of the Embassy's portal. Gold-laced footmen lined the ceremonial staircase. The coaches slowly discharged their freight of rank, beauty and fashion. There was Princess Rezzonico, the niece of Clement XIII, proud, as became a member of the great Venetian family, a *Senatrice* in her own right, beautiful withal, in ermine-trimmed brocade, a diadem of brilliants surmounting her black curls; the lovely Duchess of Santa Croce; the Princess Altieri, a rival hostess in Rome; the Donna Leopolda di Savoia, wife of Prince Doria, wearing her magnificent pearls; the Princess Rospigliosi, the famous family jewels blazing on her corsage; the Donna's sister, Princess Colonna, whose name evoked a pageant of history, wearing a collar of emeralds. The chatelaines of the famed palaces of Rome, bearing names written in the annals of the Eternal City—Orsini, Massimo, Barberini, Odescalchi, Borghese, Sciarra, Ruspoli, Chigi, Caetani—mounted the regal staircase.

And last, the centre of all eyes, came the Countess of Albany, young, slight in figure, wearing some of the Stuart and Sobieski jewels that she had not surrendered to her husband. If she had her rights, thought some in the audience, she would take precedence over them all as Queen of England. But she made no such claim, despite her husband's insistence, and was content to cede her place to the niece of the Pope. But it was her evening, whatever her rank. Her lover was producing and performing in his own play, which he had read to her long before the world had seen it. The curtain rose in a theatre lit by innumerable candles whose flames were renewed in the myriad diamonds flashing on the white throats of the noblesse of Italy.

The success of the play was tremendous. It was received with the exaggeration that greets the acting of friends, and in this case the author himself was in the cast, and the woman he loved was in the audience. Not a great play, nor one of his best, *Antigone* was successfully launched and applauded throughout Italy.

The night was cool and still when the carriages rolled away from the Piazza di Spagna. Only the staccato clop-clop of the horses along the streets, half in shadow, half in moonlight, was heard above the sound of the water falling in the fountains of Rome.

v

A few months after the production of *Antigone* the blow fell. It came out of a serene sky. In March, 1783, news of the serious illness of Charles Stuart was reported from his palace in Florence. It seemed a moment for the closing of the breach between the royal brothers, and in haste the Cardinal Duke set off towards Tuscany. At Siena he learned, to his surprise and relief, that Charles had rallied and seemed likely to recover. The Cardinal Duke continued his journey to Florence, where, by his brother's sick bed, a reconciliation took place. Charles, moreover, seemed to have re-established himself with the Church. There had always been a suspicion at the Vatican, based on a rumour when he was living with his mistress, Clementina Walkinshaw, deserted by him after she had borne him a child in Liège, 1753, that he had made overtures to the Protestants.[12] This suspicion had doubtless influenced the Vatican's attitude to Charles Stuart, never as cordial as to his father and his brother, although it permitted the latter to divert to him his pension of 12,000 crowns from the Papal Treasury and gave him the use of the palazzo in the Piazza

---

[12] 'General Redmond, a brave old Irish officer in the French service, and a Roman Catholic, told Lord Holland that the Pretender had abjured the Roman religion at Liège, and that the Irish Catholics had withdrawn their contributions on that account. This seemed to excuse the injustice of the Court of Rome, which had refused him the title of King, though his family had lost a kingdom for that Church. The Pope had withdrawn the pension paid to his father but allowed the Cardinal to give up his pension to his brother, who was now said, but I doubt it, to have £25,000 sterling a year. His marriage in a family connected with the bigoted house of FitzJames did not look as if he was turned Protestant' (Horace Walpole, April 4, 1772, *Last Journals*).

Santi Apostoli. Now all seemed well, the shadow of heresy was dispersed and the Cardinal Duke of York found his brother on cordial terms with the Archbishop of Florence and attendant priests. Though sick, the Young Pretender began to go about again. Naturally he began to discuss his grievances, particularly concerning the conduct of his wife, who, he alleged, had invented the stories of his cruelty to her in order to excuse her own monstrous conduct with Alfieri, even while she was under his roof. His indignation and disgust were shared by the Archbishop. They were all well-informed upon the conduct of the Countess and Alfieri in Rome, and the scandal of their liaison.

It was a thunderclap in the serene mind of the unsuspecting Cardinal Duke. Horrified at the story he heard, he was ready to accept the advice of the clergy thronging the Palazzo Guadagni that the scandal must be stopped immediately. The Cardinal Duke hurried back to Rome, and took precipitate action. Without challenging or in any way informing the accused pair, he went at once to the Pope and unburdened himself of his story, conveying all his own indignation. When the full tale of deceit and lawless passion was told, the Cardinal Duke asked for an order for the immediate expulsion of Count Alfieri from Rome. His Holiness, anxious to be rid of the whole unpleasant affair, responded at once. The order of expulsion was conveyed to the Villa Strozzi. A note from the Cardinal to his sister-in-law was sent at the same time, forbidding her to have any further communication with the Count.

There was an agonising scene of parting between the lovers, and then, in order not to provoke being escorted to the frontier by the Papal police, Alfieri hurried out of Rome. The always theatrical story of his life, as he wrote it later, records his emotions.

'It was the fourth day of May in the year 1783 which will always be and has been up to now my bitterest remembrance— that I then removed myself from Her who was more than half of

COUNTESS OF ALBANY, by *Xavier Fabre*
(Uffizi Gallery, Florence)

THOMAS WILLIAM COKE IN ROME, by *Pompeo Batoni*

myself. And of the four or five separations from her that I have experienced, this was the most terrible to me, since every hope of seeing her again was so uncertain and so far distant. . . . And thus I left my only Lady, my books, my villa.'

It was soon clear that the Cardinal Duke had made an appalling error in his drastic action. All Rome had known what he, in his obtuseness, had failed to discover. The sympathies of the fashionable world were with the Countess and Alfieri. Society, which had received the pair, which had applauded the production of *Antigone*, which delighted to entertain the famous young poet, dashing, handsome and aristocratic, could not suddenly turn on him because the Cardinal Duke had lost his head and victimised his pretty, ill-used sister-in-law with a scandal that, however well-founded, should have been hushed up and disposed of tactfully. Even the poor Cardinal Duke, the indignation and alarm engendered in Florence now subsiding, began to realise the mistake he had made. He asked the Countess to continue residence in his palace, and to the letters of mingled grief and indignation she wrote him, he replied in terms of affection. Throughout she refused to acknowledge herself guilty of any duplicity.

The Cardinal began to be solicitous for her welfare and happiness. He offered her some of the Stuart and Sobieski jewels in his possession, which she tactfully declined, saying the implied faith in her was more than any jewels. The old Princess Stolberg, hearing of the scandal, now proposed coming to Rome, to deal firmly with her daughter. The Cardinal Duke began to make arrangements for her visit, but the Countess peremptorily vetoed her mother's journey. She accepted for herself the Cardinal Duke's invitation to pass the summer in the Villa Muti, his property near Frascati. She was verging upon a nervous breakdown, often in tears, alternately abusing a vindictive husband and lamenting the loss of Alfieri, who maintained a trying silence.

At the end of the summer she returned to the Palazzo della

Cancelleria, and a whole year passed, her anxiety prolonged
by no sign of her husband's next move. At last he showed his
hand, through the medium of King Gustavus of Sweden. The
sight of the dropsical, maudlin Charles, once the gallant
prince of the great adventure of 1745, moved the King to
offer his services in the matter preying on the Pretender's
mind. Gustavus proceeded to Rome, and after delicate negotiations between the Cardinal Duke and the Countess, obtained, with the assent of all parties, the ratification of a deed
of separation. The Countess, finding Charles grasping in the
matter of the financial settlement, quixotically renounced
her allowance of some three thousand crowns a year, an act
she regretted later, when necessity compelled her to seek
assistance from Marie Antoinette, who procured for her a
pension of sixty thousand francs from the French Treasury.

Whatever the cost, the Countess was free now. She ignored
one of the conditions of the separation, that she should continue to reside in the Papal territory, and, rejecting the offer
of the Cardinal Duke, kind and solicitous throughout, of continued residence in his palace, left a month later for Colmar
in Alsace. Here on August 17th, 1784, Count Alfieri joined
her. All subterfuge was at an end. 'I met her and remained
speechless from excess of joy,' he wrote. The liaison was open
and avowed.

The Pretender, old and sickly, was alone in his Florentine
palace. He tried to solace himself by going out into society,
wearing the Garter, with all the trappings of royalty. Then
he found a solution. One morning the Cardinal Duke was
compelled to face a new situation created by a young lady
styled the Duchess of Albany. Charles wrote to his brother—'I
am very happy to be able to tell you myself of my very dear
daughter's recognition by Me, by France, and by the Pope:
henceforth she is therefore Royal Highness for yourself on
every occasion. I in no way dispute your own rights. They are
already established, since you are my Brother, but at the

same time I beg of you not to dispute those of my very dear
Daughter, whose title must be sacred to you.'

This was too much for even the magnanimous Henry. He
did dispute the right, regarding the whole basis of the proposal as irregular as it was immoral. Charlotte Stuart, a
plain, sensible but pushing young woman, was Charles Stuart's daughter by his mistress during his early days spent in
Belgium after the quarrel with his father and brother. He
had then called him at Ghent, Clementina Walkinshaw, a
young woman he had met at Bannockburn in 1746, now a
canoness in a convent in Holland. She joined him, lived with
him as his wife from 1752 to 1760, and bore him a daughter,
Charlotte. His cruelty to this young Scotswoman was so
great that finally she fled, with her child, taking refuge in a
convent.[13]

Poor Clementina complained that Charles Stuart thrashed
her with a stick fifty times a day, and was so jealous that he
hung bells around the bed at night to warn him of anyone
approaching. She wrote to him explaining her flight, one
month after Charlotte was born, saying she was always in
perpetual dread of her life from his violent passion and end-
ing: 'You are not yourself, your head is gone again.'

James, the Old Pretender, had done what his son would not
do: he provided six thousand *livres* for the education of Lady
Charlotte, as the child was styled. Charles refused any provision to his mistress, with whom he never again corresponded. Then, after twenty-four years, alone in his Florence
palace, he sent for his grown daughter, to nurse him in his
decline, a task she perfectly fulfilled, until, four years later,

<hr>

[13] It is singular how all the women who lived with the Old and Young Pre-
tenders sought refuge from them in convents; Queen Clementina Sobieski
Stuart, and Queen Louise Stolberg Stuart, both in the Ursuline Convent at
Rome; and Clementina Walkinshaw, in the Convent of the Holy Sacrament,
Paris. Her name being the same as Queen Clementina's, is not a coincidence.
She was born in Rome and christened there after the Queen, who had stood
sponsor in gratitude to the child's father, the Jacobite agent at Vienna, who
had played some part in the Queen's flight from Austria, in 1719.

the unhappy wreck of a once-courageous, captivating young prince, the very figure of romance, went down to the grave, burying all the Stuart hopes with him.

The bereaved Charlotte soon succeeded in gaining the favour of the old Cardinal Duke of York, taking occasion to open his eyes wide to the liaison with which the Countess of Albany and Alfieri were flouting society.[14] From Colmar Count Alfieri and his beloved Louise had moved to Paris. There, after four years of complete happiness in each other's company, came the news, in 1788, of Charles Stuart's death. Charles had returned to the old Stuart palace in Rome, attended by his legitimised daughter. The two royal brothers, in protest against the Countess of Albany's flagrant cohabitation with the poet, had addressed a joint appeal to the French Court to stop the pension she was receiving. The appeal was ignored. This action served to mark the Cardinal's break with his sister-in-law, though it was not absolute, for years later, when Alfieri was dead, they corresponded again, and the old Cardinal Duke remembered her in his Will, with the effect that her own claims on his diminished estate deprived his faithful old servants of their legacies.

When, by the death of Charles Stuart, the Countess found herself free, she did not marry Alfieri. She did not wish to relinquish the royal rank she now asserted as a 'widowed Queen,' and Alfieri, for his part, saw no point 'in having a simple Countess for a wife when he had a Queen for a lover.' In 1791 they made a visit to London, where both were well received. There the inconceivable thing happened. The widow of the Pretender to the British Throne was received at Court!

Up in Norfolk there was a man of thirty-seven, squire of the great domain of Holkham, a Member of Parliament, named Thomas William Coke. The friend of Lafayette, admired by Washington, he had throughout opposed the war

---

[14] There is a glimpse of her in Goethe's Diary, Nov. 23, 1786, at a party in Prince von Liechtenstein's palace in Rome. '. . . my good humour failed me when the daughter of the Pretender expressed a wish to see a strange marmoset.'

with the American Colonies. He had angered George III by moving in the House of Commons that the independence of America should be recognised. He had kept the House up all night until dawn, and carried the motion by one vote. He was appointed by the House to take the Address to the indignant King. He was at that time a young man of twenty-eight, but his career was only beginning. Famed as an agriculturist, he reclaimed a sea-marsh, planted it, and increased a revenue of £2,200 to £20,000 in the next twenty years. He was the magnificent host who housed one hundred and twenty guests and entertained five thousand to celebrate his annual sheep-shearing. He had already twice declined a peerage, and would decline it twice again until compelled by public acclaims, forty-six years later, to exchange the proud title of 'The Great Commoner' for that of Earl of Leicester.

Thomas William Coke must have read in his newspaper of the sensational visit to London of the Countess of Albany, widow of the Pretender. He had escorted her to the royal marriage at Macerata, he had danced with her in that memorable summer of 1772, and the portrait of him in all the splendour of his youth, painted by Batoni at her command, was hanging in his drawing-room. But his heady youth was passed, and in vigorous middle-age he was a happily married man with two growing daughters. He made no sign, and kept on his estate at Holkham. The Countess, in London, had Count Alfieri with her. She, too, made no sign across the intervening nineteen years. It was wise of both of them.

She returned to Paris with Alfieri. They had a very narrow escape from the French Revolution, and only by Alfieri's courage and persistence did they pass the barriers guarded by the menacing mob. To Florence they went, the city of their first meeting, from which she had fled eleven years earlier. They took a palace, the Palazzo Gianfigliazzi,[15] on the sunny

---

[15] The blowing up of the Ponte della Trinità by the Germans in 1944 shattered the interior of the palace. On the Via Tornabuoni side there is the Gianfigliazzi coat of arms, a lion rampant on a shield. Underneath it is a quotation from Dante (*Inferno*, XVII, 58–60 '. . E com' io riguardando tra lor

Lungarno, near the graceful Ponte della Trinità, and they settled there in serene felicity. There were some years of good work: he wrote his tragedy *Alcestis*, he taught himself, at forty-eight, to read Greek. Happy in the company of the woman he loved and the circle of a few chosen friends, the years slipped by. Then he began to fail. The flamboyant poet, the rider of the spirited horses, the great lover, grew listless and prematurely old, and at fifty-four he was dead.

'O God, what a misfortune to lose One whom one adores and venerates! A twenty years' friendship with so perfect a being, and to lose him at an age I most needed him! Consolations, support, society, all, all lost.'

So she cried on October 8th, 1803. She buried him in Santa Croce, and commissioned Canova, to whom she had sat as the figure of bereaved Italy, to carve a grandiose tomb.[16] Although it cost 12,000 *scudi* it must be accounted one of Canova's failures, but he had been overruled in the matter of the design. The first one, made in 1805, of which a plaster copy exists in the museum of his works at his birthplace, Pos-

vegno/ In una borsa gialla vidi azzurro/ Che d'un leone avea faccia e contegno. . . . And as I gazing round came among them, Upon a yellow pouch I saw azure That had the face and posture of a lion.' Dante saw in the Seventh Circle of Hell tormented figures each with a pouch hanging from his neck emblazoned with his coat of arms. A blue lion rampant on a yellow shield denoted one of the Gianfigliazzi family.

[16] 'Where has the monument to Alfieri been placed?' asked Napoleon, of Canova, in 1810, while modelling a bust of Marie Louise. 'In Santa Croce, Sire, in company with those to Michelangelo and Machiavelli.' 'Who has paid for it?' 'The Countess of Albany, Sire.' 'Who paid for Machiavelli's monument?' 'A society.' 'And for that to Galileo?' 'His relations, if I am not mistaken. I might perhaps tell your Majesty that the Church of Santa Croce is in a very bad state of repair, and that the roof lets in the rain' (*La Societa Romana nel Secoli* 18–19, Silvagni).

> In Santa Croce's holy precincts lie
> Ashes which make it holier, dust which is
> Even in itself an immortality,
> Though there was nothing save the past, and this,
> The particle of those sublimities
> Which have relapsed to chaos: here repose
> Angelo's, Alfieri's bones, and his,
> The starry Galileo, with his woes;
> Here Machiavelli's earth returned to whence it rose.
>   (*Childe Harold*, Byron.)

sagno, is much the finer. The memorial carries also the name
of the Countess, and is in effect an epigraphic notification of
their adultery, to Europe and to posterity, within the pre-
cincts of a church. It is ironical that she deputed her second
lover, Fabre, to conduct the negotiations for this memorial to
her first. In Santa Croce also, twenty-one years later, the
Countess, too, was buried, her resting place marked by one of
the most beautiful tombs in the church. It is by Santarelli,
and carries the royal arms of the United Kingdom, in a frame
of mourning cherubs.

In the years following Alfieri's death the countess was not
alone. To fill the void in her home, if not in her heart, the
French painter Xavier Fabre, as *cavaliere servente*, moved
into the palace, where she insisted, increasingly, on being
treated with royal honours. There are glimpses of her, a vivacious little middle-aged woman, more French than German
in appearance, presiding over a *salon*, seated in a chair with
the heraldic shield of the Royal House of Stuart behind her.
Her *salon* was the foremost in Italy for twenty years and not
less famous than that of Madame de Staël's at Coppet. Napoleon, desiring her prestige, invited her to Paris in 1810, but
she soon returned to Florence, where her receptions attracted
Lamartine, Chateaubriand, Canova, Byron, Thomas Moore
and Sismondi. When she died in 1824, she left almost everything inherited from the Pretender and Alfieri to Fabre, who
in turn left his pictures and belongings to his native town of
Montpellier in the south of France.[17]

When the dying Sir Walter Scott visited Rome in 1832 he
made a special pilgrimage to St. Peter's to see the Stuart
memorial. He was so ill and lame that he had to have a glove

[17] Here in the Napoleonic wars, the sick and consumptive British prisoners
were confined and found the air beneficial, so that afterwards at English seaside
resorts there was a sporadic outbreak of boarding houses called Montpellier in
memory of the salubrious French town. But that has been long forgotten, as
also that in the Fabre Museum one may see the sculptored busts of Louise, of
Charles Stuart and of Alfieri, and some books and objects from the once-
thronged *salon* of a 'Queen' who was never recognised either in Italy or
England.

tied on to the end of his stick to prevent him from slipping on the marble floor.[18] The bodies of the three Stuarts lie in the crypt in a very simple sarcophagus. The ashes of the last two Stuarts had been removed secretly from Frascati to St. Peter's. The greatest sculptor of the age, Canova, was commissioned by Pius VII to carve a cenotaph, placed on a pier in the left aisle. It reflects in its simple majesty the genius of Canova, and is a thing of much beauty. Two naked seraphs mourn by a closed portal, above which, in bas-relief, appear the heads of the royal father and his two sons. A Latin inscription below reads:

'To James III, son of James II, King of Great Britain, and to Charles Edward, and to Henry, Dean of the Cardinals, the sons of James III, last of the Royal House of Stuart, 1819.'

It is not correct, as often stated, that George III paid for this memorial. The Prince Regent subscribed £50, but it was to Pius VII, wishing to honour the Royal House that had suffered for its loyalty to the Roman Catholic Church, that the cenotaph owed its inception. Few Englishmen, even to-day, can look upon this memorial unmoved, so many memories of romance and courage for a lost cause does it evoke; and perhaps because, as Boswell remarked, 'Jacobitism was something for which both he and Dr. Johnson had a kind of liking.'

[18] Scott was amused and delighted when an Italian told him that his family had been mentioned by Dante in the *Divine Comedy* and quoted—

> Quell altro, che nei fianchi è cosi poco,
> Michele Scott fu, che veramente
> Delle magiche frode seppe il gioco.

This was the 12th century magician who created many legends. Sir Walter visited the Castle of St. Angelo, and thought of writing a story upon the Constable of Bourbon's attack, but his mind was fading, and he got home just in time to die at Abbotsford.

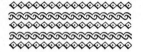

THE FORUM AND THE PALATINE

I

IN the year 1815 a remarkable woman of fashion took up residence in Rome. This was the widowed Elizabeth, Duchess of Devonshire. She was the second wife of the fifth Duke of Devonshire, whom she married in 1809. The first Duchess, the celebrated beauty, Georgiana, had been her lifelong friend. Lady Elizabeth, the daughter of the eccentric Earl of Bristol, married, first, a man named Foster, and after his death she lived for some years on the Continent with her great friend Georgiana. They wrote poetry, painted, and had a small *salon* at Lausanne. It was here, in 1787, that Gibbon met and was enamoured of Lady Elizabeth Foster. He had just finished *The Decline and Fall of the Roman Empire* in a country, he wrote, 'which I have known and loved from my early youth. Under a mild government, amid a beauteous landscape, in a life of leisure and independence, and among a people of easy and elegant manners.' Here, at Lausanne, he read to Lady Elizabeth the concluding portions of the great work. Her praise was so warm that in an excess of emotion the pernickety little bachelor of fifty proposed to her. Fortunately the proposal was gracefully declined, and he recovered his balance. Comparing Lady Elizabeth with the celebrated Georgiana he wrote:

'Bess is much nearer the level of a mortal, but a mortal for whom the wisest man, historic or mediocre, would throw away

two or three worlds if he had them in possession. . . . If she chose
to beckon the Lord Chancellor from his woolsack in full sight of
the world he would not resist obedience.'

This attractive lady, on the death of her friend the Duchess
Georgiana, married the widower, and thus, in 1809, became
the Duchess of Devonshire. We find her now, a widow,
wealthy and the centre of fashion, in Rome in 1815. Following Napoleon's downfall, Europe became again a fashionable
playground, and foremost in favour was Rome. The Duchess'
salon was the resort of a brilliant society from all countries.
Canova and Thorwaldsen were her friends, together with the
influential Cardinal Consalvi. She had been painted by Sir
Joshua Reynolds and Gainsborough, and she not only had
ambitions as a poet but she printed some fine private editions
of Horace and Virgil. It was impossible for her to escape the
prevailing interest in Roman excavations. She lavishly endowed work in the Forum. Part of it was still unexcavated,
and she was the first to suggest digging there. From Rome she
wrote, in 1816, to her son, a diplomat:

'I hear from England that Lord Byron's third Canto of *Childe
Harold* is beautiful but Lord Cowper doesn't like it much, and
Lady Blessington is sending it to me, and I long for it, as, however
odious his character, he is the great Poet. . . . I have begun a
little excavation in the Foro Romano and they found a cup or
chalice. In digging close to the single pillar, they found it to be a
column of Phocas. I am having the cup cleaned a little and put
together. At the great excavation they found a part of the plan of
Rome, which joins on to that which is preserved in the Capitol
Museum. Nothing can be greater than the interest which this
excites. I have employed poor labourers instead of prisoners which
is a charity. I saw it particularly pleased my friend Cardinal
Consalvi.'

The column of Phocas, by virtue of its isolated position in
the Forum, is extremely conspicuous. It had never wholly
disappeared in all the centuries, but no one knew what it

represented, and it was surmised that it was just a column left
over from a vanished temple. Until the Duchess dug down
and cleared the base of some twenty feet of earth, the column
was a mystery. The clue to its history was found on an inscription at its base.

It is singular that the Duchess should have missed seeing
Byron, as we assume she did, for he visited Rome in May,
1817, meditating the Fourth Canto of *Childe Harold*. He collected material for some of the Roman verses there, including
those on *The Dying Gladiator*, as it was then called, a title
that misled him into apostrophising a warrior who was never
a gladiator, was never 'butchered to make a Roman holiday'
and died far away from any Roman arena, being a Gaul who
fell in battle in Asia Minor. Byron's verses in *Childe Harold*,
with their erroneous description of the Castle of St. Angelo, as
well as of the column of Phocas and the 'Gladiator,' show that
he was a hasty sightseer. It was strange that he did not learn
when in Rome, in 1817, that a year earlier the mystery of the
column in the Forum had been solved by the Duchess of Devonshire's excavation. Not only could she have enlightened
him, but his friend Hobhouse, in whose company he was visiting Rome, and who had been pursuing archaeological studies
there for five months, should also have known about the column. Moreover, Byron dined with young Lord Lansdowne,
another amateur archaeologist. How, then, in the Fourth
Canto came Byron to write—'Thou nameless column with a
buried base'? A year earlier it had been nameless, and buried,
but now in 1817 it had a name and an exposed base.

There is one possible explanation. Byron may have worked
from a guide-book, in addition to his personal observation. He
may have seen the column, but not closely, for he tells us: 'I
have been on horseback most of the day, all days since my
arrival.' You cannot examine monuments closely on horseback. He was in a hurry and restless, for although he cried,
'Oh Rome! my country! city of the soul!' he was in it only sixteen days of the seven years he lived in Italy. In Rome he

pined for Marianna Segati, the shopkeeper's wife who was accommodatingly both his Venetian landlady and his mistress, and he returned to her in that delectable city. He spent the summer writing the Fourth Canto of *Childe Harold* at his villa, La Mira, on the Brenta, in a riot of promiscuous adventures with his crony, Hobhouse. He dropped Marianna and picked up a baker's wife, whom he dubbed La Fornarina, probably with memories of the portrait of Raphael's mistress, seen in Rome, a vixen who was to torment him for many months. In such an atmosphere he wrote the Fourth Canto.

How comes it that Hobhouse checking the manuscript and making the historical notes for this Canto, missed the slip about the column of Phocas? Well, every author who takes the precaution of having his proofs read by others as a check has had shattering experiences of how the most glaring errors get by. Three or four highly qualified proofreaders will fail to observe an error picked up by some casual reader in Australia. Yet let us be grateful. The Fourth Canto gives us much superb rhetoric and some immortal lines on Rome.

> What are our woes and sufferance? Come and see
> The cypress, hear the owl, and plod your way
> O'er steps of broken thrones and temples. Ye!
> Whose agonies are evils of a day—
> A world is at our feet as fragile as our clay!

The column of Phocas was one of the last commemorative monuments to be raised in the Forum. Fluted, and of beautiful proportions, it was originally set up by Diocletian after the fire of A.D. 282. In A.D. 608 the exarch Smaragdus imperfectly erased the inscription, replacing it with a lying one in praise of the 'worthy and clement' Emperor Phocas, who restored peace and gave the Pantheon to Pope Boniface IV. Actually, Phocas was a bloody monster, a centurion of the Byzantine army who murdered the eastern Emperor Maurizio and his five sons in order to gain his throne. When Phocas was assassinated in A.D. 610, his statue, surmounting the column, was thrown down. It is singular that the beautiful marble shaft should have survived through almost seventeen centuries, unshattered and never wholly submerged, like most of the monuments around it.

The other most conspicuous object, beyond the long platform, or Rostra for orators, is the Arch of Septimius Severus. It was erected by the Senate in A.D. 203 in honour of the Emperor. There was no way through it until Charles V was given a 'Triumph' and a new road was cut leading out of the Forum up to the Capitol. A lucky survivor through the centuries, this massive arch has no artistic merit; it celebrates the Emperor's victories in the East. His triumphal entry into Babylon and the Tower of Babel are shown on it.

We are standing now in the very heart of ancient Rome. About this Forum flowed the life of a city of two million inhabitants. Familiar here were Caesar, Pompey, Brutus, Cicero, Horace, Virgil, Catiline, Maecenas, Caligula, Lucullus, Nero and Hadrian. Let us stand here on a summer's morning in July, just twenty years before an event in Nazareth was destined to alter the calendar and start historians counting backwards as well as forwards, B.C. and A.D.[1] To a Roman on this particular morning it is A.U.C. 734—*Anno Urbis Conditae*, 734 years from the foundation of the city of Rome.

Some thirty years earlier Julius Caesar had made alterations to the calendar. He was not only a great soldier and an excellent historian, whose *Commentaries* still enjoyed a wide sale throughout the Empire and were compulsory reading in the Roman schools, but he was also an excellent astronomical author. The calendar had been a worry to him, and he had much trouble in inducing the diehards to accept a new one;

[1] But the counting from *Anno Domini* is inaccurate. Quirinius, the Governor of Syria, decreed a census for taxation purposes in 7 B.C. All Jews were re-uired to return to the centre of their tribe, hence the journey of Joseph, a rpenter of Nazareth, to Bethlehem in the Judæan hills, the city of the tribe of avid to which he belonged. It was there, in a stable, a child was born and amed Jesus. We are thus enabled to fix the year of the birth of the Saviour, which according to the Roman calendar is actually 7 B.C.

crossing the Rubicon had been child's play in comparison.
Altering the solar year had not been a simple matter of *Veni,
vidi, vici*. But now the Julian calendar was established. There
were no longer 355 days to a year—three hundreds years ago
Rome had managed with 304 days and ten months to a year
—there were now 365. Caesar had called in an Alexandrian
mathematician, Sosigenes. Between them they had worked
out a new calendar that added ten days to a year, and got rid
of lunar months. Undoubtedly this was simpler than the old
calendar, which had a first year of 355 days, a second of 377,
a third of 355 and a fourth of 378. That calendar had been
very confusing and troublesome to farmers. But Caesar had
had a little difficulty with every fourth year, and now there
was a day, called a bi-sextus, a kind of fill-up once in every
four years. It added a day to February. To honour Julius
Caesar, one of the months was now called July, quite de-
servedly.

This morning it was July 4th, and not too hot, noted
Marcus L. Hirtius, who was always very proud of the fact
that his father had carried on Caesar's masterpiece *De Bello
Gallico* by writing the story of those last two years of the
campaign, which Caesar had left unrecorded.

The whole world seemed to be out in the Forum this morning, yet there was no one declaiming on the Rostra. There
would never again be anyone to equal Cicero. Marcus was
proud to think that he had heard him thirty years ago. He
had also seen, and he would never forget it, Cicero's head and
hands nailed upon the very Rostra he had dominated, after
that dreadful slaughter at the old man's villa at Formiae,
twenty-three years ago. Antony's horrible wife, Fulvia, stuck
a hairpin through Cicero's protruding tongue. It had always
seemed to him a dark stain on the character of Augustus Caesar,
but it didn't do to say so publicly. One might think certain
things about Julius Caesar also. An inscription under his
statue here in the Forum described him as 'clement.' One
need not waste sympathy on barbarians, but when the

wretched Helvetii (Swiss) asked permission to move from
their barren land into Provence, he refused and drove them
back again. Caesar boasted that of 368,000 Helvetii only a
third got back alive. And after slaughtering them he exulted
because he had avenged himself on a tribe that had killed the
grandfather of his father-in-law.[2] Clement! Well, one must
keep one's mouth shut or get sent into exile.

By Jupiter! There was Horace standing by Maecenas's
litter as usual. What he had had out of that millionaire! He
would much like to have a word with Horace, but after that
scathing satire of his on The Bore who had accosted him it
was too risky. The new Forum Caesar had built had not relieved the traffic here. It had become a nightmare, and the
noise! Rome must be the noisiest city in the world.

Horace, walking by his friend, glanced about him. His
career, looking back now on his forty-five years, had been
singularly fortunate. No starving poet he! He had just arrived
in the Forum when he had encountered the litter of his dear
old friend Marcus Agrippa, and not that of Maecenas, as
Marcus Hirtius had supposed. Agrippa had just built the
Pantheon and given it to Rome. Everyone had agreed that it
was one of the most beautiful buildings in the city. He was
glad he had inscribed one of his Odes to him. Agrippa, seeing
him, had asked him to dine that night. He had accepted at
once. It was an excuse for not going back to his lovely little
farm just twelve miles out of Tivoli, though it was an ador-
able country retreat, small and workable for a man of such
simple tastes as he had.[3] The day the noble Maecenas had

---

[2] 'Qua in re Caesar non solum publicas, sed etiam privatas iniurias ultus est;
quod eius soceri L. Pisonis avum, L. Pisonem legatum, Tigurini eodem proelio
quo Cassium interfecerant' (Caesar, *De Bello Gallico*, I. 12).

[3] The farm would be considered a lavish establishment these restricted days,
with its five families on the estate, its bailiff, its villa equipped with everything
for entertaining, its orchards, its stream and the eight slaves in the house.

In the 19th Century so many cultured and leisured Englishmen (a breed that
has been eliminated) visited the farm, awakening echoes of their schooldays,
that the puzzled peasantry around believed Horace was an Englishman whose
descendants came to see his old home.

made him a present of the Sabine farm he had felt secure in life, come what may.

Nevertheless, it was always nice to have an excuse for remaining in town. One saw people and dined with old cronies and passed a pleasant hour or two with the latest professional beauty. Horace often laughed to himself over the serious way in which his readers discussed his love affairs. Why did they imagine his Lalages, Myrtales, Phrynes, and Glyceras, were real persons? As a youth and young man he had enjoyed himself in his hot-blooded days with the fashionable *hetairae*, and none was so pleasant and accomplished as one of these Aspasias either for conversation or dalliance. But marriage? Oh no! He had evaded that snare. What a fool old Cicero had made of himself! Among the demi-monde Cinara had been exceptional. He believed she had genuinely had a feeling for him, cash apart. Poor Cinara—*Cinaræ breves annos fata dederunt*—few years the Fates of Cinara allowed.

Waving good-bye to Agrippa, Horace watched the litters go by before crossing by the Rostra Julia. The gods be praised, no carriages, except those of the Vestal Virgins, were allowed in Rome. But it was dangerous enough still. Four huge black Nubians, carrying a litter, attended by three youths, pomaded and scented in the Greek fashion, went by. They were flirting with some creature in it. He smiled tolerantly. No more for him the tangles of Neaera's hair. It had provided him with a good *Epode*, however. How did it go? His memory was not as good as it was. Ah, yes—*Nox erat et caelo fulgebat*—'You recall the night when you swore eternal love for me? It was unhappy for you that I am not as light-minded as you. Your beauty will not tempt me back to you again. And for you, sir, my successful rival, be you ever so rich and wise and beautiful, you will be deserted as I have been, and I shall laugh at you yet.' Not bad, not bad. He could toss off things like that once, without any effort. Those amorous youths would do better sweating on the exercise

ground. They were pretty enough to look at, but he wondered
how they would figure in a cohort.

> Pyrrha, what slender boy in perfume steeped
> Doth in the shade of some delightful grot
> Caress thee now on couch with roses heaped?
> For whom dost thou thine amber tresses knot?[4]

Quis multa gracilis. . . . Yes, that had been one of his most
popular poems, so he should not sniff too much at the scented
darlings.

What memories came crowding back on him these days!
It was in this city that Virgil had introduced him to Maecenas. The millionaire had been rather cool at first. He let
nine months go by before he invited him to one of those
famous banquets where every great man in Rome was to be
met. There had been a reason for it. Horace felt hot and cold
now when he thought about it. He had nearly thrown away
everything his dear old father, born a slave, and risen to freedom and competence by his shrewdness, had achieved for
him—an education in Rome and at the University of Athens.
And, like a fool, in his rash youth he had joined the Republican party, and fought at Philippi for Brutus, on the losing
side! His property at Venusia had been seized and he found
himself destitute. Back in Rome under the general amnesty,
he had scribbled a bit and succeeded in getting a job in the
Treasury. He wasn't the last civil servant thus to subsidise the
muse. Then he had been silly enough to publish a book of
Satires. Clever young men who know everything can't resist
saying smart things, whether true or not. He made enemies
of his victims. No wonder that Maecenas had kept him at a
distance! He was wiser now. Here he was, famous, with a
nice estate, a friend Maecenas, the richest and most generous
of men, another friend Augustus Caesar, the most powerful of
men. Augustus had invited him to be his secretary. No thank

---

[4] Sir Martin Conway's translation.

you! No politics. No sword in your throat when the powerful fell. Maecenas was now his dearest friend. Why was the good fellow always worrying about things? Either it was over his marriage to a woman he could not live with nor live without, or his money, or his mistress, or his health or public affairs. How silly! Enjoy yourself, live each day as if it were the last and don't quarrel with your destiny. Life was so very brief and a day would come when king, peasant, millionaire and pauper would be all alike.

Meditating thus, not knowing he was anticipating the *Rubaiyat of Omar Khayyam* by many centuries, Horace turned out of the Forum. What a medley! Men scurrying by in togas either too long or too short, the lawyers discussing cases by the Rostra, the gossipers, the men crying their wares in the fruit-shops, the jewellers, the goldsmiths, the Jew moneylenders and changers, the fishmongers, smelling to heaven, youths with their hair bound up in the effeminate Greek fashion, with leather boots half up their legs, Lepidus reeking of scent, others of garlic. A crowd down beyond the Basilica Julia was watching a hefty young slave, stripped and bound, being flogged with a cat-o'-nine-tails while a man bawled out his offence. Noble boys in their purple-bordered chitons were going home from school, accompanied by their guardian slaves. Gyges, the fop, went by, carried in a litter, with attendant Bithynian youths, his private corps of boxers, dancers and musicians. Chloe, lovelier than ever, waved to him—very prosperous now, with a bevy of Egyptian slaves, since Lepidus the Governor had taken her up.

A cart laden with enormous slabs of marble was delaying everyone. Since they had discovered the Carrara quarries all Rome was being turned from brick into marble. Would they never stop building temples for the gods? Building was the Roman disease. Julius Caesar had spent one hundred million sesterces merely for the ground for his new Forum. Emilius Paulus had spent six millions building the Basilica Emilia. The money had come from a bribe by Julius Caesar, they

THE FORUM AND THE PALATINE

Arch of Septimius Severus

Temple of Vespasian and Titus

Temple of Antonius and Faustina

Column of Phocas, in front of Rostra

The Sacred Way

Temple of Saturn

Basilica Julia

The Palatine Hill

THE SCHOOL FOR COURT PAGES, AND RUINS OF THE PALACE OF AUGUSTUS ON THE PALATINE

said, and not from the spoils of Macedon. Now Augustus had
the mania. Not content with building the temple to his great-
uncle Caesar, he was completing a huge palace on the Palatine, and before its gates one day in every year he sat as a
beggar receiving alms because a vision had warned him thus
to appease Nemesis. But he has also put a twenty-five per
cent. purchase tax on the sale of slaves in order to raise the
money! Well, he gave excellent banquets there.

Horace turned towards the Argiletum, near the ill-famed
Subura. He had just published a book, *Epistles*, and wondered
how it was selling. It would be selling well, of course. The
first edition of a thousand rolls was already snapped up. He
had the best publisher in Rome, the Sosii Brothers, who
'travelled' his works all over the Empire.

The moment he reached his publisher's door his welcome
was effusive. All eyes were upon him, the people in the shop,
the clerks, the sixty slaves busily copying on sheets of parchment. The Sosii greeted him. The elder led him through the
bookshop and copying-room to his own den, piled up with
parchment manuscripts. Yes, trade was good, but of course he
could not make any profit these days. As for advertising by
the town herald, as one of his authors suggested, it was quite
impossible. The publisher Atrectus was doing it for an edition
of *Propertius*, but would the poet get his money? Also, there
was a new menace. These public libraries Augustus had
founded were eating into the trade and if——

'How's my *Epistles* selling?' asked Horace, breaking into
this wail.

'Oh, excellently. The whole edition's gone. We're copying
another. There's never any trouble about your work. By the
way, I've got a new poet, quite a youngster—Ovid, by name.'

'I know him. A bright young fellow. What's he written?'
asked Horace.

The publisher picked up a parchment and passed it to the
poet, who unrolled it. He read for a few minutes. It was
called *Amores*.

'Quite good, quite good!' exclaimed Horace. 'Of course, like all young poets—love! These two lines to Corinna are—well, a bit sultry, eh? He'd better be careful. Augustus is a censor of morals these days.' Horace read again. 'Excellent! excellent!' he cried.

'Can we say so? Take the copy with you. It's out to-morrow.'

'Oh, certainly, certainly!' replied Horace.

After all, you could afford to be generous at forty-five, with a large public, and Maecenas and Augustus for bosom friends. Also one should keep abreast—and collect young disciples for the day of one's apotheosis.

He bade the Sosii good-bye. Yes, he was writing very little, very little. Leaving the shop to go to the sandal-maker's, he made a mental note to invite young Ovid out to the farm. He was a bright youth and well-born.

On the way back to his town lodging Horace was held up by a noisy demonstration. It was a strike of the union of fullers (*collegium fullonum*), the men who washed togas, against paying for water which they had always had free. Why did the authorities allow these strikes and unions? They would be the ruin of Rome. Well, everything had an end. Thank Jupiter it did. He wouldn't have much longer to tarry on this silly planet.

II

Leaving Horace, let us now ascend the Sacred Way, in the direction of the Colosseum towering on the horizon. A dozen times I have halted along this ancient road, the path of the triumphant generals back from their conquests that made the Empire. Now there are no cheering crowds, only a few shattered temples, some stones; the rest is silence. But what an eloquent silence in which to dream! And always there is the brightness of the Roman day, or the loveliness of the serene evening closing in, lovely, I think, as nowhere else. The distant mountains are bathed in a violet light, their summits shining under clouds that might be the chariots of the gods. The cypresses, like black spears thrown from heaven, point the scene, and as the sun sinks an upper glory of crimson and gold catches all Rome in a pool of amber light. It is the sunset seen by Caesar and Virgil, by St. Peter and all the saints on the last evening of their lives. *Ave Roma Immortalis.*

Where the road through the Forum rises we pass the ruins of the Temple of Vesta. Here the Vestal Virgins guarded the sacred fire for eleven hundred years. In their adjacent convent they kept the store of sacred fire and water, and the *penates*, or household gods. Six Vestal Virgins of good birth were the guardians of the shrine. In the apsidal chamber of the atrium of the Vestals' dwelling were deposited those relics on which the safety of Rome and the race depended. The secrets of their shrine were never revealed, from the foundation of Rome to the fall. In all the beauty and virtue of their youth they took their vows, and if one of them broke them, the bloody rod of the high priest and the silent tomb in which she was buried alive expiated her crime. To this terrible end the fallen Vestal, lying in her hearse, was escorted through Rome, the whole city shaken with terror.

The Vestals sat in the special seats of honour at the public games; they had the rare privilege of driving in the streets of Rome. They were preceded by a lictor, and all, including consuls, must give them right of way. Any offence against them was punished by death.

After centuries of honour, the rising tide of Christianity swamped the pagan cults. In A.D. 394 Theodosius defeated Eugenius, champion of the ancient gods. The order for the banishment of the Vestals was made. To the very end they were faithful to their charge. They destroyed their dwelling so that no clues remained as to the nature of their secrets. No one has ever discovered where they carried the sacred relics and the Palladium[5] no mortal eye must ever profane. For all we know, these things were secretly buried with the body of the last Vestal.

More than fifteen hundred years later a small terra-cotta jar was unearthed beneath the house adjoining the temple in the Forum. It had been built for an officer of Pope Marinus who came to live there about A.D. 830. In the jar were found some eight hundred silver coins, almost all of them Anglo-Saxon; three of Alfred the Great, two hundred and seventeen of Edward I, three hundred and ninety-three of Athelstan, one hundred and ninety-five of Edmund I, four of Plegmund, Archbishop of Canterbury, and seven of the two kings of Northumbria. From this discovery one surmises that the Pope's officer had something to do with offerings from early English Christian pilgrims; thus the pagan shrine received homage later as a Christian one.

The congestion in the Forum and throughout Rome, of which Horace and others complained, grew steadily worse, and the independent Romans ignored all regulations. So much has been written by novelists and historians about the wickedness of Nero that his gifts have been overlooked. He was a debauchee, with some good points possessed even by dictators. Nero's celebrated burning of Rome, during which it was charged he 'fiddled' (an instrument invented thirteen hundred years later), was really a skilful piece of town planning. Seeing no way through the lawsuits and obstructions that arose whenever he tried to regulate the streets of Rome, Nero ordered his architects, Severus and Celer, to draw up a completely new plan of the city, with proper drainage and open spaces. He then secretly collected a vast quantity of wooden booths and tents. In all the harbours of the Mediterranean he had ships, laden with grain, ready to sail at a mo-

---

[5] The Palladium was a statue of Pallas Athene, and was supposed to ensure security for the town that possessed it, wherefore it was hidden. The original and most celebrated statue was said to have fallen from Heaven when Ilus was building Troy, where it was held until it was carried off by Odysseus and Diomedes, or, as Romans believed, by Æneas.

ment's notice. Insuring thus against the homelessness and hunger of the inhabitants, he then set fire to Rome with a thoroughness that swept away ten of the fourteen zones.

Not a single life seems to have been lost in this carefully planned conflagration. The crowds were housed, the grain-ships promptly appeared. Their return cargoes were the debris of the fire. When the new city was built it was according to a right-angle pattern, familiar throughout the United States to-day, with large open squares and with the height of buildings restricted and zoned. Arcades gave shelter from the sun, no wood was permitted for ceilings. Nero, of course, took his price, a square mile on which he raised his Golden House, with its woods, waterfalls, lake, a port for the imperial barges, and baths. It had walls of mother-of-pearl, sprays for scenting the guests, a celestial dome of stars and moon in circulation, and thousands of statues gathered from all over the civilised world. In the vestibule rose the colossal bronze statue of Nero himself, one hundred and twenty feet high, removed later by Hadrian with the help of twenty-four elephants.

The winding Sacred Way, between the Temple of Antoninus and Faustina and the Arch of Titus, was once a wide, handsome street decorated with shrines and statues. At the end of the rising ground we find the Arch superbly situated and silhouetted against the sky where the Nova Via merged into the Sacra Via. Nearby, earlier, had stood the portico of the Golden House of Nero. We owe the Arch's restoration to Pope Paul II. We are told it is not on its original site, but that it was moved by Hadrian to accommodate the porticus and twin temples he built. We can only marvel at such a feat. The Arch once served as a buttress to a tower built in the eleventh century for the safekeeping of the papal archives, and was incorporated in the medieval fortress built by the Frangipani. In 1093 they gave protection in it to Pope Urban II. Of this tower and fortress nothing but the base remains.

The Arch is isolated and superb. Through it there is a stu-

pendous vista of the great Colosseum, in the building of
which twelve thousand captive Jews were used, and which
was inaugurated eight years after the return of Titus from
the siege of Jerusalem. This Arch is one of the most beautiful
specimens of its kind in Rome. It marks a terrible catastrophe
to the Jewish nation, dispossessed and dispersed from A.D. 70
until A.D. 1949. Under the Arch passed the Roman emperors
and generals proceeding in triumphal procession down the
Roman Forum and up to the Capitol, with their cohorts and
trains of chained prisoners. Under it also passed the newly
created popes going in solemn state from the Vatican to St.
John Lateran.

The Jews, humiliated by this memorial to their downfall
and exile, had to purchase their immunity from passing
under it. In the days when the Forum became a builders'
quarry so much debris was dropped here that the Arch was
buried to a depth of twenty feet. To-day it is one of the best
preserved monuments of the Forum. Let us examine its decoration and the events it celebrates.

III

In 65 B.C. Pompey besieged and took Jerusalem. Eleven
years later it was again plundered by Crassus. Herod the
Great, having taken refuge in Rome, was replaced on the
throne of Judæa in 37 B.C. He was a despot who tried to found
a dynasty with the acquiescence of the Roman overlords. He
built up his kingdom culturally and politically. Inspired by
Roman architecture, the friend of Antony and Augustus, he
built a temple, a palace, a theatre, a gymnasium and strong
fortifications. As Solomon had turned to Tyre, so Herod
turned to Rome. He fought all opposition ferociously, and
when a few days before his death in 4 B.C. he discovered his
son was conspiring against him, he obtained the permission
of Augustus to put him to death. His power and his beautiful
city passed to Archelaus and, later, to a Procurator.

Rome watched Judæa with a sharp eye. When Herod

Agrippa began to extend the city walls, Rome stopped him. Intrigues and rebellions followed. Judæa had the opportunity of becoming a great power. On each occasion the nation in its folly deliberately rejected it. In A.D. 66 Rome, alarmed again, had to proceed against the defiant Israelites. The campaign was conducted by Vespasian and his son Titus. In this war Flavius Josephus, the Jewish historian and general, played a singularly dramatic rôle. He had always advocated a working alliance with Rome, following his visit there in A.D. 64 to intercede for 'some priests, his friends.' In vain he expostulated with his countrymen, and as a Jew he found himself drawn into a war against the Romans. His known hostility to the policy of the Sanhedrin drew upon him the enmity of John of Giscala, who called him a traitor. In Josephus' battle with Vespasian he and his colleagues, left to the mercy of the Romans by the wild flight of their forces, retreated to a last hiding-place after bravely defending Jotapata, where forty survivors, rather than commit suicide, drew lots to kill each other progressively. When the last lot fell upon Josephus he persuaded his destined victim to surrender, along with himself, to Vespasian. Brought before the Roman commander, he prophesied Vespasian's ascent to the throne. On the fulfilment of this prophecy he was liberated, joined the Romans and took the name of Flavius, the family name of Vespasian. Later he returned to Rome and received a pension and an estate in Judæa. He was destined to play a beneficent rôle in the siege of Jerusalem, saving many lives.

When Vespasian was elected emperor he went back to Rome, leaving his son Flavius Titus to finish the war. Titus found himself before the walls of Jerusalem, the last stronghold of the defiant Israelites. He pitched his camp on Scopus, the Tenth Legion invested Mount Olivet, his other forces lay to the west. Jerusalem was crammed with refugees and pilgrims, it being the Paschal season. It is calculated that two million seven hundred thousand people were within the city, a computation arrived at by the fact that two hundred and fifty-six thousand lambs were sacrificed at the Passover; there were ten partakers of each lamb, and in addition there must have been many ceremonially unfit. To house this swollen population tents had been pitched all over the city and its suburbs.

Titus first attacked the Herodian outer walls of Jerusalem, using a special battering engine, 'The Conqueror.' These soon fell, and he advanced into the New Tower and took up a position on the very corner where the Assyrians under Sennacherib had formerly encamped. He extended his forces to the Kedron ridge, familiar in the attacks, centuries later, of the Saracens, Crusaders and Turks.

Five days after the reduction of the first wall Titus attacked the second, the outer boundary of the lower city. Soon he had breached it with a thousand men, and began to prepare the attack on the inner wall, the Jews holding the upper city, the Temple and the Antonia. Before doing this, aware of the great strength of their position, Titus despatched Josephus to parley with his countrymen and propose terms of surrender. Unwisely these were rejected. The forces in the city were torn with dissension and senseless rivalries. They had even destroyed each other's granaries, vital to their defence.

Titus now took merciless steps. Many hundreds of Jews had escaped to his camp, seeking to avoid the famine within the city. These, in full view of the besieged, he stripped, bloodily scourged, and crucified, the most painfully protracted of all forms of death. After this terrible warning he told the Jews that they would compel him to destroy the city and their sacred Temple. They replied that they preferred death to slavery and that their Temple would be saved by Him Who dwelt within it.

The siege proceeded ruthlessly. In order to starve out the Jews, Titus built in three days a containing wall of wooden stakes and mud. Behind this encircling wall famine gripped the millions within. The dead reached such numbers that the besieged were compelled to throw their bodies over the wall into the ravines. The stench become terrible. Stories of cannibalism came out of the starving city. The hypocritical Titus, seized with disgust and horror, called upon God to witness that it was not his doing.

Another breach was made, and the outer city was invested. The Jews, retreating into the Temple, fought in the outer courts. For six desperate days, fighting with tremendous valour, they kept the Romans from forcing the western gate. Enraged, Titus ordered the gates to be set on fire, but the next day he relented and had the fires extinguished, hoping still to procure the rich Temple and its fabulous riches as a trophy. Covered with plates of gold, it shone upon its summit, one of the glories of the world.

A council of war debated whether it was possible to take this last outpost of the enemy without destroying it. While the council was sitting a Roman soldier threw in a burning brand that started a fire soon out of all control. Within an hour the Romans had gained admittance. A scene of terrible slaughter followed, the Jews fighting with fanatical bravery until they fell in their own blood on the Temple pavements. Then the Roman Eagles were set up in the Holy Place of Israel. The treasury was sacked, the sacred vessels were seized, but the Holy of Holies was empty; the Ark of the Covenant was not there. Titus, surveying his victory over the fortress-city, was amazed at his achievement. 'God most certainly has fought on our side,' he declared. 'It was God that cast down the Jews from these bulwarks, for what could human hands and engines of war avail against these mighty towers?'

Neither humility nor mercy were part of the Roman character. Ruthless, implacable, cruel, they butchered their vanquished foemen no matter what valour they had shown. The Holy City and Temples were fired and razed to the ground. All who attempted resistance were put to the sword. The tall and handsome youths were rounded up for the Roman triumph. Others were despatched to slavery in the Egyptian mines, many were distributed throughout the provinces for

gladiatorial shows. One million one hundred thousand perished in the siege, one hundred thousand were made prisoners
of war. Four hundred thousand fell in the five years' fighting
in Judæa and the five months' siege of Jerusalem. The prophecy of Jesus Christ after He had wept over Jerusalem was
fulfilled:

'For the day shall come upon thee, that thine enemies shall cast
a trench about thee, and compass thee round, and keep thee in on
every side, and shall lay thee even with the ground, and thy
children within thee, and they shall not leave in thee one stone
upon another, because thou knewest not the time of thy visitation.'

How many recalled this prophecy made thirty-seven years
earlier?

When Titus returned from Judæa, a year later, he took
with him the leader of the Jewish defenders, Simon Bar-
Gioras and John of Giscala, together with seven hundred
young Jews selected for their handsome appearance. The tremendous spoils included the holy relics of the Temple. A
Triumph was given to Vespasian and Titus. It was the 320th
of these spectacles witnessed by Rome, and it was the most
magnificent. Vespasian and Titus, having offered prayers to
the gods, rode through the Triumphal Gate to pass down the
Sacred Way to the Forum and up to the Capitol. They rode in
state chariots, crowned each with laurel and clad in the an-
cestral purple. Behind them marched the Praetorian Guards,
the Legions from Judæa, and a company carrying the displayed spoils of the conquered Jews, the gilt table, the golden
seven-branched Candelabrum, the Book of the Law, the ceremonial bowls and cups. Behind these, jeered at by the delirious mob thronging the processional way, walked the seven
hundred Hebrew youths in chains. Chief of all, their general,
Simon Bar-Gioras, rode high on a chariot, naked and pinioned. When the victors and vanquished reached the foot of
the Capitol there was a pause. Simon and his men were de-
tached while the procession went on up to the Capitol. Bound

and scourged, Simon was taken into the dungeon of the
Mamertine Prison and executed. His death was announced
to the acclaiming multitude. After him the leading Jewish
warriors were put to the sword. Thus in a welter of blood and
exultation ended the Triumph.

The Senate voted the erection of two commemorative
arches to Titus and to Vespasian. Only one was erected, after
the death of the latter. The Emperor had given back to the
people most of the ground taken by Nero, and Vespasian built
with Jewish slave-labour the Colosseum on the site of Nero's
lake. It was on part of the land once belonging to the Golden
House that the Arch of Titus was built.

The vault and the arch mark a great contrast between
Greek and Roman architecture. The Greeks scarcely knew the
existence of these two assets of building. They used the horizontal lintel and gave it direct supports. The arch and the
vault are missing from their constructions, and within the
limitation of vertical masses, carrying horizontal masses,
they achieved an infallible sense of proportion. The Greek
temple is a triumph of rectilineal architecture.

This form imposed limitations on decoration. The Greeks
had only the capitals of the columns, the pediment, and the
cornicing with which to vary their simple lines. The Roman
temples achieved a much greater freedom, and the most
famous of their buildings are not the temples, but such edifices as employ the vault and the arch—the Pantheon, the
Colosseum, the Basilica of Constantine, the Baths of Caracalla
and of Diocletian. It was the discovery of the varied possibil-
ities of the arch and the vault that gave birth to Gothic art,
and stamped our own architecture. The Greek temple,
limited to column and architrave, had no future. From
Roman usage of the vault, from experiments in lateral thrusts
and curves, European architecture took its birth. No ancient
Greek could have thought of or built St. Peter's or St.
Sophia's dome. The Romans also developed domestic architecture. They mastered the use of stone blocks. They invented

a concrete made from volcanic earth found near Naples whose great strength enabled them to build gigantic vaults. The Romans blended magnificence and utility. They learned how to group and extend buildings with saloons, corridors, and communicating rooms.

There is to-day, for public buildings, nothing that surpasses or equals the Roman temple plan, with its dignified lines, its vaulted ceilings and soaring domes. The Renaissance extended the Roman tradition. Palladio derived his tradition from the Roman architect, Vitruvius. All the propaganda of Pugin and Ruskin for the Gothic style has not shaken the supremacy and utility of the Roman design. The use of the arch created also a nation of great bridge-builders. The Romans brought water on viaducts over immense distances, spanning ravines and valleys. They carried roads through Europe and crossed rivers and swamps. They used the arch for decoration. The Doges' Palace at Venice is founded on it, as also the Cloth Hall at Ypres. Departures from the Roman tradition often reveal a reduction in both utility and beauty, as we may see by contrasting Sansovino's simple and noble library with the ornate Doges' Palace at Venice.

The Romans placed at points throughout their Empire the triumphal arch. It was a symbol of their dominion, as later the winged lion on the column marked the dominion of Venice. It still commands our admiration wherever we find it, often isolated, but always noble amid the decay surrounding it after many centuries of Roman rule have passed. To-day the Arch of Titus, the Arch of Septimius Severus and the Arch of Constantine are enduring memories of Rome. It was once adorned with twenty-one arches.

When the Senate decreed the triumphal arch to Titus it created a thing of beauty. It was not completed until after his death in A.D. 81. It was copied frequently, as at Benevento. An inscription records its dedication 'to the divine Titus,' and the Emperor is depicted as being carried to Heaven on the wings of an eagle. The keystones bear representations of the army's two deities, Virtus and Honos, abstractions of manliness and honour. On the north side Titus rides in his triumphal car, accompanied by lictors, while Victory crowns him, and Rome herself holds the bridles of the horses. The two reliefs are specially notable, as they mark an advance on Greek art. What baffled the Greek sculptor was triumphantly solved by the Roman. The Greek reliefs showed a blank ground, their figures moved against a wall. When, in a late era, they attempted to show a landscape behind, they achieved only a flat picture. The Roman sculptor in these reliefs has figures and background naturally related, producing a three-dimensional illusion. The two reliefs strikingly set forth the triumphal procession, the carrying of the destroyed Temple's sacred relics, the Table, the Golden Trumpets, the seven-branched Candelabrum. It is Roman soldiers who carry the spoils, and title-boards listing them.

Jerusalem had fallen. The nation was scattered and in bondage, and yet who had triumphed? The Jews were first brought to Rome as captives after Pompey's conquest of Jerusalem in 65 B.C. For two thousand years these Jews and their descendants, augmented and diminished in numbers from time to time, have lived by the banks of the Tiber, on one side or another.

One late afternoon, wandering down by the ancient Theatre of Marcellus, I saw a string of bright balloons quivering above a crowd of children gathered under the solitary Porticus of Octavia. In the wide street behind there was unusual activity. Tables, laden with wine-bottles, were spread over the pavements, and a smartly dressed crowd spilled over them and out of the houses. It was some time before I realised that these smart Romans, with their beautiful children in the daintiest attire, were Jews, and that this was their festival, and that I was in the Ghetto. So here they were, as long in their Roman descent as the Pope across at St. Peter's, who was created in a sense by their forefathers' refusal to accept the credentials of a Galilean Messiah.

What a price in blood and tears they had paid through the centuries for their survival here! They had set a price on the Gentiles also for their captivity. Within seventeen years of their deportation in bondage they had become a power in Rome. They liked Julius Caesar because he borrowed money from them and repaid it at forty per cent. When he died they maintained his funeral pyre in the Forum for a week, lamenting the loss of a benefactor. By the time of Tiberius they had increased to fifty thousand, with colonies in Naples and Genoa. In the reign of this emperor, Jesus of Nazareth was crucified by Roman law in the year 782 A.U.C. (from the foundation of Rome). This incident neither then nor for three centuries afterwards affected their standing.

The Roman Jews mourned heavily when they heard of the overthrow of the Temple and the renewed subjection of their fatherland. They saw members of their own race, bound in chains and led in a Roman triumph. The Arch of Titus, with its display of the holy relics, was an insult and an humiliation, and they paid large sums to avoid passing under it. But the detestation in which they were generally held by pagan Rome had nothing to do with their rejection of Christ. In that they were one with their masters. Tacitus tells us they were a race hated by the gods. Their kings, Herod and Herod Agrippa, were sustained by and owed their power to the Romans. Herod Agrippa I, partly a Jew, changed his name to a good Roman one, as did Josephus. His granddaughter was loved by Titus, who would have married her but for the scandal it would have provoked. Nero's wife, Poppaea, later kicked to death by him, had a Jewish lover, a handsome comedian named Aliturius, employed by Nero. It is said by St. John Chrysostom that St. Paul tried to persuade Poppaea to leave Nero, since she had two husbands living, and become a Christian. When St. Paul and St. Peter were imprisoned by Nero, it is alleged that Josephus, later conductor of the negotiations between Titus and the Jews in the siege of Jerusalem, besought Poppaea, through his friendship with the actor

Aliturius, to influence Nero on behalf of the two prisoners whom Josephus described as 'certain priests of my acquaintance, very excellent persons, whom on a small and trifling charge, Felix, the Procurator of Judæa, had put in irons and sent to Rome to plead their cause before Caesar.' The prisoners were released, but later, it is alleged, Nero, hearing of the attempt by St. Paul to convert Poppaea, clapped the apostles into gaol, on capital charges.

Now favoured, now persecuted, the Jews became a thorn in the Roman's flesh. A magistrate wished Pompey and Titus had never conquered Jerusalem and left the Jews in their native land, 'since the contagion of the cancer, cut out, spreads wider, and the conquered nation grinds its conquerors.' Again and again they were uprooted and suppressed, but vainly. Industrious, frugal, adroit, their fingers touched many trades as well as money-lending. They never lost their faith or their tribal loyalties. They set up in their synagogues copies of the ravished symbols. It is believed that these, after the sack of Rome in 1527, had been thrown into the Tiber, and the Jews petitioned the Pope for permission to search the river-bed, which was refused. They infiltrated into non-Jewish territory, and every Roman had his favourite Jew, or was indebted to one. A day came when a Jewish family held the Castle of St. Angelo. One of them, Pier Leone, a Jew turned Christian, drove out Innocent II, and, while Louis VII opposed the Pope, ruled in Rome as anti-Pope for eight years, A.D. 1130–1138, until his death.

Politically the Jews were always inept, and so they never succeeded in consolidating their position when they achieved power. They excelled as physicians, and were held in such high repute that one always dwelt in the Vatican, and thereby had considerable influence. The Jews were confined to the Ghetto, but this was often a protection against the savage persecution of the mob. With the rejection of the pagan gods and the official recognition of Christianity, their position in Rome became critical, but they survived. The Church was more tolerant than the civil authorities, and as late as 1943, when Fascists and Nazis combined to hunt them, they found safety in the shade of the Vatican. And now, two thousand years after the Romans first devastated Jerusalem and took them into slavery, from that city, a nation again, free and re-established, they send envoys to the Italian Government in Rome, and to the Vatican.

The great Arch of Titus commemorates the downfall of the Jews. In another sense it marks a circle of history. It would be completed perfectly if one day, somewhere in Rome, the seven-branched Candelabrum, the Table, the Trumpets and the gold and silver vessels were excavated.[6]

IV

A path leads from the Arch of Titus up to the Palatine, the plateau overlooking the Forum that was long the site of the palaces of the Emperors. It was in a cave at the western angle that legend declared that the wolf in her lair, the Lupercal, nourished the twins, Romulus and Remus. It was on the Palatine that Romulus created Rome, with its sacred enclosure. It was always a place of the favoured, aristocratic, and never, even in the last days of the Republic, occupied by plebeians. The palaces of the Caesars and the mansions of the nobility covered its plateau. It is to-day an impressive space, revealing colossal brick foundations and a sunken hippodrome. Here

[6] The whereabouts of the Temple spoils has been much debated. After the Triumph a Temple of Peace was built and they were placed in it. In less than a century, soon after the Flavian dynasty ended with Domitian, the Temple was burned to the ground. There was a legend that the Golden Candlestick was lost in the Tiber when Maxentius, after his defeat by Constantine, attempted to cross the Milvian bridge. The arch of Constantine, built to commemorate this victory, reveals no Candlestick as the Emperor bears down upon Maxentius struggling beneath him in the water. A thousand years later the Jews asked the Pope permission to dredge the Tiber in search of the relics, which he refused. Gibbon is in error when he states, 'The holy vessels of the Jewish Temple, after these long peregrinations, were respectfully deposited in the Christian church of Jerusalem.' He does not name the church, and they have never been found. The Arch remains, witness to a Christian empire, which, by sapping a pagan civilisation, succeeded the fourth great Roman monarchy. One can well understand why Romans under Diocletian and Maxentius regarded Christians as the Communists of the day, a peril to be remorselessly stamped out.

Augustus was born, here lived Augustus, Tiberius, Caligula, Claudius, Nero, Domitian, Marcus Aurelius, Commodus, Hadrian, Septimius Severus and Heliogabalus, and many distinguished patricians, such as Mark Antony, Cicero, his forensic rival Hortensius, his bitterest enemy Clodius, and Catullus the poet. It became the sacred hill of patriotic memories, and, like the Forum, is a repository of Roman history.

I spent many weeks there, investigating, through enchanted days that left unexhausted its resources. It is a place of singular and pensive beauty. It commands a great panorama of distant mountains and valleys. It is unique whether one visits it in the morning when the light is crystal clear and the early silence emphasises its vanished glories, or in the late afternoon when the incomparable Roman sunset, in tones of violet, rose and gold, falls over it, and every brick and broken wall becomes a lute sounding the threnody of vanished splendour. Happily, it is always open until sunset, and one may watch the last golden light flush the temples and pillars of the Forum, while the waning day glows in purple and crimson above the Alban hills until a last runner of gold seals the vista of the visible world.

In the Republican period the palaces of the Caesars had not spread over the Palatine. Being the best residential district, Cicero had his house here, with a magnificent view over the scene of his forensic triumphs, but he suffered much from his neighbour and enemy, the vindictive Clodius. The latter lived in a house built on the corner of the Palatine, where Livius Drusus, who was murdered in his own hall in the presence of his mother, had once dwelt. Drusus was an upright man, with a good opinion of himself, who asked, as he lay dying, 'When will the Commonwealth have a citizen like me again?' After his death Crassus lived there in great luxury, having spent six million sesterces on improvements. He adorned it with bronze floors and ivory ceilings and six columns of Sicilian marble, whereupon he was nicknamed 'the Palatine Venus.' He was particularly proud of his fish-ponds, in which he kept lampreys. When his favourite lamprey died he wept. To Ahenobarbus, who sneered at him for this, he retorted that it was more than he had ever done on the death of his three wives.

Cicero possessed a nearby villa. It happened to be just below that of his enemy, Clodius, whose view of the Forum he could block by building. A day came when Cicero was banished and had to flee to Greece as the result of the power of his enemy. This enabled Clodius to ransack and destroy the orator's villa, driving his wife to take refuge in the cloister of the Vestal Virgins. He also destroyed the portico of the house belonging to Catullus, the poet, and because another neighbour blocked his plan to possess all the Forum side of the Palatine, he had him poisoned and then bought his victim's house. Later a political change enabled Cicero to return. The State compensated him for his demolished villa, and he rebuilt it. The blackguardly Clodius hired small boys to shout offensively outside Cicero's house, and even molested his neighbour in the street. His life was one long scandal. A man of great wealth, he stopped at nothing. Caesar's wife was not above suspicion, Clodius was her lover. One day, with her assistance, he dressed himself up as a woman and got into the house where the sacred rites of the Bona Dea were celebrated, so sacred to women that, says Juvenal, 'not even a male mouse dare show itself there.' Inside, Clodius got lost in the passages and was discovered. The scandal shook Rome. Caesar divorced his wife. The judges found Clodius guilty. He attempted to establish an alibi, which Cicero easily demolished. This started the lifelong feud. Clodius escaped any penalties by bribery. He met a violent end in 52 B.C.

Another luxurious house was that owned by Catullus, with its domed roof, later acquired by Clodius. Nothing could exceed the splendour of these private residences, which came to be known as palaces from their position on the Palatinus.

After the murder of Julius Caesar, Augustus bought the

villa that had belonged to the orator Hortensius, and enlarged it, adding to it Catiline's villa. He created here the first palace of the imperial Caesars. A man of simple tastes, for twenty-eight years he slept in the same small bedroom. The palace was destroyed by fire in A.D. 3, whereupon a voluntary subscription was raised throughout the Empire, restricted to one denarius per citizen, to build a new home for the Emperor. A magnificent palace took the place of the old one. It was later enlarged by Caligula and Domitian. On the southwest end there was a loggia from which the emperors could look down on the games in the vast Circus Maximus.

A feature of the palace in the time of Augustus was its great library of Greek and Latin books. Rome to-day is well equipped with libraries. There are no fewer than seventy-eight official ones, from the Vatican downwards, covering all domains of knowledge. This does not take into account branch libraries or private ones.[7] These libraries have always been a great tradition of Rome, dating back to the Emperors. Asinius Caius Pollio, the orator, poet and historian, who accompanied Caesar when he crossed the Rubicon, built and opened the first public library in 39 B.C. He was the friend of Horace and Catullus. His library stood on the Aventine and contained Greek and Latin literature. There were private libraries in Rome previous to this. Among the loot taken by the Roman conquerors, manuscripts were not neglected, and the most valued slave was often the Greek amanuensis who wrote from dictation, copied or translated. Sulla the Dictator, in 86 B.C., brought home from Athens, along with the columns of pentelic marble he had stolen from the Olympeion, the library of Apellikon, which had once belonged to Aristotle. The genus of book-borrower has not altered through the centuries. When Cicero's librarian was asked by a Rhodian

[7] When I first planned the writing of this book and reviewed the resources I discovered that twenty-one of these libraries would aid my research. I was overcome by the statement that, in the bibliography of Rome alone, there were 274,678 books. The writing of yet another seemed almost an act of effrontery.

confrère to check a passage in Aristotle's *Works*, he could only get permission by bribing Sulla's librarian, who jealously guarded his master's books.

Lucullus brought back from his conquest of Pontus a library which he generously permitted scholars to consult. Plutarch, remarking on the epicure's liberality, said his house was a temple of the Muses. Cicero and Atticus, the bookseller, were two bibliophiles who exchanged volumes and notes. Nothing is more human than Cicero's request to Atticus to send him two bookbinders with a supply of parchment. Atticus despatched to him his two best workmen. They repaired Cicero's whole library with such skill that the orator sent his friend a special letter of thanks. When one of his slaves ran away with some books, he was more distressed by the loss of the volumes than by the loss of the slave.

A private library was considered essential in all great houses. Special rooms were built facing east because that aspect gave the best protection from mildew. A good library contained two or three thousand rolls of papyrus. Finely written *editions de luxe* would contain the whole of the *Iliad* in pocket size. Illustrations were not unknown and a good copy would fetch as much as £400. There was no copyright.[8]

Fake editions were often on the market. When Horace walked down to the Argiletum—the book market—he had the choice of a dozen bookshops, usually publishers' offices as well. Publishers competed for leading and popular authors. They corresponded with capitals like Athens, Alexandria and Lyons in search of talent.

The public library opened by Pollio was soon copied. Lanciani is of the opinion that some of these were lending libraries, and he relates how at a Roman villa near Tivoli, on

---

[8] Fifteen hundred years later printed books, when they first began to appear, were regarded as vulgar. The libraries of the Italian courts prided themselves only on manuscript copies. The Duke of Urbino, Raphael's early patron, kept forty scribes constantly employed. 'I libri tutti sono belli in superlativo grado, tutti iscritta a penna, e non v'è ignuno a stampa, che ne sarebbe vergognato,' wrote Vespasiano—'All the books are superlatively beautiful, all hand-written, and none is printed, which would be a matter for shame.'

a hot day, a discussion arose on the wisdom of drinking iced water. Someone quoted Aristotle on the subject. The quotation was challenged, whereupon one of the company ran to the public library in Tivoli, borrowed an Aristotle, and read out the passage condemning iced water as injurious to the health, whereupon the company decided to give up the use of ice or snow in water.

When Augustus built his palace on the Palatine he added on to the west side of the portico, behind the Temple of Apollo, Greek and Latin libraries, with a great reading-room between them. Here he housed for public use a large collection of books, specialising on civil law and the liberal arts. It was carefully selected, with a learned librarian in charge. The size of the reading-room may be judged from the fact that in the centre stood a colossal bronze statue of Augustus as Apollo, sixty feet high. The walls were decorated with gold, silver and bronze medallions, in relief, of poets, historians, philosophers, etc. Meetings were held here of the learned societies, and lectures were given. The Emperor Claudius enforced attendance at some of these lectures, and keeping awake in the warm Roman day was a great trial. Pliny has recorded one of these sessions. 'We approach the hall as if we were compelled by main force; many of us sit outside of the door, and try to overcome *ennui* by discussing the gossip of the town. Messengers are surreptitiously sent in to enquire whether he had finished his prologue, or how many sheets are still to be read. Then, when we hear that the moment of deliverance is not very far off, we come in slowly, sit on the edge of our chairs, and do not even wait for the end of the discourse to slip or steal quietly away.' Whether it is 10 B.C. or A.D. 1950, lecturers and lectured have not changed their natures.

The palaces of Augustus had a simple plan. It was in the form of a square, with a colonnade all round the central courtyard. The south-west front opened on to a semi-circular terrace surveying the Circus Maximus in the valley below.

The palace was approached from the Forum side through a magnificent gateway, which was crowned by a quadriga, four horses driven by Apollo and Artemis, cut by Lysias from a single block of marble. Beyond it was a large rectangular portico, with the temple of Apollo, flanked on each side by the Greek and Latin libraries. It was built entirely of white marble from the newly discovered Carrara quarries, and it was faced with bas-reliefs in Parian marble. In the temple, between columns of African marble, stood fifty statues of the daughters of Danaüs, and fifty equestrian ones of their doomed husbands. The altar was flanked by four gilt-bronze oxen. Here also was a statue of Apollo playing the lyre, the god reflecting Augustus in the beauty of his youth. The gates of the temple were of ivory. Over the pediment Apollo drove the chariot of the sun, the whole executed in gilt-bronze. The temple shone with gold, bronze, and thirty different rare marbles. It had innumerable hanging chandeliers and a collection of gold plate. Two golden chests held the oracular Sibylline Books. The cost of this was met by the melting down of all the silver statues to Augustus in the provinces, set up against his will.

The world has probably never seen anything as magnificent as the group of buildings raised by Augustus on the Palatine, and to this creation were added the palaces of Tiberius, Caligula, Nero, Vespasian, Domitian, Hadrian, Septimius Severus and Heliogabalus. Each of these palaces equalled that of Augustus, 'if not in pure taste, certainly in wealth, in luxury, in magnificence, in the number and value of works of art collected and stolen from Greece and the East, from Egypt and Persia,' observes Lanciani. Of all this splendour and the subsequent superstructures of the emperors, nothing remains except the cavernous brick foundations with their interminable chambers and corridors. The temple and palace were gutted with fire in A.D. 363, and were not rebuilt.

In approaching these sites across the levelled space now intersected by a sixteenth-century convent, let us recall an incident in June, 17 B.C. Augustus had revived the Secular Games, and to celebrate the occasion had asked Horace for a poem. The poet wrote the *Carmen Saeculare*, to be sung on the third day of the festival. It was a part-song, chanted by a white-robed chorus of boys and girls who sang fifteen alternate verses, and a prologue and epilogue together. The custodians of the oracular Sibylline Books, the fifteen Commissioners, had defined the nature of the ceremony. We can stand to-day by the portico of the temple and see the winding way up which came the white-robed procession, singing, led by Horace himself, wearing his laureate's wreath.

How vivid it all is across the lost centuries! We have, too, a singular link with this June day of almost two thousand years ago. In the beautiful cloister of the National Museum, situated in the Baths of Diocletian, there is a pilaster with an inscription which records this revival of the *Ludi Saeculares* by Augustus. Found in many fragments in 1890, when making the Corso Vittorio Emanuele, it tells us that Horace wrote the song, and appointed the singers, twenty-seven boys and twenty-seven girls (the mystic numbers, three-times-nine) of great beauty and chosen from living parents, who performed on June 3rd, in the year of Rome, 737 (B.C. 17).[9]

Descending through the foundations of Augustus's palace, we come out into a great oval stadium. It looks to-day, sunk deep below the general level of the ground, like a giant's swimming-pool. It was a stadium for foot-races, games and military exercises, one hundred and sixty yards in length, and fifty wide. Domitian and Hadrian made a garden of it, but in A.D. 379 the Emperor Theodosius turned it back into a stadium. The imperial box still towers over it.

[9] Phoebus and Diana, grant the prayers duly offered at the sacred season. O Sun, ever-changing yet ever the same, let Rome's pre-eminence be as changeless! Dian, birth-goddess, guard our mothers! Bless our new marriage laws to the increase of our people that each generation may find us still celebrating this festival. O Destinies, fulfil the happy oracles, and add future to past blessings, fertility of earth and cattle, seasonable rain and pure air. Apollo, hear us boys! Dian, hear us girls!' (First thirty-six verses of Horace's *Carmen Saeculare*).

Beyond the stadium, on a tremendous foundation of tufa and brick arches, the Emperor Septimius Severus built himself a new palace with baths. It rose majestically on the cliff's edge, dominating the valley of the Circus Maximus. On the side of the Way of Victory, looking southwards, he built a six-storey colonnade called the Septizonium. The Emperor was born near Leptis, in Africa. He built this façade to impress his countrymen arriving from Africa by the Appian Way. It survived until 1588, when Sixtus V, the pope who proposed making a woollen factory of the Colosseum, pulled it down, using parts for the new wing of the Vatican, for the base of the obelisk in the Piazza del Popolo, for a staircase in the Lateran Palace, and for a public workhouse for poor women. It is almost impossible to find where many pieces of ancient Rome went, or what purpose they served. Building, patching and restoring made demands on all kinds of monuments. Dog ate dog. There was a famous patcher named Montorsoli, a sculptor-monk, recommended to the Pope by Michelangelo for repair work. He was established in the Belvedere, where he had his workroom. 'He made a missing left arm for the Apollo and a right arm for the Laocoön, both of which statues are placed there, also proposing to restore the Hercules,' records Vasari.

Adjoining the ruined palace occupied by Septimius Severus and by Hadrian there is a wide belvedere projecting from the Palatine. It is a large platform carried by gigantic arches of brickwork. The sunset hour there offers a scene of inexpressible grandeur; the gardens, hills, churches, bell-towers, the blue shadows of the Campagna and the soft violet-hued mountains spread themselves before us.

v

In the last golden glow of a late autumn afternoon I made my way down from this belvedere into the lofty brick foundations and empty, roofless chambers, their arches framing lovely vistas of the Alban hills, until I reached the ground

level with the long Circus Maximus, once the scene of delirious crowds cheering the charioteers. The path ran in and out
of these ruined arches. In a wilderness of shrubs a solitary
artist was happily engrossed before his easel. I stumbled upon
a pair of young lovers, ecstatically locked in each other's
arms, their passionate moment oblivious of the centuries of
ruins encompassing them.

At the end of the long path, under the Palatine, I came to a
roofless, one-storied building of eight small rooms grouped on
either side of a hemispherical chamber. One of the pillars still
retained the fragmentary torso and broken thigh of a naked
boy, the white marble warmed by the rose of sunset after
some eighteen centuries. The solitary mutilated figure was
not inappropriate. The ruined building in the long grass,
with its crumbling, tessellated floor, its broken walls on
which the frescoes were still visible, was the *pedagogium*, the
training-school for the imperial pages in the emperor's household above. Boys never alter in their nature, thank God. They
blossom in mischief eternally, and because of their passion
for scribbling on walls we can recapture a little of their lives
in this school, believed by some to be for refractory pages,
since one small room, from remarks scribbled on the walls,
seems to have been used as a confinement cell. Good boys or
bad boys, they found life here pleasanter than at the school
in the Street of the Head of Africa (*paedagogium ad caput
Africae*), down which we may wander to-day, the select
school in the aristocratic Coelian section.

There was no softness about Roman schools. It was a severe
drilling, with no sparing of the rod. An obstinate boy was
stripped, mounted on the back of another and flogged with an
angiulla, a whip made of eel-skin because of its stinging quality. Well might one of the pages, delivered from such discipline, scribble on the wall, as we may see it to-day,
Corinthus exit de paedagogio and *Marianus Afer exit de
paedagogio*. Happy Corinthus and Marianus to be out of
school! One of these *graffiti* scratchings with a nail on plaster

rings admonishingly even so long after. It is written under a sketch of a donkey turning a cornmill, and runs: *Labora, aselle, quomodo ego laboravi et proderit tibi* ('Work, work, little donkey, as I have worked myself, and thou shalt be rewarded for it.')

One cannot help wondering what scenes, splendid and terrible, magnificent and bloody, these pages witnessed in the halls of the Caesars, what messages of good or evil, of life or death they carried to others on the whim of an emperor. Graceful and agile, well-born and now well-placed, they might become governors of a Province, tribunes, or victims of the edict of exile or the assassin's sword. Intrigue was ever abroad, and jealousies were rife in this thrusting crowd of courtiers. In a great household of six thousand servants a page's feet must have run swiftly over the marble floors, along the vaulted corridors, through the secret apartments. Their golden limbs, naked save for the brief chlamys thrown over one shoulder, must have marked a note of innocence on that heavy score of crime. Ovid wistfully recalled how Mercury, seeking to make a conquest, smoothed his hair and arranged his chlamys.

> *Chlamydemque, ut pendeat apte*
> *Collocat: ut limbus, totumque appareat aurum.*[10]

Out of their vanished lives comes back a boyish taunt scribbled on one of these walls. What an insight it gives one into the strife growing between the Pagan and the Christian worlds! We know from St. Paul that followers of the new faith were members of Caesar's household. Since a great majority of its servants were slaves, the new teaching, offering them rewards in the next life, in compensation for the miseries of this, naturally appealed to this multitude in heavy bondage. It was not only a new religion, propagated by renegade Jews who made preposterous claims, it was a danger-

---

[10] He drapes his chlamys in order that it may hang suitably and wholly reveal its golden border (Ovid, *Met. II*, 735).

ous doctrine of communism, adopted by the have-nots, the slave order and the rabble. To profess Christianity was, at the best, to invite ridicule. Did not the wretched Jews worship an ass? Had not Tacitus related how the custom grew from the services rendered by wild asses to the Israelites in the wilderness? Jews and Christians were all of the same order, thought the orthodox Roman.

When, therefore, it leaked out that the page, Alexamenos, was a Christian, it was a thing for mirth and derision among the other boys. One, with a neat gift for caricature, drew on the wall in the pages' quarters an ass with large ears on a crucifix, and scribbled derisively underneath: 'Alexamenos worships his God.' One can hear the shouts of laughter and see poor young Alexamenos, crimson before their derision.

In Rome legend and superstition surround us. We can reject everything, and thus feel we avoid error, but the most sceptical will admit that in these voluminous legends, often quite preposterous, traversing the centures, there must have been a basis of truth on some occasions. We can follow here an interesting supposition. In a later epoch these rooms, as inscriptions on the walls suggest, were occupied by soldiers of the Praetorian Guards on special service at the Imperial palace. St. Paul, chained to a soldier while awaiting his second trial, referred (Phil. i. 13) to the fact that he was known throughout the Praetorium. 'The soldier to whom he was chained to-day might have been in Nero's bodyguard yesterday; his comrade who relieved him might have been one of the executioners of Octavia, and might have carried her head to Poppaea a few weeks before,' writes Coneybeare. It is a series of 'mights' with which speculation can play.

Opposite the pages' school are the ruins of the house of Gelotius. It was acquired by Caligula not because he wanted more space, but because it lay near the Circus and was quickly and unobtrusively accessible from the palace. Here he housed the charioteers and grooms for the races. His passion for these was such that he spent days and nights in the company of these young darlings of the Romans, sharing their maddest exploits. These *agitatores circenses* were the equivalent of our own jockeys and football players. They were worshipped by the crowd. A State institution, they lived in princely style. Caligula had a stable of 'greens,' Domitian had six stables. They wore coloured caps from which they took their names, the Greens, the Reds, the Whites, the Blues, and, added by Domitian from the privy purse, the Gold and the Purple. Juvenal records the excitement they aroused. 'The whole of Rome has flocked to the circus to-day, and the uproar of the crowd can be heard miles away.' Bulwer Lytton gave us the spectacle of these chariot races in *The Last Days of Pompeii*. The charioteers made great fortunes. Crescens, the leader of the Greens, Caligula's favourite, aged twenty-two, made £20,000. Diocles, the foremost of all, left £300,000.

Ascending to the Palatine again, we pass a small altar from which is derived our term the *genius loci*. From this altar in 310 B.C. came 'the wandering voice' (*Aius Locutius*), warning Rome of the Gallic invasion. It was restored by Sextus Calvinus about 100 B.C., who thereupon dedicated it to 'the Being who spake and uttered.' A staircase leads to a platform once occupied by the Temple of Jupiter Propugnator. In the foundations are vast cisterns for the storing of water. Beyond lies the palace of Domitian, partly constructed by the Flavian emperors. There is sufficient left for the imagination to reconstruct its splendour. It was faced by a great arcaded portico. Through bronze doors the emperors entered a state reception hall, lined on each side by fluted, violet-hued columns of Phrygian marble supporting a coffered gilt vault, and decorated with basalt statues. At one end on a dais, in an apse, stood the throne. On the right was the Basilica or Imperial Tribunal, whose nave, aisles and throne in the apse, set the form for the basilicas of the Christian churches. It was lined with precious marbles from Egypt and Libya, and had a ceiling painted to represent the starry heaven, in pursuance of the practice for Roman magistrates to sit under the open sky. Here St. Paul, fettered, came for trial before the tribunal of Nero, and, on the first occasion, was acquitted.

From the basilica we enter the big open court, arcaded and once filled with statues. The marble floors in the colonnades were specially polished so that the apprehensive Domitian might detect the reflection of any approaching assassin. It was in vain. The fate of which he was so terrified overtook him. A freedman, whose patron had been condemned to death, struck him in the groin. A desperate scuffle ensued, in which Domitian clutched the assassin's dagger, cutting his hand to the bone. Shrieking, he beat his assailant on the head with a goblet and tried with bloody fingers to gouge out his eyes. Accomplices of the assassin rushed in and finished off their victim.

The columns of *portasanta*, flesh-coloured marble from Chios, often used for the door-jambs of basilicas, were surmounted by an open gallery with porphyry and granite columns. The state dining-room, the *triclinium*, follows next. Here had dined Hadrian, Antinoüs, Aurelius, and Pertinax. The last received here the news that his guard had revolted, and, going out, he was assassinated on the threshold of the palace. Tacitus has left us an account of a banquet at which the Emperor Tiberius dined, his aged mother, the Empress Livia, the firm-handed widow of Augustus, on one side, his niece Agrippina, who died of voluntary starvation, on the other. The pavement of the apse, made of slabs of porphyry and coloured marbles, is in good preservation. Beyond the dining-room is a nymphaeum where fountains played into a large oval pool, its refreshing sound coming through the open arches.

Near the Flavian palace, at a lower level, is the enchanting little house of Livia, consort of Augustus, a modest dwelling built round an enclosed atrium, with painted rooms, panels of birds, fruits and animals, and a perfect heating system. To the left of this is the palace in which Tiberius lived in the earlier part of his reign. It is largely unexcavated, its vast ruins spread under the former Farnese gardens. Here lived Livia, aged eighty-six, so able and domineering that Tiberius retreated to the island of Capri to escape her; here also he lamented the loss of his son Drusus, poisoned by his wife and her lover; here, in its libraries, the young Marcus Aurelius studied.

Along the eastern side, stretching from the palace of Tiberius to the tremendous ruins of the palace of Caligula, which dominated the Forum and had a magnificent view of the Capitol, is a long, subterranean passage, the *Cryptoporticus*. One walks along it, now lit by the vivid blue sky where the vaulted roof has fallen, recalling the grim murder enacted here on the morning of January 4th, A.D. 41. Caligula, already at twenty-nine notorious for his capricious cruelty, had been at the theatre witnessing one of the Palatine plays instituted by Livia in honour of her husband, Augustus. About noon he left the theatre, with his attendants, and walked back to his palace. Instead of entering the courtyard and proceeding with Claudius up the staircase, past the guards, he turned aside and went along the dim corridor. It led to some bathing apartments. Here he visited a company of dancers, young noblemen from Asia, his guests at the Imperial Court for the purpose of learning Roman hymns and Pyrrhic dances. Having spoken with them, he passed on, when he was challenged by Cassius Cherea, the captain on duty and leader of the conspiracy, to give the password of the day. Caligula swore at him, and immediately was struck by a dagger. He ran towards the terrified Asian youths, but was knocked down by another conspirator who held him until all life was stabbed out of his body. The conspirators then tried to escape. Fearing to encounter the guard at the end of the passage, they went out by the other end and took refuge in the house of Livia, where Caligula's own father, Germanicus, had formerly lived.

VI

As the golden, level light of sunset gilded the ruined palaces of the Caesars, a bell tinkling somewhere warned me that the attendants were rounding up the visitors. There was just time to proceed to the Casino Farnese that enjoyed one of the loveliest sites in Rome, and one of the most historic. It was now sadly neglected. Here in the early afternoon, in a part of a garden run wild, I had stumbled upon an astonishing scene. Hearing the lively music of a guitar nearby, I emerged from a pergola, and saw two youths and two maidens capering before a broken fountain to the music played by a young man sitting on a stone lion. I retreated somewhat, not wishing to spoil this Theocritan scene. I can only imagine they were for some purpose rehearsing a dance. A little change of costume —the two maidens in white girdled gowns, the two youths draped in the brief chlamys, the guitarist laurelled, and I had stepped back into a pagan era when the fauns and nymphs danced to the pipes of Pan.

Nor was the scene historically inappropriate. Here, as late as the eighteenth century, had come the Roman *dilettanti*, calling themselves the Academy of the Arcadians, making this deserted Casino and gardens their headquarters. It was all a little self-conscious. Its members took Grecian names, the emblem was the pipes of Pan. Music and letters held séances here; the Maestro Marcello came from Venice to be crowned with laurel for his music, the young Metastasio recited his verses. Dressed as Paris and Helen, Endymion and Diana, they held their revels amid the ilex and cypress. The fashion passed. With the sterner events of the nineteenth century there was no time for light folly. The shadow of Napoleon fell over Europe.

It is the shadow of another Napoleon that is the last to fall on this deserted Palatine, nursery of more than two thousand years of Rome's rise, triumph and fall. By singular circumstances the Farnese Villa, casino and gardens, and a great part of the Palatine, property in the sixteenth century of the Farnese family, passed to the Neapolitan Bourbons. It was they who sold the property in 1861 for £10,000 to the Emperor Napoleon III, who made disastrous excavations. The only shred of his empire left to him, he lost it, when, exiled in England after Sedan, he was glad to sell it to the city of Rome.

EPILOGUE

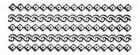

WHEN the heat of summer comes, when the oleanders, white, pink and magenta, are in bloom, when the sound of fountains is most refreshing and the deep shade of ilex groves offers a cool retreat, Rome takes its siesta in the afternoons. The traffic ceases, the streets are quiet and shuttered. Only the ardent tourist crosses the burning piazza. But towards evening, when the blue sky merges into the rose, purple and jade-green of sunset, then the shutters open and the life of Rome floods through its streets and squares. This is the season of evening music, for which the ruins of the Caesars have been adroitly converted into vast auditoriums for opera and symphony concerts. In the warm, starry night the tall cypresses guard the horizon of a moonlit world wherein the ruins become vaster and mysterious memorials of a vanished greatness. The walls of the Baths of Caracalla echo back not the ghostly voices of Romans, centuries dead, but those of living singers and orchestras presenting Verdi or Puccini from a stage built within gigantic bastions of crumbling brick and broken vault.

On a plateau, from which it commands the ancient Roman Forum, stands also the massive ruin of the Basilica of Maxentius, or Constantine, taking the alternative name from the emperor who dedicated to Christian use the unfinished basilica of the pagan emperor he conquered. Built in A.D. 306, it was originally a great law court, with a central nave, three

273

hundred and twenty feet long, and two aisles. The principal apse was at the western end, but in the north aisle are three great arcaded bays. Into the central bay a concert platform has been ingeniously fitted. The tremendous vault was carried by eight colossal Corinthian columns of Hymettus marble. None of these exists, but the north bays retain parts of their tremendous vaults, majestic in their soaring strength. This colossal basilica, of which only a fragment remains, reveals in every line the grandeur of the Roman genius for scientific construction. The south aisle has completely vanished, and in the roofless nave the modern audience listens, its back turned to the open Forum and the wooded heights of the Palatine beyond.

It was here on a warm, moonlit night of July that I heard the tenor voice of Gigli rising up to those broken vaults, still bearing their embossed panelling, *soffitti*, once marble-covered and adorned with gilded roses; a panelling that has set the pattern of the embossed ceilings of Europe for the last sixteen hundred years.

As Gigli's pure tenor voice rose in the still night, I recalled the occasion on which I had first heard it, some fifteen years earlier, wondering which setting had been the more beautiful. One summer evening, returning from a friend's house in Venice, long after midnight, I had turned into the empty Piazza San Marco. The tall campanile towered in the sky, the four bronze horses on the moonwashed Byzantine façade of the church stood poised in their arrested movement. The long arcades and windows of the vast Piazza enclosed a deserted arena. And then, to my surprise, I saw that this arena was not deserted. At the far end there were three or four rows of mellow lights revealing shadowy forms, while, faint in the stillness of the scene, I heard a silver voice singing to the accompaniment of an orchestra.

What could it mean, this spectral orchestra and singer in the hushed, empty Piazza? I stealthily approached, apprehensive of breaking the magic. As I drew nearer I saw stand-

ing before the orchestra a little stout man. He had thrown a
muffler aside and wore a black beret. To a muted accompaniment he sang, silver-voiced, under the open sky, so that one's
flesh thrilled in the listening night. I knew that singer at
once: it could be none other than Gigli, whose advent to
Venice had been announced. For this was a nocturnal re-
hearsal of Verdi's *Requiem Mass* to be given in the Piazza
on the morrow.

Much tribulation has encompassed the world since that
magic hour in Venice and this in Rome. Under the spell of
that voice again, I lapsed into a reminiscent reverie in this
ruined basilica of the emperors. Soon I should be departing
from this city of so much ancient splendour and history. My
task was finished. Through eager days of autumn, winter,
spring and summer I had tirelessly pursued my quest. In a
sense I knew it could never be finished. The riches of Rome
are inexhaustible. A man might spend his whole life within
the limit of one hundred square yards of its soil and then not
complete, or in any way approach completion of his task. I
recalled how Ferdinand Gregorovius had come here, a century ago, an eager young man, and had spent twenty years
writing his monumental history of Medieval Rome. His work
finished, the day of departure arrived. 'I look back with satis-
faction on this long space of time,' he wrote, 'during which,
amid troubles indescribable, I have worked my way up-
wards to the light. My life task is ended, and my work at the
same time had been recognised by the city of Rome as worthy
of its subject. Never have I felt myself so free or happy.'

So he departed, elected an honorary citizen of Rome, his
name in that honourable roster holding those of Petrarch,
Raphael, Michelangelo and Canova. How great, known and
unknown, is that army of patient scholars whose lives have
been absorbed by this wonderful city; and to what happier
bondage could a man's destiny direct him? I also knew it, in
some degree. Like Gregorovius, I had walked in its streets in
the coolness and stillness of dawn and midnight. I had ex-

amined, questioned, followed clues and taken voluminous notes, until they were many times the size of the book I had planned. Every day some exciting diversion presented itself, so that one was side-tracked from the first objective. Every journey was rich and rewarding, and the horizon ever receded.

On this very day I had gone into an old street of Rome, trying to check, as was always my custom, some fact concerning Raphael's Fornarina. Seeking the Palazzo Sassi, I had peered into an arcaded courtyard where a tailor sat sewing in the waning light. He could not answer my query, but he took me to a door labelled 'Biblioteca.' Within, in a dark library of crumbling folios, a little old man approached me. He told me where I should find my palazzo, and, my curiosity aroused concerning this biblioteca, courtyard and house, he proceeded to show me the surprising treasures of this *palazzetto* in which he worked. Known as the *Casa di Sisto V*, its story had been obscure until 1931 when my guide had lowered a plumbline into history.

Later, in the library, he stood revealed. He was an old professor, Carlo Astolfi, seventy-five years of age, whose whole life had been passed in the investigation of his beloved Rome. He had written some books, he had filled portfolios with clippings of his published contributions to learning. Like Browning's Grammarian, he had fought a lifelong campaign elucidating some obscure point; he had explained how the circular staircase within the column of Trajan had been made, why Ovid had been sent into exile, why Raphael should be accepted also as a sculptor. Finally, he had conducted me to the Palazzo Sassi, and I there bade farewell to this modest old scholar. Soon he will have vanished from the scene, taking with him so much treasure of the mind gleaned through the long years. He had transformed an enquiry of a few minutes into a pageant of human history lasting two hours, in which he had opened for me unending vistas of knowledge.

Gigli's voice, rising to the vault of the basilica, set me wondering when last the pagan chant and when first the Christian hymn had been heard in this ruined fane. Constantine
had conquered Maxentius at the battle of the Milvian Bridge,
where he had seen in the sky the Sign of the Cross—a not
unusual meteorological phenomenon. *In Hoc Signo*, I.H.S.
In this sign he had conquered, Maxentius had been destroyed,
and with Constantine's conversion a struggle, century-long,
had begun between the pagan Senate and the Christian emperors. He had been aided by the reforms of the Emperor
Diocletian, a persecutor of Christians who, paradoxically, restored the Roman administration, and thereby made possible
Constantine's official adoption and foundation of the Christian religion in the West.

Applause broke my reverie. Gigli bowed, retired. The
opening strains of a Rossini overture filled the air. I glanced
over my shoulder, sensitive to a pervading aura, not of present time but of this ancient place. Behind me was an astonishing floodlit panorama. Through an arch of the basilica rose a
segment of the towering Colosseum. Nearer, I saw the thir-
teenth-century Romanesque bell-tower of the church of
Santa Maria Nova, decorated with discs of enamelled pottery
that preceded Majolica ware. It adjoined the site of the Temple of Venus and Rome, planned by the Emperor Hadrian in
honour of Eternal Rome, whose beautiful cornice still bears
witness to the last pagan temple in use in the city. There
stood, in the rise of the Sacred Way traversing the low valley
of the Forum, the glimmering Arch of Titus, the ruins of the
house of the Vestal Virgins, and, dominating all, the Palatine.
It seemed like the drop-scene of a theatre, floodlit, a long
wooded ridge of inexpressible beauty, with its dramatic tall
pines, its slim, dark cypresses tipped with stars, its dense ilex
groves and exotic palm trees.

It was all so soft in the summer moonlight, a mysterious
repository of so much history, that the mind could not assimi-

late all the magic it held. There Rome had come to birth. Around that hill Romulus had driven his furrow demarcating the future city. Upon that height had stood the temples of the gods, the palaces of the emperors and the aristocracy. Sacrosanct, no plebeians had been permitted to dwell there. To the end of the republic it had been the domain of the governing nobility. Augustus Caesar had been born there, in the consulship of Cicero. On that wooded mount had stood the Golden House of Nero. Even now the great bastions of brickwork, a brown honeycomb, revealed the foundations of the palaces of Tiberius and Caligula. In those dark pinewoods by the cliff's edge had stood Cicero's dwelling whence he could see the Forum and the Rostra from which he spoke so eloquently. The steep paths, woods, palaces, temples and villas had been known to Virgil, to Horace, to Tacitus and Plutarch. Its memories had been wistfully evoked by Ovid, who, from the far north, sent to the imperial library by the hand of a friend, a copy of his book. In sick exile he fancifully followed its journey up the hill, noting the temples, palaces and monuments it passed, thus giving us for all time a picture of its splendour.

Yet was it ever lovelier than on this July evening, with its floodlit slopes, its umbrageous crest silhouetted in moonlight, remote and mysterious, in which perhaps, even now, the ancient gods kept vigil? I knew then why, listening to the music in the basilica, I had been conscious of another presence. It seemed to me that on the verge of that woodland, high above the ruins of the silent Forum, a thousand ghosts had thronged, to look down across the centuries and wonder at our diversions; and perhaps while Gigli's voice soared to the stars the sad shades listened: shades of emperors who had travelled and conquered in far lands to build an empire, and who had come to violent deaths at the hands of assassins; shades of patricians, proscribed or exiled; of philosophers, historians and poets whose words have not yet died; of architects and sculptors whose genius still pulsates in shattered temple and broken torso. I seemed to feel them there, sentient in the warm night. And when the music ended and the lights went out, I felt that it was I not they who departed. For around us the arch, the column, the statue, in their diurnal orbit through Time, abided still, witnessing the immortal spirit of Rome.

INDEX

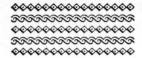